The Saga
Of The Outlaw
Harry Tracy

James J. Nystrom

So Right Press

Bothell, Washington

ISBN-13 978-1456373504

ISBN-10 1456373501

For Mary S.

Mary N.

Adam N.

Lesley N.

Chris N.

Hal N.

Thanks to Bob W., Val, Greg, Don, Bob D. and Pat

And the Memory of

Wally

Dave

Bob

Isobel

Contents

Introduction:

The Man and the Element

Few legends thrive in the Pacific Northwest. The legend of the outlaw, Harry Tracy, however, is one of the most enduring and fascinating of the region. This legend, one of the last of an era, occurred in the often ignored and sometimes unappreciated section of the United States that does not have the bleak, sweeping landscapes or wide-open skies more widely associated as backdrops for the tumultuous theatre of human drama that has come to be known as the "Wild West." There are no immortalized and lawless towns like Dodge City or Tombstone. There are no celebrated hideouts like Hole-in-the-Wall, Robber's Roost or Brown's Park. In the early days of the development of this untamed territory, the ethereal beauty of the land and the incessant demands of daily life in the wet and cloudy climate were omnipresent; the struggles of mere mortals were often ignored or have faded into the mists of the past.

The generation of residents here, both native and immigrant, both transient and permanent, have left enumerable tales and stories as legacies to their lives. However, nature occupies the center of attention with her awe-inspiring scenery, her lush fertility and her fickle climate. The identity of Pacific Northwest inhabitants, from the gentle, low-key indigenous Native Americans to the restless European settlers from the east coast of the continent who arrived in large numbers only as recently as the late nineteenth century, to the recent multicultural inflow of emigrants from all parts of the world, has always been relegated to minor significance compared to the dominating presence of the land and the weather that nurtures it. When some individual has risen above the struggle of everyday life to force the mark of their personality in some significant event, no matter how seemingly important at the time, a few years later, the trees, the water and the mountains are still ever-present and somehow, they make the memory of that individual and that event fade into oblivion, as forgotten and obscure as the last winter's rainfall.

The Pacific Northwest as a geographical and topographical region is limited to a thin strip of land which begins at the Pacific Ocean shore and ends in the Cascade Mountain heights and which stretches from the giant redwood forests of northern California to the cold reaches of northern British Columbia. Every inch of this land is literally swarming with growth. Evergreen forests stretch out across the land like thick carpets of variegated texture. Where there are no trees, there are thickets of vine maple, salal, cottonwood trees, Oregon grape, sword and bracken ferns and blackberry brambles. Where there is no brush, there are shoulder high wild grasses and weeds. In the spring and summer, there are glimpses of bright color dotted in and out of the undercover, placed like paint splashes in an impressionist's canvas, giving momentary brightness to the constant green and gold cover.

Confused, that is the Pacific Northwest natural milieu in a single word; as disorienting as the myriad web of rivers, streams and creeks splashing down from a glacial spawn of menacing, craggy peaks and angel-down mountains; and as undefined as the undulating landscape of rolling hills, sand dunes, towers of granite, valleys carved by relentless glaciers and slopes covered with rows of Douglas Fir and Western Red Cedar trees. The Pacific Northwest, despite the consistent shades of grey and white cloud-filled skies, is still full of its own variety of color; color that has a mood, a moment and manner which can represent a regional originality: a dirty, dingy, oyster Depoe Bay grey, the deep brown of stagnant Skagit Flat sludge, a hypnotic blanket of Willipa Hills green, a dramatic yet mournful Quinault orange sky as the sun sets quietly in the flat, steel-blue Pacific. Yet, on those marvelous, rare and beautiful days when the sky is as clear as a newly mined blue sapphire and the sun is as yellow as polished gold; on those days, the color of the Northwest can only be described in terms of emotion; an incomparable feeling of joy that nowhere else in the world could life by quite as pleasant and good and right.

The seasons are present in the familiar circle of progression but with a difference that is linked to the climate; there is a recalcitrant spring, a lingering summer, a resplendent autumn and a dismal winter. They hold none of the normal sharp divisions that might characterize other northern regions; they are blurred into one another by the temperance of ocean currents sweeping over from Japan and a persistent tropical weather pattern, called the "pineapple express," blowing north from Hawaii. There is also a lack of temperature extremes - no long, hot summers or bone-chilling winters reminiscent of continental climates as the Southern or Northeastern regions of the United States. The Pacific Northwest has its genesis in the relentless kinetic energy whirling out of the wide eastern expanse of the boundless Pacific (though the weather almost always comes from the west) to blow with an abandoned freedom across the unfathomable green sea of landscape in cloud-whorls of moisture. The rain is the inspiration. Without its constant and humbling presence, the earth would not burst forth in such abundance. Trace the flow: the uncontrolled misty journey from sea level grey fogs to majestic white mountain heights, dropping back down through the glistening glaciers, crashing creeks and rushing rivers to return, once again, to the ocean source.

But description falls short. The Pacific Northwest defies precise definition. Despite numerous attempts, it exists, immune to certitude. Deep within the watery mist, under a forest of anonymity, its true nature remains hidden. It is more a feeling than a fact, a sense that is no normal sense, a place that is no ordinary place. It is a culmination of all the unique sensations that this land has to offer. There is an essence of every region within its murky boundaries, and although this deprives it of a complete homogeneity, the compensation is a subtle mystery which gives neither hint nor clue to the secret and is there, finally, only to be experienced.

It is, perhaps, ironic then, that this hidden corner of America should serve as the unlikely backdrop for the story of a man living outside the law, a "bad man" against good men, an uncivilized individual fighting encroaching civilization during a time when those men who answered to no one and came to be known as "Outlaws" or "Banditos" or "Desperados." Men such as these have figured prominently in the lore of his era of American history and, even today, they still command the public's imagination and attention. Harry Tracy was perhaps, the boldest and "badest" outlaw of them all. The all-out search to hunt him down became one of the most desperate manhunts of the times and when it ended, it likely signaled the end of the era. While this manhunt would seem to be more a part of the action-packed heritage of the Rocky Mountain mining country or the cattle ranches of the arid Wyoming plains, this drama of legendary proportions was played out in the sparsely settled forested areas of Washington and Oregon during the second year of the new century, 1902, and despite what would appear to be a distraction from the events that happened, the Pacific Northwest countryside was not a hindrance to the events, was not even a passive backdrop to the drama as it unfolded, it was, instead, a major character in the play, in many ways an accomplice in the outlaw's depredations. For it was only in the thick vegetation of the Pacific Northwest landscape, that Harry Tracy could have carried out his incredible two month march toward escape with such style and ease.

Largely on foot, he repeatedly slipped through the cordons of hundreds of lawmen and posse members using the natural growth as ally to such an extent that the efforts of his pursuers seemed at times hopelessly futile and at other times even farcical. It was as if man, Harry Tracy, had inadvertently found a land that could combine forces with his natural abilities to help him avoid escape. He was able to walk into a farmhouse or cabin, demand a sit-down meal, casually change his clothing, supplement his ammunition and weapon arsenal and disappear into the woods before a posse could be notified with enough time to track him down.

As wild and unkempt as the countryside still is today, it was so much more so in 1902. It was a veritable wilderness to the settlers who had made the difficult choice to try to scratch out a living among the trees. The small towns and scattered farms seemed but a temporary mark upon the vastness of the sprawling and towering forest. To the men who were sent out in this impenetrable thicket to find Harry Tracy, the ever-present canopy of tall trees and low clouds were as foreboding as the outlaw himself. Within this sinister fold was concealed their worst nightmare, a man with no fear of any man or any kind of gunplay, a man who had killed men in his past as an outlaw in the famed Hole In The Wall Gang in the Wyoming-Colorado border country, a man who had systematically shot and killed three prison guards while escaping from the Oregon State Penitentiary in Salem and a man who was determined to let no one stand in his path to freedom. He inspired mortal fear by the mere mention of his name. So great was the effect of this match of man and the elements that shielded him upon the nascent population of the Pacific Northwest that for years after children would whisper the name, "Harry Tracy," in their play with each other to foster screams of fright.

The Pacific Northwest and Harry Tracy proved a pair to be to be reckoned with. It was not until Tracy had passed out of his western fir fortress across the imposing peaks of the Cascade Mountains and down into broad, high desert of the Eastern Washington plains that the seeming magic was broken. When Harry Tracy took to the flat land and sparse landscape to speed his escape, he imagined himself to be on the verge of freedom; instead, he had only hastened his meeting with destiny.

Chapter 1:

First Encounter

Harry Tracy was first introduced to the Pacific Northwest region where the final dramatic episode of his life would take place early in 1896. At twenty-five he had already established a trail of criminal activities, including everything from petty thievery to murder, which stretched from Illinois to Colorado. In the tri-state area of Wyoming, Utah and Colorado he had fallen in with the Hole-In-The-Wall Gang otherwise known as "The Wild Bunch." In his first short stay at the outlaw stronghold in a hidden valley in the vast wilderness in the Green River area, he had had contact with such outlaw luminaries of the time as Butch Cassidy, Kid Curry, Elza Lay, Ben Kilpatrick and Harry Longabaugh (AKA The Sundance Kid). Tracy had also participated in various cattle raids, train robberies and other illegal activities of the group until he ran into a lawman in Utah who put him in prison.

After a short term at the Utah State Penitentiary, he migrated to the Pacific Northwest with the hope of making an honest living. He realized that the days of outlaws committing crimes with impunity were over. But having grown up in the seamy backstreets, bars and brothels of the "Tenderloin" Districts of large Midwestern cities, he was heavily schooled in the knowledge of best methods to exploit human weaknesses and it was this previous experience rather than his good intentions that was to mark his life in this recently populated region of the country.

Harry Tracy was of medium height, lean and in extremely good shape from his years of outdoor living. As a young man recently released from the rigors of harsh prison routine, the fresh atmosphere of booming Seattle, Washington seemed just far enough away and had just enough potential for success to satisfy his hope for the future. Like so many young men who inhabited the western United States at that time, he was ambitious. He thought he would only have to be in the right place at the right time to make his fortune. But Tracy was more determined and sure of himself than most because he had previously experienced the fast life of an outlaw.

Harry Tracy was possessed with the demon of ex-convict frustrations: the inability to see beyond his own past punishment and misery. Yet, revenge upon an unfeeling world was not what he had in mind. He wanted certain amenities from life, felt that his boldness and intelligence deserved those amenities, and imagined that no one or nothing could stop him if he pleased to take them rather than earn them. However, despite inherent ruthlessness, he was not wantonly cruel. He did not go out of his way to harm people and considered such behavior despicable. He responded to women with a kind of frontier knight-errant fealty, perhaps because of his ignorance of the fair sex or out of his lack of contact with them. The opposite nature of this near-chivalry versus overt ruthlessness seemed a direct contradiction of character, but one that was consistent with his set of criminal values.

Women were attracted to Harry Tracy. At 5'8" he wasn't

exceptionally tall, but his leanness made him look taller. He was not what could be described as classically handsome, his rawboned cheeks and ruddy outdoor complexion making him seem rough and rugged. However, his thick, sandy hair tinged with a hint of red and his piercing grey-blue eyes, at once both cold and warm, made him attractive in a wild and adventurous way. Coupled with this facial magnetism, was his wiry tightly-coiled body, slim yet sinuously powerful - as if every muscle was charged with abundant energy. His appearance alone was enough to attract the feminine eye, but his polite manners and ready wit made him an exceptional man - especially in the rough bars and dance halls of the Seattle "Tenderloin" District.

Seattle was a city in its infancy. Although it had grown into the most important city in the Puget Sound area, it still only had a population of around 40,000 citizens. The economic recession that had followed the panic of 1893 had hit the Pacific Northwest with particular impact. The one major event that was positive since the panic was the arrival of the Great Northern Railway in 1893 giving the city a railroad terminal and putting on the same footing as the city of Tacoma which had been chosen as the terminus for the Northern Pacific Railway. The Great Northern was the dream of the so-called "Empire Builder," James J. Hill who had put together a transcontinental railway system in a combination of deal-making and visionary opportunism.

Dress was always a matter of convenience, or rather inconvenience, for Tracy. He wore what it took to blend into his surroundings. A conservative blue sackcloth suit (three piece), a worn, grey, homburg-style hat and heavy, all-purpose black logging boots melted him nicely into the turn-of-the-century Seattle street crowds. Somewhere in his travels, he had dropped his real surname, Severns, and had adopted the simpler and more brutal name, Tracy. It was an apt choice. The name, "Tracy" was as lean and cruel and tough as he imagined himself to be. Upon his arrival in Seattle, however, he returned to his given name of Severns - the one he had been born with in his hometown of Minong, Wisconsin – hoping to escape his outlaw past.

It did not take Tracy-Severns long to settle into a pattern of living. He rented a small room at a 1st Avenue hotel near the center of town and for one of the few times in his life he set out to find legitimate employment. In the labor-hungry Seattle boom economy, it did not take much time for the strong and quick-witted young man: he was hired as a student fireman on the Northern Pacific Railroad. He was determined to make an effort at earning a living by honest means. Not being wanted or known in the Pacific Northwest, if there was ever a chance that he could start his life anew, this was it. His life in Colorado as an outlaw had been exciting and full of monetary rewards, but it was hard going and held little in the way of safety or material comfort. A good railroad job, stable and secure, seemed to be just the thing he needed at the time.

The reason this undisciplined young man could accept the daily routine and physical toil of railroad labor was the result of one nightmarish experience; the short term he had served in prison. The level of cruelty meted out in the name of justice by guards was of such a desperate nature that made him determined not to do anything that might cause him to be returned to prison again. To be locked up for years at a time and be at the mercy and whim of such arbitrary men in order to keep living, was more than his rebellious and free-spirited nature could endure.

Even with all of his good intentions and fearful memories, Tracy could not deny himself the pleasure of nightly outings to Seattle's "Red Light" District south of Yesler Street. Even in those days before the Yukon Gold Rush of 1897 that would turn Seattle into a boomtown, the nightlife in the "Skid Road" District of Seattle was well established. In his book about Seattle, *Skid Road*, Northwest author Murray Morgan outlined the origin of the term "Skid Road." It was the name used for the road, Yesler Street, down which local timber literally skidded into Puget Sound from the forested hills above the city. The name "Skid Road" eventually came to be used as a term for the down and out sections of other cities and towns in turn of the century America.

The "Skid Road' area of Seattle was the section of the city now known as Pioneer Square. Originally it had been owned by "Doc" Maynard. He in turn handed over some of his land to the irascible Henry Yesler who built the steam-powered saw mill that contributed heavily to the city's early success. Maynard and Yesler favored a wide-open town with gambling parlors, dance halls and houses of prostitution to attract the rough-hewn fishermen, loggers and bachelor farmers who had arrived to make their fortune on America's far coast.

The city of Seattle was divided into two camps: the original pioneers, the conservative church-going faction led by the Denny Party who were generally tea-totalers, serious and tight with their money, and the boom-towners who were there to make money first, have fun second and devil-take-the-hindmost. There was a constant struggle between the two groups as to who had control of the direction of the city in its early days.

Harry Tracy's tastes did not lean toward gambling and alcohol, both of which were in good supply. In fact, his outlook toward drinking was almost puritanical. As a result of a week-long binge in Utah, he had let himself reach such a low level of physical condition that he had been arrested and sent to prison at the state penitentiary before the effects of his alcoholic stupor had worn off. He blamed this misfortune on the debilitating effects of drinking and swore never again to let it have control over him.

Tracy could not, however, stay away from the women of the dance halls. Having grown up in similar environment, he knew how to treat the dance hall girls and prostitutes and how to impress them. It was, nevertheless, no easy matter to achieve his desires. The worldly-wise girls were not satisfied with mere attention. They demanded gifts which could not be supplied by the paltry wage of a student fireman.

The thought of being deprived of female companionship outweighed Tracy's fear of capture and prison. To finance his amorous adventures, he began prowling the hotels at night to relieve the more prosperous guests of a portion of their wealth. His previous outlaw life had taught him not to be too greedy. He tried to spread out his criminal efforts so that he would not arouse excessive suspicion.

The Seattle Police Department had received a number of complaints about thefts from irate visitors to the city so they sent a detective to investigate. The man assigned to the case was King County Deputy Sheriff Jack Williams. A family man and a diligent worker, Williams was chosen because of his close association with businesses and people in the "Skid Road" area. His brother, Jon Williams, owned the Alhambra Saloon and Dance Hall and he could provide valuable information regarding strangers who were spending large sums of money.

Deputy Williams received almost immediate reports from his brother that a man calling himself Tom Bliss had been frequenting various saloons and was heaping both attention and lavish gifts upon his favorite girls. Bliss was described as "quite a sport," a man who dressed conservatively, drank little and spoke with a bold tongue. After several fruitless nights of searching through saloons and dance halls for Tom Bliss, Williams decided to concentrate his efforts on the railroad station. The hotel guests who had been victimized were all newly arrived in town and vulnerable to a sharp criminal's predatory eyes. Someone who watched disembarking railroad passengers could easily pick out a wealthy mark for his evening's prowls.

Williams set up an observation post behind the baggage wagon at the Northern Pacific Station and spent hours looking over the crowd. After a few weeks, he began to notice a smiling, sandy-haired young man who periodically took the 1st Avenue streetcar to and from the railroad station and downtown hotels. The young man always stepped off the car and walked around the station, smiling and tipping his grey hat to the ladies. When the streetcar reloaded, he would board once again and would ride back to the hotel area.

Williams' suspicions were aroused. He decided to the press the investigation to discover the young man's name. It did not take long to discover that suspect's name was Harry Severns, a student fireman living at a hotel where several of the burglaries had taken place. Severns' description matched the one given by Williams' brother of the man who called himself Tom Bliss. Convinced that Severns/Bliss was in fact the room prowler but without enough direct evidence to prove the assertion, Deputy Williams turned over his information to Seattle Police Chief, Charles Reed.

Police Chief Reed was a man who did not want to waste either time or money trying to prove a burglary case against a young, unknown criminal. He preferred a more direct, if less than legal method of keeping the peace. Severns was brought to the police station and told by Reed, in no uncertain terms, to leave town immediately, if he knew what was good for him. Severns replied with the arrogant retort, "I'll leave town when I'm good and ready." Without sufficient evidence Reed could go no further, but he warned Severns that if the burglaries continued, he would be forced to have him arrested.

The case was filed away and soon forgotten. Chief Reed had more important things to worry about than another case of a Skid Road hotel prowler. Seattle was a wide-open town in those days and Reed preferred to keep it that way as long as the situation did not get out of hand.

Later that summer, there was an incident which rekindled Reed's interest in Harry Severns. A pack peddler, a Jewish man by the name of "Old Tom," was robbed of jewels and valuables and was murdered out in the Seattle suburbs. A clerk at a 1st Avenue hotel told police that a stranger who had been occupying one of the rooms had tried to sell him some expensive jewelry the next night after the murder. The same stranger had packed up and left town the next day, complaining that his room had been ransacked and burglarized while he was asleep.

Deputy Williams was asked to rejoin the investigation because of his familiarity with Severns, but when he went to question the young man, he discovered that his suspect had fled town.

The Seattle Police Department was ready to accuse Severns of the crime of murder. Williams had another theory. He guessed that Severns had unknowingly burglarized the room of the pack peddler's murderer and when he discovered the jewels, had decided to take the first train out of the city in order to avoid being implicated. A police bulletin was sent out seeking Harry Severns for questioning, but it was lost in crush of more serious matters in a matter of a few weeks.

Williams, however, did not forget his encounter with Harry Severns. There was something in the young man's manner that made the deputy take notice; maybe it was the bold and unconcerned attitude, the air of invulnerability which Severns had shown during process of the investigation or maybe it was just a good lawman's hunch about a difficult and dangerous person. Whatever the reason, Williams filed Severns' appearance in his memory and a year later when Severns-Bliss-Tracy had been sentenced to a term in the Utah State Penitentiary, he nodded his head in appreciation for the efforts of the authorities there.

For the moment Harry Tracy was out of his jurisdiction and out of his hair. There would only be a short sojourn of six years until Deputy Sheriff Williams and Harry Tracy would cross paths again and when they did, it would be under more desperate circumstances.

Chapter 2:
The Outlaw Trail

In the late 1800s, as more and more settlers arrived in the Colorado, Wyoming and Utah region, scattered towns and cattle ranches sprang up along the foothills of the Rocky Mountains. The area was good range land for raising cattle and other livestock with rivers draining the mountain snow melt, but the terrain was rugged and the vegetation, while available, was sparse in areas away from the river canyons. As a result, ranches were widely spread out and animals were allowed to roam free. There were many opportunities to "exchange" ownership of these animals by branding strays and by "rebranding" the unguarded, leading to constant and sometimes violent arguments about whose stock was whose. Intermittent feuds and out and out wars sometimes flared as these disputes grew. Some of the hands hired as cowboys for these ranches saw a better opportunity in rounding up the scattered cattle and horses and setting up their own independent operations. They soon became known as outlaws and in order to avoid capture, they began to search out and find places to hide in the time between their cattle roundups. The ranchland had a number of natural rock formations that combined with the steep river gorges to create hidden ravines and valleys that were virtually impenetrable to any others than those who knew safe passages to the protected areas that became "hideouts."

Once the cowboys had become recognized as "outlaws," they

drifted to a life of crime that expanded to activities like holdups and robberies. The outlaws formed into groups, or gangs, in order to be better able to execute the bigger and more complex crimes focused on mines, stagecoaches, trains and banks. The gangs were loose associations with minimal leadership which contained members that came and went with their own individual whims and plans. "The Wild Bunch" of Butch Cassidy, the "Curry Gang" led by Kid Curry, and "Black Jack" Ketchum were among the most well-known of these groups. Over time, the hide-outs gradually became complete living areas with cabins, livery barns and livestock to maintain the outlaws between forays out into the civilized world to obtain their ill-gotten gains.

"The Outlaw Trail," as it came to be known, ran from Mexico to Canada along the base of the Rocky Mountains. An careful examination of the lives of most western outlaws most likely would reveal a lifestyle that included night-riding, scattered meals, close pursuits by posses, poorly treated wounds, tenuous relationships, and intermittent economic deprivation. They were usually broke or in hiding, unable to spend the money they had stolen. There was little glamour in their daily lives. They experienced difficult family situations, long periods of time on the trail, and a fear of treachery with the knowledge that, regardless of the cause, they were outlaws and that anytime they might be betrayed for the price of reward money placed on their capture, or, very often, a sudden death. Yet it was reported that these cowboy outlaws often acted as gentlemen. Outgoing and friendly, they posed little threat to the average citizen.

By the selection of large targets for robbery, they maintained identification with the common people while becoming hated enemies of big businesses. Outlaws were products of their times and gained, if not the respect, at least the tolerance of their ordinary citizens.

The area surrounding the Colorado, Green and Dirty Devil Rivers was one of the wildest stretches of land in the West and it was crisscrossed with steep-walled canyons and hidden draws. The three most advantageous places in the rugged area were Robber's Roost, Brown's Park and Hole-in-the-Wall. The hideouts stretched out over two hundred miles, more or less in a north and south line.

Robber's Roost was the southern most of the three strongholds, located in southeastern Utah. It was in this place that Butch Cassidy and Elza Lay first formed their gang which would come to be known as "The Wild Bunch." It was remote, rugged and virtually impossible to navigate without prior knowledge. It never was successfully penetrated by lawmen.

The Hole-in-the-Wall was literally a "hole" or small opening in the red stone cliffs of central Wyoming that led to a fertile valley. The opening was the only entry from the east and was easily defended by even a small group of armed men. From 1880 on it was used as a safe hideout for a loosely associated group of men who operated outside the law. Initially, it was a place to hide rustled cattle during raids on local ranches. As time went by, a number of gangs located there, drawn by the unchallenged safety provided by the area.

The gangs formed a coalition, each planning and carrying out its own robberies with very little interaction with the other gangs. At times, members of one gang would ride along with other gangs, but usually each gang operated separately, meeting up only when they were each at the hideout at the same time.

The "Hole" had all the advantages needed for a gang attempting to evade chasing posses or authorities attempting an arrest: it was easy to defend and impossible for lawmen to access without detection. Each individual gang supplied its own food and had its own herd of cattle and horses. A corral, a livery stable, and a number of buildings were constructed over time. Each gang had their own cabin or group of cabins. Anyone operating out of the "Hole" had to adhere to certain rules of the camp which included a method of settling disputes with other gang members, a pledge to never steal from another gang's supplies and a promise not to take another gang's livestock. There was no overall leader, with each gang answering only to themselves.

Gang members, who came and went each to their own whim, included such infamous outlaws as Butch Cassidy, Harry Longabaugh (The Sundance Kid), Kid Curry, "Flat Nose" Curry, Sam Carey, "Black Jack" Ketchum, and Harry Tracy. No lawman or posse ever successfully entered Hole-in-the-Wall to capture outlaws during its more than fifty years of active existence.

Brown's Park was a mountain valley along the Green River in the border country of Moffat County, Colorado and Daggett County, Utah. It was an isolated valley that began in far eastern

Utah, approximately 25 miles downstream from Flaming Gorge that followed the river into Colorado ending at the imposing Gates of Ladore. The power of the river had cut out a canyon thirty miles long and five miles wide. Encircled by mountains and surrounded by desert, the only access was from the north and south on steep, rocky trails. These trails limited travel and offered early warning of impending intruders. While the landscape was rough, it was still suitable for cattle with ample feed, a mild climate and plenty of water. Brown's Park was the largest of the hideout areas and many of the outlaws preferred it as a long term location for hiding from the law. Because of this, there was frequent interaction between the outlaws and the local farmers and ranchers.

There were few settlers in the area, and those who operated farms and ranches were most often Mormons (Butch Cassidy, Matt Warner, David Lant, Wilbur Meeks and roughly one third of the outlaws who operated in the area were descended from Mormon families). The Mormon ranchers were encouraged by their spiritual leader, Brigham Young, to pursue an agrarian lifestyle and, in doing so, spread out from Salt Lake City to acquire land. Mormons, for the most part, abhorred violence and crime, yet many of them were on friendly terms with the outlaws. An explanation for this was the area's economic situation in the late 1800s. Mormons had long been outcasts - socially, politically, and economically - and in the late nineteenth century they had suffered severe persecutions at the hand of the government over their practice of polygamy. Mormons felt resentment and distrust toward outside interests, whether

government or big business. They had little use for the strictures of
normal law at that time but instead relied upon their Mormon faith
and the precepts of the Church of Latter Day Saints to guide their
path. They adopted a "laissez-faire" attitude toward the outlaw
gangs who flocked there for protection against authorities. The
only exception was the crime of murder; there was no sanction for
this unforgivable crime for the pious Mormons.

The focal point in the isolated valley of Brown's Park was the
Jarvie Ranch. It was established in 1880 by John Jarvie who had
emigrated from Scotland. He married a woman known locally as
"Pretty Little Nell' and the two set about running a farm and raising
a family in the Brown's Park area. Jarvie became the shopkeeper of
a general store, the postmaster and operator of the only ferry that
crossed the nearby Green River.

His store, the Jarvie Trading Post, was the only general store
within seventy miles. The trading post was the main meeting place
and source of goods for those who lived in the remote location. He
sold nearly everything required for survival in that harsh land
including Indian flour, saddles, boots, wagon supplies, clothing and
canned food; he even had a pile of teepee poles for the Indians
stacked outside the building. Liquor was available and it was a
popular item for the outlaw gangs who were in a mood to celebrate.

Inhabitants of the area were inclined to turn their heads and
mind their own business when it came to the loose accumulation of
shady characters that had gathered and had occupied cabins in the
isolated area. The outlaws appreciated the relative safety provided

by nature and the open attitude of the settlers.

In 1895, in a gesture of appreciation, the outlaws decided to repay their neighbors for their principle of coexistence by holding a special Thanksgiving dinner that became a legend. According to Ann Basset, born, along with her sister Josie, in the Brown's Park area to one of the more prominent ranchers, a girlfriend to more than one of the outlaws and the so-called "Queen of the Cattle Rustlers," the Thanksgiving banquet was the only truly formal affair ever held in Brown's Park. Billie Bender, Les Megs, Butch Cassidy, Elza Lay, Isom Dart (one of several black cowboys to join the outlaw gangs), the Sundance Kid and several others in the gang (including possibly Harry Tracy who was known to be in the area at the time) "put on a spread" that would become known forever after as "The Outlaws' Thanksgiving Dinner."

Since it was billed as an "elegant occasion" men wore dark suits, vests, starched collars and bow ties while the ladies wore long tight-fitting dresses with puffed sleeves and high collars over taffeta petticoats and taffeta underwear that supported lacey silk and cotton lisle stockings that were fragile, precious ($3.00 per pair) and worn only at parties.

The dinner was held at the Davenport Ranch on Willow Creek. The best silver, linens and dishes had been provided by the Brown's Park rancher's wives and one of the Basset sisters provided a silver candelabra. The guests were received at the door by Les Megs, Billie Bender and Elza Lay. Butch Cassidy and the Sundance Kid, dressed in white butcher's aprons, waited on tables.

While Isom Dart, as chief cook, wore a tall chef's hat as he directed the activities in the kitchen.

The guests were varied and included many immigrants from such faraway countries as Scotland, England, Ireland, Austria, Sweden, Yugoslavia, Wales, England, Mexico, Italy and Germany.

There was a entertainment program to mark the occasion. The invocation was given by John Jarvie from his position at the head of the long table. This was followed by the performing of "Then You'll Remember Me" and "Last Rose of Summer" by two local singers accompanied by Jarvis on the accordion. Josie Basset played "The Cattle Song" on her fiddle accompanied by an additional fiddle and a guitar. Ann Basset gave a short reading on the "meaning of Thanksgiving."

After all the guests were in their seats, Jarvie asked for a blessing and dinner was served. The meal included blue point oysters, roast turkey with chestnut dressing, giblet gravy, cranberries, mashed potatoes, candied sweet potatoes, creamed peas, celery, olives, pickled walnuts, sweet pickles, fresh tomatoes on crisp lettuce, hot rolls and sweet butter followed by coffee with whipped cream, Roquefort cheese, pumpkin pie, plum pudding with brandy sauce, mints and salted nuts.

Butch Cassidy was uncomfortable with the job of pouring coffee according to Ann Basset.

"Poor Butch, he could perform such minor jobs as robbing banks and holding up pay trains without the flicker of an eyelash, but serving coffee at a grand party - that was something else. He became panicky and his nerve was shot to bits. He became frustrated and embarrassed over the blunder he made when he was told that it was not good form to pour coffee from a big black coffee pot and reach from right to left across a guests plate to grab a cup."

The dinner party lasted almost six hours after which the group adjourned to dance. They danced all night long until the sun came up the next day. No one, neither citizen nor outlaw, ever forgot the party.

******

In early 1898 an event took place which changed the atmosphere at Brown's Park. "Speck" Williams, who operated the Jarvis' Ferry was asked to look after the seventeen year old son of a local rancher, while he went to the Trading Post for supplies. The young man, Willie Strang, soon grew tired waiting on the banks of the river and joined another young man named Pat Johnson who was working as a ranch hand at the Valentine Hoy ranch on upper Red Creek. Willie spent the night drinking with other cowboys on the ranch: Pat Johnson, "Judge" Bennett (so nicknamed for portraying a judge at a mock trial for a doctor who arrived too late to save a wounded outlaw), Charley Teeters and Bill Pigeon. Throughout the night, the men laughed and talked and played jokes on one another. In the spirit of the party, Willie reportedly pulled a chair from under Pat Johnson, early the next morning. Johnson was nursing a hangover and was not in the same jocular mood as he was the night before. As Willie ran out the door after the prank, Johnson pulled his pistol and shot the boy in the back.

The Blairs, Hoy's in-laws, heard the shot and ran to the window of their upstairs' room. Mrs. Blair saw the young man stretched out in the snow. Willie Strang was dead from the gunshot. Johnson had violated the one unforgivable law of Brown's Park: commit no murder.

Johnson, accompanied by Bennett, took horses from the Hoy ranch and immediately left for Powder Springs. There they met Dave Lant and Harry Tracy who had recently escaped from the Utah State Penitentiary. Since all were now wanted, they joined forces and headed for Robber's Roost, the outlaw stronghold to the south.

Bennett separated from the other three men in order to pick up supplies and they arranged to meet later near Douglas Mountain.

Sheriff Neiman and Deputy Ethan Allen Farnham of Routt County, Colorado, arrived in Brown's Park on a separate issue; they had come to arrest Bennett and Johnson for some other illegal activities which had taken place in Colorado. Learning of the Strang killing, they quickly formed a posse of Brown's Park men including Eb Bassett (the father of Ann and Josie), Valentine Hoy, Jim McKnight, Joe Davenport, Longhorn Thompson, and Bill Pigeon and the manhunt began.

The posse tracked the fugitives to a camp where they had hastily left horses, blankets, and food. Sheriff Neiman reasoned that the outlaws would not last long without any supplies during the freezing March night. The posse gathered up the abandoned gear and headed to the Bassett ranch for the evening.

The following day the posse approached the apparently-trapped outlaws. Valentine Hoy was in the lead. Two shots rang out and he slumped to the ground. Within seconds, the snow surrounding his body was crimson and he lay dead on the frozen ground. Unfortunately for Bennett, he arrived on the scene with the supplies just after the shooting. He dismounted, fed his horse some oats, walked to a knoll, and "discharged his six shooter three times, waited a few moments as if for an answer to his signal and fired his rifle once." Instead of the four men from Powder Springs which he had hoped to meet, he was captured by Eb Bassett and Boyd Vaughn, taken to the Bassett ranch, and put under guard by Deputy Farnham.

The next day, after the posse left to retrieve Hoy's body, McKnight's small son, Crawford, cried out, "Mommy, look at the funny men!" A small party of seven men with hastily manufactured masks had ridden up to the ranch. Vigilantes had formed in order to take vengeance on Hoy's killers. They found Farnham and Bennett and demanded that Farnham turn over the outlaw to them. They took Bennett to the coral where he guessed his fate. He begged for his life, promising to reveal the real killer if he was allowed to live.

The Hoy corral had posts framing the gate. They reached a height of about twelve feet and were tied together at the top by a cross member consisting of a substantial pine pole. Bennett was destined to hang from the crossbar for the murder.

An article written in "Steamboat Magazine" gave this account from one of the posse members:

"They stood him up in a springboard buggy, put the noose around his neck and when they were all ready, pulled the wagon out from under him and let him hang. The drop was too short to break Bennett's neck and for three or four minutes he danced a lively jig in midair, gyrating and pirouetting grotesquely. Then . . . there was one less trouble-maker in Brown's Park."

Sometime later, a poem was found in Bennett's pocket. It had been written by fellow outlaw Dave Lant and described his escape from the Utah penitentiary.

"We left the Salt Lake pen
As the sun was setting low;
And walked along the railroad track
Until our legs refused to go.
But we reached Park City early
Where the morning sunbeams lit
On our striped pantaloons
Where a happy party sit.
Its there we took our refuge
And watched the brave policemen
While around us they did tear.
Its there we ate our lunches
And our weary limbs did rest
Until the sinking was sinking
In the far and distant west.

When we started on our journey

From our home we call the wall;

Where very few detectives

E're dare to make their call."

The killing of Hoy brought men from three states pouring into Brown's Park to join the manhunt. The Colorado group was led by Neiman and Farnham. The posse from Vernal, Utah, was under the direction of Sheriff Preece while the men from Sweetwater County, Wyoming, followed Deputy Sheriffs Peter Swanson and William Laney.

The Rock Springs newspaper forecast "there is no doubt that the murderers will be shot or lynched as soon as captured."

It did not take long, however, for the freezing, starving outlaws to give themselves up. Their feet were bare and bloody. They had had to kill a colt for food.

A member of the posse offered this account: "Johnson was the first to throw his hands up then Lant did likewise, but Tracy made him pull them down again under a threat of killing him right there. Shortly afterward, however, both gave themselves up."

A hearing was conducted by Justice J.S. Hoy, brother of the murdered Valentine, in the Bassett living room. Johnson was taken to Rock Springs and Tracy and Lant were taken to the Routt County jail at Hahn's Peak.

The governors of the three states met in Salt Lake City to congratulate themselves for the joint effort at law enforcement and to formulate plans for future action against other outlaw gangs. During the conference, a message was received from the outlaws at Brown's Park addressed to the governors. As Governor Adams put it, they "intimated they were ready for us and we could not surprise them."

During his incarceration, Tracy wrote a poem, which he gave to Sheriff Charley Nieman. It was kept in his possession and was later released by his widow. It bears a striking resemblance to the poem supposedly written by Dave Lant that was found in the pocket of the hanged Bennett, giving supposition to the possibility that Tracy had also written the first peom.

> "But we struck Park City early when the Morning
> sunbeams lit
> On our striped pantaloons where the happy party sit
> It's there we took to refuge in some jungles which stood
> thear
> And watched the brave policemen while around us they
> did tear.
> It's there we ate our lunches and weary limbs did rest
> Until the sun was sinking in the far and distant West.
> When we started on our journey for our home they call the
> wall
> Where very few detectives ever dare to call.
> For their we have no sheep to hear and corn we
> not hoe

And for other kind of labor old sheats is rather slow.

Joe Bush is also harmless with his double barreled gun

For when he came to Powder Springs he was prepared to
run.

He is out for notoriety and not atal for gain.

He may arrest a school boy or pull a hobo from a
train.

We claim to no poets but the truth we will plainly
tell

Of those two brave detectives who have by the
wayside fell.

Now just one word to cite some who for protection
cry

Just vote for braver officers when the swallows
homeward fly.

      Yours with Kind Love and Best Wishes

      Harry Tracy"

On March 24, 1898, Dave Lant broke through the wall separating his cell from Harry Tracy's cell. The Sheriff had briefly left the jail in order to get breakfast. When Sheriff Nieman returned with the food and opened the cell door, Tracy clubbed him over the head, took his keys and locked him the now vacated cell. The two outlaws then made their escape. They had taken the keys with them, so it was sometime before the jail lock was pried off and the Sheriff was released from the cell. He immediately pursued the escapees and succeeded in capturing them in short order a few miles south of Steamboat Springs.

J.S. Hoy wrote a letter of thanks to the people of Uintah County who helped so courageously to capture the murderers.

"Lant and Tracy surprised Sheriff Neiman in the Hahn's Peak jail, beat him into insensibility, robbed him, and fled. They were recaptured after a few hours of freedom as Neiman knew every escape and cut them off. Certain Routt County citizens, fearing the cost of an extensive trial in their county, urged that Lant and Tracy be sent back to Utah to finish their prison terms before the trial was held. However, popular sentiment favored a Routt County trial. The prisoners were moved from Hahn's Peak to the jail in Aspen since the cost of their incarceration there was only $2.00 per day instead of the $3.50 to $4 per day at Hahn's Peak."

Johnson was tried for the murder of Willie Strang and was freed by the jury citing self-defense.

Harry Tracy and Dave Lant were transferred to Aspen, and held in the Pitkin County jail, a more secure location, to wait for the next term of court in September. They did not wait to be tried. On June 22, 1898, they broke out of jail again. This time, in a bold bluff, Tracy found his way out of the maximum-security section of the jail with a wooden gun, which he had carved in his cell and covered with tinfoil. Dave Lant, as usual, followed him to freedom.

Short of money, they proceeded to the nearest town which was Breckenridge, Colorado. Once there they broke into a saloon and robbed $165.00 from John R. Etzler's craps table. Bartender

Theodore Stonacker chased them out before they could get into the safe. A week later on July 3, they robbed the saloon at Kokomo, fifteen miles from Breckenridge. There they netted $300. While in town they visited the home of George W. Steve, treasurer of the Odd Fellows Lodge and stole $460 from the lodge treasury.

Tracy told Lant that it was getting "too hot" for him in the Rocky Mountains; he was headed west. Lant, a Mormon, reportedly decided to leave behind the outlaw life, enlisted in the army, was cited for bravery in the Philippines, and lived out his life as a legitimate businessman in California.

Chapter 3:
The False Face Bandits

Sitting in a saloon after recently arriving in Portland, Oregon, Harry Tracy faced an uncertain future. At the bar across the room from his table, Tracy noticed a nervous young man with a fleshy face and beady eyes shuffling his feet against the bar rail while fingering the glass rim of a foamy glass of beer. He was dressed in a cheap brown sack cloth suit and wore a large diamond ring which stood out incongruously on his small, thick fingers. The nervous young man with the diamond ring was watching the progress of a poker game in another corner of the bar at a table with men obviously intent on the contents of their hands. After a short period of time, one of the players got up to leave. When he stood up, the nervous young man eagerly approached the table, flashing a pocket full of shiny dollars, and asked if he could join the game. The other men looked him over, sensed an easy mark and asked him to sit down..

Tracy followed the young man with interest. He surmised that he must be some kind of thief due to the contrast of his cheap clothes compared to the large bankroll and diamond ring. He watched the progress of the game and cut back his intake of whiskey from his table in the shadows at the back of the room. No one dared to sit within any proximity of him; his glowering presence was enough to keep any of the patrons away from his table.

A large sailor lunged from his chair at the poker table and stared straight down at the nervous young man who had just joined the game. He had been planning to join the game before being supplanted by the young man's approach. He did not appear to appreciate the newcomer's intrusion. Pulling his derby hat down over his eyes in an attempt to avoid the blazing glare of the large sailor, the nervous young man reached meekly for his pile of chips which were neatly stacked near the center of the table. The sailor was poised to strike when suddenly, in single, swift motion a knife flashed into the sailor's hand. Seeing the glint of the blade, the young man dropped his chips to the floor and jumped away from the chair. Slowly the sailor tracked the motion of the young man who was trying to back away from the threat. They had unknowingly intruded upon the space that Tracy was occupying. With seeming ease, Tracy rose, picked up a chair, swung it over his head and down onto the unprotected skull of the sailor. The sailor collapsed in a moan of pained dismay. He jerked his shoulder to the left and then was still. Tracy loosened his grip on the chair and it fell to the floor beside the unconscious sailor. It had been a brief altercation, but it served Tracy's purpose.

The nervous young man who had been rescued from the brink of disaster introduced himself as Dave Merrill. He offered his benefactor bewildered but heartfelt thanks.

Tracy did not acknowledge the man he had just saved but instead turned to the table full of astonished poker players as if ready to offer an explanation for his behavior. The men at the table did not wait for him to speak. They quickly gathered up what chips were left on the table and headed for the door. Tracy moved to the nearest chair and fell into it.

Dave Merrill invited his new acquaintance home for dinner with his family and Tracy nodded his acceptance. A new criminal partnership had begun.

******

During the next few years Harry Tracy and Dave Merrill participated in an unprecedented wave of criminal activity in the Portland, Oregon area. Throughout the late part of 1898 and the early part of 1899, the Portland newspapers were filled with accounts of robberies later attributed to them. They were nicknamed the "False Face Bandits" for the practice of wearing masks during their robberies in order to conceal their identity.

Their first crime was to hold up the 2nd Street trolley car at 2nd Street and College Street, taking the conductor's watch and relieving the passengers of their available cash and jewelry. The next robbery was at Dr. Plummer's Drug Store at 3rd and Madison. They bound and gagged the old doctor and stole his receipts and his pages of postage stamps.

They then staged a series of bold daylight robberies in the downtown area: they robbed Russell's Saloon and Magoo's Saloon of their days proceeds, they strode into the Jennings Saloon with guns drawn demanding all cash from the saloon and from the patrons. Then they moved down to Nueston's Saloon at 11th and Washington, Way's Butcher Shop at Front and Globe and Offner's

Grocery at 4th and Lincoln. They were a two person crime wave. Their method of operation was simple and brutal: they would brazenly walk in off the street in broad daylight and, in view of many bystanders and witnesses, steal as much as possible within a few minutes. It was not a plan to get rich, as no one carried much money with them into the saloons and businesses during the afternoon, but it was safe for the perpetrators and it held little chance of failure. As Harry Tracy had learned in years of outlaw activity, it was better to steal a little regularly rather than large amounts all at once. It attracted less attention from the police and, in such manner, a man could live comfortably off the proceeds of his labors without the ever-present fear of jail..

Despite the somewhat limited scope of their robberies, the wave was unprecedented for Portland, which was still very much a small town with almost all law-abiding citizens - not at all like Seattle with its boom economy from the Klondike Gold Rush and the criminal element that accompanied it. Soon every shop owner and saloon proprietor kept a loaded shotgun near his side during the hours his business was open. The police quietly began investigations in the small "Tenderloin" district of the city in order to see if criminals were attempting to convert stolen jewelry into cash.

Dave Merrill, not believing his luck, was trying to press Tracy into increasing the frequency of the robberies. He was a small time thief and sometime con artist who had never met a man quite like Harry Tracy. The outlaw seemed to show no fear and he could inspire acquiescence in his victims by merely staring them down. He could handle firearms like they were extensions of his body. He was not afraid to use violence and intimidation but usually they were not necessary. With Tracy's bold nature and cunning intelligence, there seemed to Merrill to be no limit to what the partnership might accomplish.

David Merrill was born in Cowlitz County, Washington in 1875. When his father, Benjamin Merrill died in 1880, his mother moved the family to Vancouver, Washington and shortly thereafter, she married a man named Lem Robinson. Young Dave grew up with a bad reputation around town. His stepfather had no use for his wayward ways and, in return, the boy had no affection for him. Dave Merrill was described by other locals as "a tough case." His schoolmates described him as a bully. The boys who grew up with him often fell into fistfights caused by his taunts and boasts. When Lem Robinson's house was burned to the ground one night under suspicious circumstances, Vancouverites suspected that Dave Merrill had been the arsonist, but there was no proof that this was the case, so the matter was dropped. A stepbrother, James Robinson, remembered Dave as a boy who was always away from home at night and who was off running around the woods during the day when he supposed to be at school.

Mrs. Merrill-Robinson grew tired of Mr. Robinson and moved her family across Columbia River to Portland. She took with her Lem Robinson's daughter, Mollie Robinson. Mollie changed her name to Rose Merrill when Mrs. Merrill took back her old name.

She became a dance hall girl in the "Tenderloin" district of Portland but she was too innocent and shy to take to the wild life and gave up her job to live at home. Mrs. Merrill made her earn her keep by making her a virtual domestic servant. With the hope of further solidifying their partnership, Dave Merrill introduced Tracy to Rose hoping that since she was still young and pretty, that the outlaw would take a liking to her and would want to marry her. Some accounts say, he did in fact marry Rose Merrill. Tracy himself denied the union saying, "the girl ... in Portland is not my wife. I took pity on her. Her family is not treating her right."

******

As the crime wave pressed on, the pressure on the police grew stronger. Detectives were assigned permanently to find the two men who were terrorizing the city. Acting on an anonymous tip, Portland Police Department Detectives Cordano and Ford went to the Merrill household investigate reports that the family was holding and selling stolen merchandise and jewelry.

As they approached the house, Ford heard someone running out the back. A surprised Dave Merrill opened the back door to find himself staring into the barrel of Cordano's drawn revolver. He quickly slammed the door in Cordano's face, turned the key in the lock and ran back into the center of the house. Cordano wasted no time in breaking down the door. He met Ford coming the other way.

"Where's your man?" asked Ford.

"I don't see him," replied Cordano.

Additional city policemen arrived to cover all exits. The two detectives decided to make a thorough search of the house. Mrs. Merrill and her other son, Benjamin Jr., looked on nervously as they moved from room to room. She made no objection to the search but refused to unlock a spare bedroom claiming no one used it anymore.

"There's nothing to be seen there," said Benjamin nervously.

"If you don't open that door, we'll break it down," threatened Cordano.

Benjamin relented and opened the door to reveal a small room containing only a bed stand, a worn carpet and a bureau. As Cordano moved in the search the room, he saw a shoe sticking out of the bottom drawer of the bureau. Suspecting that this was Dave Merrill's hiding place, Cordano pulled out the top drawer of the bureau as a shield against his body. He drew his revolver and announced, "give up or you die right here."

"Throw up your hands," yelled Ford from the doorway of the room.

Dave Merrill sat quietly for a full minute inside the bottom bureau drawer tightly gripping his .44 caliber pistol and hoping that there might be chance that he had not been found. He finally resigned himself to the prospect that his situation was hopeless.

"I surrender," Merrill called out.

Cordano hastily disarmed his prisoner and placed cuffs on his hands behind his back.

"Don't take my son that way," pleaded Mrs. Merrill in tears.

"He is not a criminal."

Ford and Cordano smiled at each other. Dave Merrill had been known to them for years as local thief and Mrs. Merrill was known in the area as "Mother Merrill" the leading dealer in stolen merchandise. Evidence of the thefts was strewn about the house. Seeing that her crying would do no good, Mrs. Merrill motioned Detective Ford into the corner of the room and whispered a proposition. She wanted to know that if she provided information which would lead to the arrest of the other robber, would she collect the reward money.

Ford made no promises.

"Well, when you went into that room after Dave, I wouldn't have given a red cent for your life," she said.

In a few short additional sentences, she proceeded to tell Ford all about her son's partner, Harry Tracy.

As Dave Merrill was being led away, Benjamin Merrill expressed a concern that "my brother often told my mother and me that if we gave him (Tracy) away to the police that he would take our lives."

At the police station under questioning, Dave Merrill gave the impression that he thought Tracy had something to do with his capture and that he had broken the "honor among thieves" code that was supposed to help keep them safe. He proceeded to give the police enough information to lead them to believe that Tracy would visit the Merrill home on February 6. To keep the element of surprise, Merrill's arrest was not revealed to the newspapers.

On February 6, Detectives Ford, Cordano and Weiner took up positions inside of the Merrill home as planned. Late in the afternoon, Ford and Cordano left to get something to eat and Weiner was left alone. Without knocking Tracy walked into the Merrill house and found Weiner alone. Weiner recognized Tracy by the black Mackintosh he was reported to be wearing.

With great presence of mind, Weiner introduced himself as a friend of Dave Merrill's. Cautious conversation ensued with Weiner offering to buy Tracy a drink at the bar down the street. The detective hoped that his fellow officers would be on their way back from eating and would be able to arrest Tracy on the street. Tracy agreed to the suggestion but he was becoming increasingly suspicious.

Weiner and Tracy walked side by side down Market Street. At the corner of 4th and Market, Tracy stopped. His eyes were fixed upon a Southern Pacific passenger train as it slowly chugged its way along a track out of town.

Tracy calmly turned to Weiner and said, "See that train? Well, I guess I'll take it. So long."

As he broke into a run, Weiner shouted after him, "I guess you won't," and proceeded to draw his revolver hidden inside his coat.

Tracy, however, had drawn his revolver first. He quickly fired off two bullets which whizzed past Weiner's head. The detective returned fire but did not have a chance to take good aim. Tracy ran for the engine of the train and jumped aboard. Pointing his pistol at the engineer's head, he ordered the man to speed up.

A crowd gathered to see what the shooting was all about. One of the men in the crowd was a railroad worker who guessed what was going on. Without hesitation, he climbed onto one of the passenger cars and pulled the emergency brake. As the train began to lose power, Tracy ordered he engineer to either resume speed or lose his life. When the frightened engineer explained that control of the train was no longer in his hands, Tracy abandoned the hijack and jumped back into the street. By that time the entire neighborhood had been aroused.

Albert Way, the local butcher who had ironically been held up by Tracy and Merrill just a few weeks before, came running down Harrison Street with his shotgun loaded and ready. When Way saw the crowd pursuing a lone man and someone yelled to him that man they were pursuing had tried to shoot Detective Weiner, he joined the chase. Way caught a fleeting glimpse of the outlaw about one hundred feet in front of him. He stopped took aim and fired both barrels. Although his shot was slightly off the mark, one of pellets of buckshot struck a glancing blow off Tracy's forehead. Dazed, but not seriously hurt, Tracy ran into the nearest yard seeking shelter. Unfortunately for him, the property belonged to a Constable Wilkinson who was off duty at the time and who was in his yard watching the commotion. Tracy reeled back into the street still trying to regain his senses. He was immediately stopped by both Wilkinson and Detective Weiner who finally made the arrest.

The dramatic chase through the streets of Portland was not Tracy's last attempt to avoid the penitentiary walls. While at the courthouse jail awaiting sentencing after being convicted of robbery, he took one last desperate chance.

Jailer Ned Dougherty opened the outer cell door of the small courthouse jail one morning to find Harry Tracy pointing a pistol at his head. Where he procured the weapon was a mystery, but it was later thought that it had been smuggled in by Rose Merrill, a frequent visitor to Tracy's cell. Seeing the gun aimed in his direction, Dougherty dropped to his knees and pleaded, "It won't do you any good to kill me, Harry. I won't open the doors anyway. I won't." Tracy tried his best to convince the jailer that it would be better to open the doors than to die there on the floor, but the stubborn and foolhardy Dougherty refused to budge. When Tracy hesitated to pull the trigger, Dougherty jumped from the floor and ran for cover behind a wall. Tracy let the man escape because he realized that it would do him no good to kill the poor man while he was still locked up. He had taken a liking to the old fellow during his weeks of confinement and he did not want to harm him.

The ability to give a convincing bluff was one Harry Tracy's most potent weapons. Jailer Ned Dougherty was one of the few men to call his bluff. However, despite his fondness for old Ned, the outcome might have been different if Tracy's path had not been blocked by bars of steel.

As soon as Dougherty saw that he was reasonably safe, he yelled to Deputy Sheriff Jordon in a guard position outside the cell area.

"Tom, fire." he shouted.

Jordan wasted no time. He guessed that Tracy was trying to break free and fired two shots into the cell. Tracy returned fire and ducked down for cover behind his cot. As he moved to fire again, he lost his grip on his revolver and it fell to the floor. As he stooped to pick it up, his foot kicked the handle and it skittered across the floor. Tracy cursed his turn of bad luck. Without a gun he was powerless to attempt an escape. With resignation, he called out his surrender. He realized that his last hope of avoiding the Oregon State Penitentiary, a place known as one of the most brutal prisons in the United States, had disappeared.

Harry Tracy went before the judge to be sentenced. He was given an extra seven years for his abortive escape attempt to go with his thirteen year term for robbery. Finally, one of the last of the notorious outlaws of the old west had been apprehended and sent to jail. Everyone thought that this was the end of the story for Harry Tracy. Instead, it was just the beginning of the legend that he was about to create.

Chapter 4:

The Living Grave

Harry Tracy's arrival at the cold, grey Oregon State Penitentiary was unceremonious; he was only another one of one hundred and fifty inmates. Located to the east of the capital city of Salem, Oregon, the prison stood among the scattered peaceful farms in the lush Willamette River valley like some feudal remnant of another age and another continent. It was as out of place in the gentle landscape as a thistle in a cultivated garden. It was here, in this foreboding institution out of the public's sight, that the most dangerous criminals in the state were locked up.

Flanked by two guards, Tracy was first taken to the outside guard called the "Turnkey." A tall, powerfully built man with past history as a semi-pro baseball player, he introduced himself as "Guard McCormick." He took no special notice of the new prisoner and ordered him to strip, throw his clothes into a garbage container and march naked across the prison yard to the tailor shop. It was a long, cold walk on a damp afternoon for Tracy. At the tailor shop, he was ordered to take a bath in small tub of ice-cold, murky water at the bottom.

Tracy accepted this initial degradation with the stoic calm that comes from maturity and experience. Having spent two short sentences in the Utah State Penitentiary, he was used to the harsh, dispassionate treatment meted out by the guards in an attempt to break down the entering convict's usual resistance to authority and to the prospect of a long period of confinement.

After the bath, which only seemed to make him feel dirtier, Tracy was issued some ill-fitting prison clothes (his black and white "Stripes" that were so named for their appearance) and two threadbare blankets. Still not dressed, he was led to his assigned cell.

To his surprise, he was assigned the same cell as his former partner in crime, Dave Merrill. When Merrill saw Harry Tracy walk into his cell, he tried to conceal his fear that his partner might have learned of his betrayal at the Portland Police Station. Seeing that Tracy was ready to greet him heartily and sensing no treachery, Merrill took his new cellmate's hand and pledged further friendship.

Tracy thought his assignment to Merrill's cell to be a fortunate but foolish oversight on the part of prison officials. There was no one better than a former partner with whom to plan an escape. Tracy had no intention of spending the next twenty years or more in prison. Escape was the first thing on his mind. He planned to spend only as much time as necessary to discover the best method of getting over the high walls that surrounded the prison grounds.

The second morning Tracy's indoctrination by the prison guards was completed. He began the day with a normal prison breakfast consisting of foul smelling beans and wheat squashed together in a ugly grey mash and served upon a tin plate accompanied by a mug of muddy coffee. He watched the other prisoners gobble up the meager gruel as if it was a delicious as ham and eggs. Soon, he too would eat it hungrily, but on that day he only forked in a few mouthfuls, washing it down with a large gulp of coffee. He left the remaining portion untouched.

After the meal, Tracy was marched back to the tailor shop were his measurements were recorded and his hair was cut to a close crop. It took only a few strokes of the barber's wrist to reduce his sandy-red thatch to bristly stubble. Looking into the mirror, Tracy saw his nearly bald reflection staring back at him in the same half-set resentment he had seen on other prisoners' faces.

The final part of his indoctrination took place at the prison chapel. He was placed upon his knees on the altar. An overweight yet muscular guard who introduced himself as John Stapleton stepped up to the altar to address the prisoner. Stapleton was known by the inmates as the "Jack of Clubs" because of his unofficial position as the "Man Of Flogs," the guard who performed the punishment whippings.

Stapleton read solemnly from a scrap of paper he held in his hand:

"You must take off your hat when you come to chapel. You must hold your head down when you walk. You must lie like hell when your friends come to see you. You must puff up the screws if you don't want to get flogged or hung up all night on your cell door (a punishment exacted by attaching a pair of manacles to cell door handle and stretching them over the top of the door where, on the opposite side, they were clasped around a prisoner's hands so his feet could not reach the floor)."

To dramatize his speech, Stapleton reached under the altar and displayed a flogging club with four blood-stained leather strips studded with prongs. With a flick of his thick wrist, he made the whip snap with a loud crack that echoed off the chapel walls. A thin smile curled across his lips as he gingerly and almost reverently placed the whip back into its storage place.

"Now that you're a convict," he continued, "and at our mercy, your word don't go for nothing. You're supposed to be dead. We can make you say or do anything we want. We can kill you if we want to. We are all one, our word is all one. The guards are like brothers."

Tracy listened to this harangue trying not to show his contempt for the obligatory show of strength which the guards felt was necessary in order to establish their hegemony over the more numerous if less powerful prisoners. He knew prison guards and their ways from his stay in the Utah penitentiary. Some were a decent sort, but they were nearly always subdued by the more aggressive types like Stapleton who preached a doctrine of rule by corporal punishment and fear. As a convict, one either went along with this doctrine or suffered the brutal consequences. Tracy, against his nature, vowed to be acquiescent until his chance came to make his escape.

******

The Superintendent of the Oregon State Penitentiary was man named Lee, a political appointee by reason of his marriage to Governor Geer's sister. He was known as an honest man, a regular church attendee and a fine head of his family. However, as was usually the case, he had very little to do with inner workings of the prison.

The conditions at the penitentiary at the time Tracy and Merrill were incarcerated there had improved somewhat over previous years. A man named Patrick Brofield had been the warden only a few years before and he had ruled the prison with a cruel hand. Vestiges of his regime still remained and were secretly still implemented by the guards. Brofield was reported to have promoted Guard McCormick to "Turnkey" for shooting a prisoner named Oska twice in the heart from long range in a "set-up" escape attempt.

The incident which brought about Brofield's dismissal was still vividly impressed into the prisoners' minds. The memory of it hung like a pall over the entire prison population. The prisoners were required to serve two masters: the freeman contractors who ran the stove foundry and profited by cheap labor and the guards who were assigned to oversee them during their work. A French Canadian boy named Delmane who had been sent to the penitentiary at the tender age of twenty for burglary became the victim of the "two masters" system and of the "flogging as punishment" policy.

Delmane was ordered to perform a particular task by one of the contractors and while he was at it, Shop Guard Stapleton asked what he was doing. When Delmane replied in a contemptuous tone that he was busy, Stapleton marched him off to Warden Brofield for disciplinary action. When the Warden found him to be insolent in his attitude, Brofield ordered him to be taken to the chapel to have a little respect flogged into him.

The boy was delivered to the chapel and to Guard Sherwood, the "Man of Flogs" at the time. Sherwood stripped Delmane to the waist, knocked him to the ground, strapped his wrists and legs in leather thongs and strung him up on the whipping post with his bound hands above his head.

Only a few other guards were in attendance, but the whole prison knew what was happening.

Backing up slowly, Sherwood uncoiled the cudgel he had removed from its storage place under the altar. He set himself, measuring the distance between the boy and him with his eyes, then took two long strides, jumped two feet in the air and brought down the whistling flog so hard that the force drove the leather thongs deep into Delmane's flesh. The crack of the lash against the boy's back was instantly answered with a high pitched scream of pain which reverberated throughout the prison.

Sherwood took no notice of the scream and calmly repeated the action nine additional times. Delmane replied to the whipping with nine more screams. As blood oozed from the wounds laid open by the lashes, Delmane was let down from the posts. Sherwood took particular pride in inflicting as much damage as possible during a lashing. He believed that once a prisoner suffered the force of his lash, he would never again make trouble.

In a fit of rage, Delmane struck out at Stapleton with almost useless fists. Sherwood pushed aside the punches without much trouble, but he told the boy that for his insolence he would not be given medication to treat his wounds.

Delmane was incensed. No medicine meant poor healing and scars. Again he struck out at Sherwood, this time surprising the guard so thoroughly that he was knocked off his feet. Sherwood called for the other guards to assist him and when Delmane had been brought under control, the "Man Of Flogs" ordered the boy to be bound to the posts again so he could suffer additional punishment.

As Delmane was being prepared for the second whipping, Sherwood's face tightened in grim purpose. The first whipping was for the official punishment, this one would be for personal revenge.

The cudgel struck out again, even more cruelly, at the boy's already bloodied back. His screams increased in intensity with each succeeding stroke.

The lash count mounted: ten … fifteen … twenty … and still it continued with Sherwood's muscular arms pumping with no slack in his fury. In a gesture of sympathy, the other prisoners began howling and screaming with the Delmane. It became an eerie chorus. At the height of the furor, some men were screaming and cursing even louder than the boy suffering the blows. Other inmates started butting their heads against the hard stone walls and began kicking at the locks on their cell doors.

After the count of fifty five, Delmane's shrieks turned to low moans. At the count of seventy eight, he was silent, his limp unconscious body slumping against the bloodstained chapel post. Still Sherwood did not stop the punishment, he continued methodically until the count reached one hundred. Showing no compassion, Sherwood ordered the other guards to let Delmane down and take him to solitary confinement cell. He also told them not let the boy have any medication.

Delmane was locked up for thirty days with only crusts of bread, some thin broth and water to sustain him. When his punishment was finished, the door was opened to his cell and, to no one's surprise, his wounds had not healed. He was in terrible shape mentally as well as physically. In the short span of the thirty days, he had been reduced from a normal man to a raving maniac. After an examination of this back, he cowered in a corner of his cell and cursed and spat at the guards.

A doctor was finally called in and it was discovered that Sherwood's lashes had cut into Delmane's spine. To stop his violent thrashings, his hands were manacled to his back and his feet were fitted with lead-weighted boots. He was put back into solitary confinement until something could be done with him.

A few days later, a guard was delivering a bucket of water to his cell when Delmane lunged out with his head and knocked it to the floor. It was his last act of defiance.

The guard grabbed the emptied bucket, swearing at the top of his lungs at the prisoner's stupidity, and began pounding it down upon the boy's head to subdue him. Delmane struggled toward the guard, seemingly impervious to the blows. Finally, he collapsed under the guard's increasingly heavy pounding with the bucket. His head was bloodied and battered; a strange, thick fluid oozed from the cracks in his skull.

Delmane was removed to an insane asylum shortly thereafter. A few days after that, he mercifully died having suffered spinal and brain damage from his altercations with the guards.

Delmane's gruesome death caused a storm of controversy throughout the state's penal system. The public, as was usual in these cases, was not informed. Quietly and unobtrusively, Brofield and Sherwood were dismissed.

The man appointed to assume the job of Warden after Brofield was J.T. Janes. His assistant was a former guard, A.C. Dilley. Shopguard John Stapleton, the man who had begun the entire episode by first reporting Delmane for a minor infraction, was promoted to "Man Of Flogs." Warden Janes believed that a little flogging was necessary to the maintenance of order (it was a seldom-questioned way of doing business throughout the prisons of the West at that time), but he thought that it should only be used in extreme circumstances and never to the degree which led to Delmane's death. Dilley was succeeded by Warden Lee, who had even less inclination toward flogging.

The prisoners were not reassured. The threat of that horrible kind of death was never far from their minds. As long as whipping was a possible punishment, they could not be sure that it would not happen to them. The guards, the men who held the threat of death as a deterrent, were feared and hated by the inmates to such an extent that the possibility of gaining revenge against them was a bigger wish than the possibility of escape. Harry Tracy was biding his time and planning to do both.

Chapter 5:

Breakout

Despite his determination to escape from the Oregon State Penitentiary, Harry Tracy spent nearly three years languishing inside its walls, working daily in the hot prison foundry making stoves for the private contractor. He and Merrill had planned several escape attempts during the three years but the opportunity to carry them out never arose. A "break-out" seemed to have the best hope of success since the heavy guard prevented an opportunity to sneak out over the walls.

The man who gave Tracy and Merrill the idea for a "break-out" was an aging train robber named George S. Jackson. Jackson, under a life sentence, was known throughout the prison as "The Old Hero." He stood in high esteem among the inmates for his courage and his intelligence. There was only one way, according to Jackson, that a prisoner could escape the penitentiary: first, he had to procure guns and ammunition from the outside, get them past the guards and have them hidden for easy access; then, he would have to retrieve the guns and ammunition without anyone's knowledge and proceed to shoot his way out of the yard and over the wall. He said that if a man was not prepared to kill the guards and accept the risks to his life, he should forget any hope of every getting out until his sentence was complete.

Tracy thought "The Old Hero" made sense; no fancy maneuvers, just a quick shoot-out and then over the walls to freedom. Merrill voiced his objection to the risks, but Tracy's insistence that a "break-out" was the only way, finally persuaded him to agree.

Before they were able to carry out a "break-out", they were overheard making plans by the head "Stool Pigeon" or "Snitch" and were fitted with lead-weighted boots, called "Oregon boots" by the inmates. This boot was special kind of punishment which originated in that institution and was used virtually all over the West at that time because of its success at limiting the movement of any inmate wearing it. It was made by attaching a heavy lead weight to an ordinary leather boot. Because the weight was fitted with a wrench-set screw, many prisoners were crippled by trying to walk with the tight fit. Tracy, after his month of punishment was completed, suffered no ill effects, but Merrill did not fare so well. From that point on, he walked with a slight limp.

The wearing of the "Oregon boot" only heightened Tracy's desire to attempt a "break-out." As soon as it was possible, Tracy made a deal with a soon to be released inmate and promised him a large sum of money if he would smuggle rifles and ammunition into the prison. The man agreed to the proposition and told the two men to look for the rifles in the stove foundry in late May or early June.

Not knowing when the exact day the rifles and ammunition were going to arrive, Tracy and Merrill had to force their way to the front of the prison line every morning as they were marched from their cells to the foundry. They wanted to be sure that they would reach the rifles before anyone else. The three shop guards,

John Stapleton (the "Man Of Flogs"), G. E. Girard and Frank Ferrell, should have been alerted by this unusual action, but they chose to ignore it, chalking things up to Tracy's usual aggressive behavior.

Tracy had promised a good deal of money to the former inmate, Charles Monte, who had been released from the prison the previous month, to help set up an escape. In fulfilling his part in the plan, Monte had accomplished an amazing feat - probably one of the few times a former prisoner has broken back into jail.

On the night of June 8, 1902, Monte drove a buggy to a secluded spot near the prison wall. Toting a large bundle of ropes, grappling hooks, and guns, he approached the prison wall under the cover of darkness. Throwing a grappling hook high in the air, he secured it fast to the catwalk above. Hand over hand; he made his way up the rope to the top of the wall. Drawing the rope up quickly, and letting it down inside, he lowered himself into the prison yard. Moving silently, he crossed the yard, entered the foundry shop, and planted two loaded, short barrel 30-30 Winchester rifles beneath some foundry patterns in packing cases. Stealthily making his way back to the outer wall, he had climbed over it and was gone. No one had seen him. It was a bold action - one that later earned him a life-sentence.

On the morning of Monday, June 9, 1902, after mandatory chapel, Tracy and Merrill again pushed their way to the front of the marching line. By this time, the other inmates were aware of their behavior and let them crowd to the front with little resistance.

When they entered the foundry, the two men quickly removed their coats and moved to the area where the stove patterns were located. There, on one of the tables, were two "short" Winchester rifles (guns sawed off at the barrel to provide ease of handling) and several boxes of ammunition. Holding the weapons in their hands, the two men looked at each other with wide eyes. The escape was on.

Guard Ferrell took his post by the rear door of the foundry. The prisoners had all filed in by that time and he yelled, "all right," to the Stapleton and Girard. Ferrell yawned sleepily and began the work day in the usual way by rolling himself a cigarette. It would be the last one he would roll.

Before he could put the homemade cigarette in his mouth, he heard a commotion and turned around to see what was happening.

"You've had your day, now it's mine," yelled Tracy.

Ferrell began to raise his rifle to answer the challenge, but before he could Tracy aimed the Winchester and shot him through the back of the head. Groaning his last words, "Oh my God," Ferrell fell forward onto the foundry floor.

For a moment, there was no movement in the foundry. The inmates looked on in stunned silence at the blood oozing from the head of the dead guard. The remaining shop guards were too shocked to move. Tracy and Merrill could scarcely believe their escape was at hand.

Tracy recovered first. He had planned to kill all of the shop guards in retribution for his three years of suffering. Swearing an oath, he began squeezing off shots on the run as he attacked Stapleton and Girard.

Merrill moved to the nearest window, broke out the glass and started firing at the guards on the wall.

Startled by the sudden outbreak of gunfire, Stapleton and Girard (unarmed as was the rule inside the foundry) assumed they were witnessing the beginning of a full scale riot and mass escape attempt. They took flight through the shops using every object in their path as cover against the bullets flying at them from Tracy's rifle.

Seeing that the shop guards would get away and warn other guards, Merrill abandoned his long range efforts and joined Tracy.

One of the prisoners, a man named Luther Ingram serving a life sentence for killing his brother, was trying, as were other inmates, to move out of the way of the two gun-wielding inmates when he accidentally bumped Tracy's shoulder. With no time to waste, Tracy hastily pushed Ingram out of his way and inadvertently into Merrill's line of fire. One of Merrill's bullets struck the unlucky Ingram behind his knee and sent him writhing to the floor in pain.

In the weeks that followed, Ingram was called a hero who supposedly tried to save Guard Girard by grabbing Tracy's rifle. According the Ingram, he was simply a bystander who got in the way and was shot by mistake. Governor Geer, in an attempt to salvage some state pride out of one of the bleakest episodes in Oregon history, magnanimously released Ingram, who lost a leg as a result of his wound, under a full pardon for "extreme heroism at the risk of his own life."

Guards Stapleton and Girard managed to escape from the foundry unharmed. As soon as they were out of the door, they ran across the prison garden tearing up onion plants in their wake. They were in a mad scramble to reach the prison chapel where the guns were stored.

"Run," called out Stapleton to the other guards walking the yard, "there is going to be a war after we get the guns."

"Turnkey" McCormack stood at the chapel door letting all of the panicked guards inside. Stapleton had outdistanced the shorter Girard across the prison yard and reached the chapel door first. McCormack closed the door and locked it, thinking that all of the guards were safely inside. When Girard finally reached the door and found it locked, he began pounding wildly on the door and shouting for someone to let him in. McCormack reopened the door and Girard was in such a hurry to reach safety that he knocked down the larger McCormack and scrambled over him.

John Stapleton said later:

"The prisoners had just come in and were going to work at 7:00 AM. Girard and I were standing thirty feet away from where Ferrell was. The first thing that I knew (that) there was trouble was when I heard the report of a gun and saw Ferrell fall forward. I saw that he was killed and Girard and I ran for safety to give the alarm. The convicts followed firing several shots, none taking effect. There is no doubt that their intention was to kill all three shop guards."

With most of the guards locked in the chapel, Tracy and Merrill only had to worry about the guards on the wall. Other convicts, meanwhile, were running in every direction trying to find cover from the bullets being sprayed all over the yard by the wall guards. Before venturing into the yard, Tracy and Merrill took cover and began riddling the southwest and northwest guard posts with rapid rifle fire. None of their shots did any damage but the barrage of gunfire gave them time enough to move to a better position close to the wall.

From this new vantage point, Tracy took aim and waited for the first guard to appear from cover. Guard S.R. Jones raised his head to see where the convicts were located, but before he could aim his rifle for a shot, Tracy fired in his direction. The bullet found its mark. It smashed into Jones' chest and sent his dying body slumping over the back of the wall.

Without blinking an eye at the success of his marksmanship, Tracy turned his Winchester on wall guards, Tiffany and Ross. Several shots were exchanged with Merrill joining in the shooting in between bouts of fear. The only casualty in this gun battle, with the exception of Merrill's nerve, was Ross' hat which was blown off by a speeding bullet in a near miss.

Tracy decided that their only chance was to get over the wall before the other guards recovered and joined the fight. Bullets were raining around them, but Tracy and Merrill removed a ladder from the top of one of the shop buildings and placed it against the east wall of the prison. Miraculously escaping injury, they mounted the ladder and climbed up on the wall. They were now on the same level as the remaining wall guards.

Realizing that the escape was nearly complete, Guards Tiffany and Ross desperately fired shot after shot hoping that at least one would find the mark. Their excitement in the action adversely affected their aim. It was a one on one battle at that point and they had lost their advantage.

The guards did not know that they were really at a distinct disadvantage. Harry Tracy's secret weapon in any gun battle that he was involved with was his inner calm and his complete lack of any sense of fear. While other men, like Merrill, were not only fighting a gun battle but a also an internal battle with their own nerves, Tracy's cold, calculating instincts were honed by years on the run as an outlaw. He had been in life or death struggles before and he was able to maintain remarkable control of his emotions as a result of that experience.

In order to make themselves smaller targets for the rapid fire of the guards, Tracy and Merrill hugged the sides of the prison wall. After a few shots aimed at keeping the guard's heads down, Tracy reached down and grabbed the top rung of the ladder they used to climb the wall, pulled it up above his head and threw it down on the other side. He pushed Merrill down the ladder and then lowered himself down after him leaping the last few rungs to reach the ground.

Tiffany and Ross hurried to the spot where the convicts had

gone over the wall and, seeing no sign of them, also climbed down the ladder in pursuit. Following the wall, the two guards turned a corner and were met face to face with the escapees. Tracy and Merrill stood smiling with their rifles pointed directly at the guard's chests. Not expecting such trickery, the guards were not prepared and they were forced to give up their weapons.

The captured guards were forced to raise their hands and march in front of the convicts as shields against any other guards who might be out searching the grounds. After they had moved a short distance, Tiffany glimpsed the figure of another guard on the wall. The men in the chapel had reorganized themselves and had reached the vacated guard positions. Tiffany, trying not to draw attention, gently motioned for the guard to shoot. The guard answered with a bullet that narrowly missed the group. Tracy was enraged. He turned toward Tiffany and calmly shot him in the head. Ross, sensing that he would be next on the list of execution, wisely fell to the ground and feigned being hit by one of the many shots that were increasingly being fired as the other guards as they reached the wall. The bulk of the guards were joining the fight but they were too late.

Tracy and Merrill sent a few shots toward the wall and turned to disappear into the thick brush which surrounded the penitentiary. In a few violent minutes, they had made their escape from a place where no other prisoner had ever escaped.

******

The Oregon State Penitentiary that Tracy and Merrill left in their wake was a scene of total panic and confusion. The guards lost all sense of organization and they ran around the prison yard, trying to ascertain what had happened. The prisoners, of course, had less of an idea about what had occurred than the guards. They huddled inside the foundry hoping that the prison officials would not order a charge with guns and clubs. Luther Ingram, the wounded inmate, lay bleeding on the foundry floor waiting for the warden to decide what he was going to do. Warden Janes decided, with much delay, to lock down the inmates, still cowering in the stove foundry, until the situation settled down.

After a few hours, the guards sent a trustee into the foundry with a flag of truce and the convicts quickly agreed to return to their cells.

Deputy A.C. Dilley later gave his account of what happened that day:

"At 7:00 this morning we sent the men into the shops. Warden Janes and myself counted the men before they went in. Mr. Janes and I stopped in the yard after the men had gone into the shops and discussed business affairs of the prison when the first shot was heard - when Ferrell was killed. This was followed by more shots and the alarm was given. Janes, McCormack and myself hastened to the arsenal and secured rifles expecting a general outbreak. When we reached the wall at the first post, McCormack fired five shots at the men. I hastened to post two where I found Jones dying. By this time, the men had rounded the fence and firing was heard from there. Before we could get to them, they disappeared into the brush."

Warden Janes, realizing that at least two convicts had definitely escaped, telephoned for assistance from Sheriff Durbin of Marion County in Salem, ordering him to bring all available men. However, Janes, in his haste and confusion, had neglected to tell Durbin why he needed the men. It took some time, but the sheriff arrived with fifty men piled into wagons, buggies and carryalls armed to the teeth and ready to put down a full scale riot.

The Salem men were disappointed to find that nothing of such magnitude was going to happen; only a tedious search through the countryside for two convicts who had escaped hours ago and were probably already miles away.

After a brief and unsuccessful search of the nearby area, Durbin and his posse went back to the prison to await the arrival of Superintendent Lee who was expected to arrive from Salem. Lee wanted to look things over personally before the manhunt began in earnest.

By the time Lee arrived, help had also been called in from the nearby "insane" asylum farm (the same asylum where the tortured prisoner, Delmane, had died), a reform school and a deaf school. Marshal Gibson, the town marshal of Salem, and Sheriff Durbin were designated by Lee as heads of two separate posses. Both men quickly went to work by spreading their men north and south to cover the ground between the penitentiary and the town to the west. An added incentive to the posse members was the $1,000 reward set by Lee for the two convicts' capture.

Superintendent Lee gave this statement on the escape of Tracy and Merrill:

"The outbreak was entirely unexpected and could not be prevented. The men were supplied with rifles from the outside - probably brought over the wall that night and cached in a place where tools in the foundry are kept and where the prison secured them. This would be possible at night. I was not at the prison when the outbreak occurred but came soon afterward and directed the pursuit. I have sent for a brace of bloodhounds from Pendleton and they will arrive tomorrow when murderers will be run to earth. It is an awful affair and I will not rest until I run the fiends down."

******

Dave Merrill limped on the run to a shallow, rushing creek. There, he fell forward into the fresh water and drank until his he his fill. His heart was beating as fast as he thought it could and he was so out of breath that he was gasping. He rolled back out of the stream and looked up at the bright, blue Oregon sky and sighed with relief and joy. It was summer. The air was sweet and pure and, more importantly, he was out of the dark penitentiary walls and into open country.

The man who had helped him accomplish this feat and, indeed, was responsible for it, slowly emerged from the thick, green brush and sat down beside him. Merrill could not believe that he was not thirsty, nor even a bit out of breath. The exertion that he undergone the past few hours was enough to make most men weak with exhaustion, but Harry Tracy was as calm and as collected as if he were off on an afternoon walk.

Tracy looked at Merrill trying not to show his contempt. He wished he had a partner like himself. Through the progress of the escape, he felt that Merrill had shown his true cowardly self and that he would never be much good when another dangerous situation presented itself. Tracy knew he had to make do, for the moment, with what he had. What really mattered was that he was free from the hated Oregon State Penitentiary. However, he would not allow himself the luxury of celebrating his freedom, as Merrill was, because he had been hunted before and he knew no freedom was assured until the last man had stopped searching for him.

It took a day of careful running and hiding for the men to reach the city limits of Salem. Once there, they contacted an ex-convict named Louie Butler who gave them food and told them where they might steal a team of horses from a barn. Merrill wanted to stay the night there, but Tracy cautioned that the house of an ex-convict would be one of the first places a posse would investigate and that it might be best to put as much distance between them and the posse as possible during the first twenty four hours after their escape.

On the way to the barn, Tracy and Merrill met J. W. Roberts, a local resident, who was returning from his job in town.

Roberts gave this account of the meeting:

"I had just returned home at about 10:00 that evening from downtown and as I entered the gate at my house I observed two men approaching me. I presumed they were members of the searching party returning home and I paused to question them. In an instant, I found myself covered with two rifles and I obeyed the command of 'hands up and be quiet.'"

"The men were both dressed in the garb of convicts and asked if I was an officer of the law. They then stated that their names were Tracy and Merrill, the escaped prisoners from the penitentiary. They made me remove my hat, coat, vest and trousers which they divided between themselves, having discarded one convict's shirt and a pair of trousers. After warning me not to reveal any secret or alarm the police, they left. They had the latest modern improved rifles with plenty of ammunition and said they were prepared to fight to a finish for they would never be taken alive."

After leaving Roberts, Tracy and Merrill passed quickly through the residential district of Salem into Cartright's Section, where they stole a team of horses from the barn pointed out to them by Louie Butler. The barn was located one block east of East Salem School and A. M. Southwick, who lived one block from the barn, saw the escapees pass by his house on horseback at 11:00 PM. Southwick called the night watchman at the Marion County Courthouse to report the sighting, but, for some reason, no mention was made of the call to Sheriff Durbin.

A few farmers thought they saw Tracy and Merrill "skulking around the brush" on their property that day.. One man who said he saw a man answering to Merrill's description limping badly as if wounded (the limp that had been exacerbated by the Oregon boot) and supported by another man who might have been Tracy.

Outside of these reports, the convicts were not to be found.

Sheriff Durbin gave up his search for the night, posting guards on all railroad crossings and county roads leading out of Salem, but he knew that there was no hope of finding the men and returning them to the penitentiary easily. The men that they sought were too resourceful and too dangerous to capture without a thorough and organized hunt.

Chapter 6:

The Oregon Posse

Sheriff Durbin sat impatiently in his office the day after the prison breakout. He was waiting for the arrival of Guard M. E. Carson and his team of bloodhounds. The dogs were needed before a serious tracking effort could begin.

Guard Carson was traveling from the Washington State Penitentiary at Walla Walla. Normally he was not required to participate in out of state manhunts, but because he was the master of the only quality tracking animals in the area and because this was a priority case, he was ordered to Salem by Governor McBride of the state of Washington at the request of Governor Geer of Oregon. Geer had taken a personal interest in the search for Tracy and Merrill and had called out the National Guard to aid in Sheriff Durbin's search in any way possible.

J. W. Roberts, heeding the warning of Tracy and Merrill not to reveal their visit to his house until the next morning, rushed into the sheriff's office to tell his tale. Durbin was pleased to learn that Roberts' clothing was being worn by the convicts since it would provide a scent for the bloodhounds to follow.

A working posse was formed from the men in the Salem area who were able to use a gun and who were familiar with the surrounding countryside. The men gathered in the streets of downtown Salem preparing for what they hoped would be a short, productive search. The community was very excited about the attention the escape had brought upon them. Reporters and photographers from as far away as Portland and Seattle were arriving on each incoming train to give on-hand accounts on the progress of the manhunt. Children stood together in small groups on the corners of the streets watching in admiration as their older brothers and fathers prepared for the forthcoming search. Bird guns, Civil War vintage pistols, small bore .22s, deer hunting rifles and virtually anything else that could be fired were being oiled and cleaned in anticipation of being used in a direct confrontation with the desperate escaped convicts who had already killed three men. There was much talk among the men as to the best course of action. Many thought that capture was out of the question and that shooting them was the only hope of stopping them since they had already vowed not to be taken alive.

Late in the day, at about 5:00, Guard Carson finally arrived on the California bound Southern Pacific train. He climbed down from the baggage car with a small suitcase and his two well-bred bloodhounds, Dan and Hunter. Guard Carson was an all business kind of man, tall and thin with ramrod straight posture. With evident pride, he paraded his two well-trained dogs to the sheriff's office. Carson was dressed in clothes suited to tramping around the brush: a light colored uniform with pants tucked into his leather boots like the ones worn by campaign soldiers in the Spanish-American War. On his head he wore a well broken-in white Stetson, rolled up on the sides in cowboy fashion and pulled down on his forehead almost over his eyes. He looked his part.

After introductions, Sheriff Durbin - offering a strange contrast to Carson with his vested business suit on his short, dumpy physique - put Carson and his bloodhounds to work immediately. He thought the posse still stood an good chance of catching up with Tracy and Merrill that night because of the double good fortune of having fresh scents leading from both the Roberts' house and from the stable where the team of Clydesdales had been stolen.

The large group of armed men moved down the street toward the Roberts home with Guard Carson holding his bloodhounds in the lead. He was followed by Sheriff Durbin, Marshall Gibson, deputies carrying issued Winchesters and various Salem citizens dressed in everything from business suits to blue jeans and carrying every kind of firearm imaginable. Adolescent boys in knickers and caps pedaled on two-wheeled bicycles as an escort. It was a large and unwieldy crowd and stood little chance of catching the convicts by surprise.

The bloodhounds picked up the trail near Roberts' house and quickly lost it near the School for the Blind. They were then taken to the stable where they just as quickly lost the trail in the dust a few yards outside the barn door.

Tracy and Merrill had been on the move the entire day. On the outskirts of Salem, they surprised a woodcutter named August King whom they asked for food. King was not aware that they were the escaped men and did not see fit to report sharing a meal with two wanderers. After leaving King, the two men entered the town of Gervais. They walked stealthily through the alley in the back of the town drugstore, passed the Post Office to Main Street, climbed the fence in Edward Bupease's back yard and calmly walked by the two town hotels without being noticed. At the northern edge of town, they took refuge with a plan to wait until nightfall.

At 12:00 noon that day, August King's employer, Mr. Miller, arrived to pick up some wood to take with him back to Salem. When he learned of King's unexpected visitors, he immediately guessed that they must be Tracy and Merrill and he hurried to notify the authorities.

Word of Miller's discovery did not reach Sheriff Durbin until he was investigating the trail at the stable. With renewed hope of success, he ordered the posse to King's cabin.

Arriving at the first shades of dusk, the bloodhounds were put to the trail and seemed baffled. Finally, they found a scent and rain it down for a mile into the woods. When they lost the trail near a patch of timber, Durbin suspected that the convicts were hiding in the heavy cover provided by the tall fir trees. He formed a skirmish line around the area believing that a direct confrontation at that time would mean certain death for some of the more inexperienced members of the posse. As it grew darker, Durbin became increasingly convinced that he had the men trapped in a place they had chosen for the night. He posted a few guards around the timber patch and told the majority of the men to go home for some rest with orders to return in the morning before dawn.

Two posse members, Dr. F. S. White and Edward Bupease,

drove their buggy into Gervais ahead of the other men who were searching on foot. They did not know that Tracy and Merrill were still hiding in their day-long resting place. Realizing that they had been accidently discovered by the homeward-bound posse members, Tracy and Merrill jumped up from their concealed position and flagged down the buggy. Tracy pointed his rifle at Dr. White and ordered the two men to step down onto the road. Merrill relieved them of their coats, a rifle, a shotgun and several boxes of ammunition. While other returning posse members were well within rifle range of the robbery, it was much too dark to see what was taking place. Tracy and Merrill were speeding down the road which led out of Gervais in the stolen buggy before either White or Bupease could call for help.

As soon as the other men understood what had happened, they regrouped and took up the chase. Several miles outside of town, they found the abandoned buggy next to a field of ripening summer wheat. Sheriff Durbin was notified and he quickly moved to the field.

He ordered the posse to surround the field and bed down for the night. Pickets were posted in key positions around the field to prevent any escape. Durbin thought he had his quarry in his grasp.

The posse did not know that Tracy and Merrill were not within the surrounded area. They had jumped from the moving buggy only a few blocks from where they had stolen it. Seeing that the posse had fallen for the ruse, they then followed them at a safe distance to the wheat field. They saw the Sheriff surround an empty area. Tracy decided that he wanted to keep an eye on the posse's movements and reasoned that the best way to do so was to remain nearby for the night. Since Tracy knew that Durbin thought he had surrounded them, it would be an easy proposition to stay out of sight and watch what took place.

Both Tracy and Merrill took a turn keeping watch on the posse. Just before daylight, Tracy and Merrill surprised the pickets by breaking through their lines into a clump of timber just beyond the wheat field. Since they emerged from the opposite direction than was expected, the men on guard were unable to do anything other than fire a few ineffective shots after them into the woods. By the time the alarm had been sounded and the other posse members had been aroused from their slumber, Tracy and Merrill had made wide circle around the woods and as the still-sleepy men spread out to search for a sign of the trail, the convicts doubled back on their original tracks, encountered a few straggling posse members, took their guns without firing a shot and started back toward Gervais.

Sheriff Durbin was exasperated at the convicts' unpredictable actions. He decided to let the posse have breakfast before continuing the chase.

Tracy knew what he was doing. He had a sense of how a posse acted and reacted in a search situation. He had been hunted before and knew all of the tricks necessary to cover his trail, to hide his scent from the dogs and to confound conventional wisdom by doing the opposite of what was expected. The posse was no match for his experience, especially in the rough country where the chase was taking place. Tracy used the natural cover as an ally which no posse could overcome.

Dr. White did not return to the posse that morning. He was busy searching for his guns and ammunition that had been taken from him the night before. He eventually found his weapons in a small creek which ran alongside the town. He also found an old, ragged overcoat which had been stolen from the stable in Salem.

After the posse had finished its small breakfast, Durbin received word that August King, the woodchopper, had again been visited by Tracy and Merrill. Once more the posse returned to the cabin to question King and to see if they could pick up the trail left by the resourceful convicts.

When they arrived, King gave them this account of his second meeting with Tracy and Merrill:

"They came to my place an hour ago and wanted something to eat. They were very polite and offered to pay any price I wanted for some food. When they opened the door, Tracy said to me, 'Partner, I suppose you know who we are by now.' I told him I did and said it would be best to leave since the posse was near. He said they would not stay long and all they wanted was food. All I had was a loaf of bread which they received. They did not sit down as they did yesterday morning but held their guns all the time and even poked the barrel of a rifle into a bunk to see if I had anyone concealed there. They left after telling me not to alarm or notify officers."

When the dogs were put out on the trail, they again were

baffled shortly outside the cabin. Tracy knew how to cover the trail and make the dogs lose the scent. Sheriff Durbin decided that there was little possibility of capturing the men by continually chasing after them. The two convicts had made fools out of their pursuers on more than one occasion already. Instead, he decided to make a systematic search of the area backed by a cordon of armed men. He hoped that this strategy would cut off their route of escape.

The citizens of Gervais were becoming quite amused by the back and forth frantic movements of the posse through their town. Sheriff Durbin was not taking the situation so lightly. He posted pickets on all roads leading into Gervais and then brought the bloodhounds back once again to try to raise a scent at August King's cabin.

After a few false starts, the bloodhounds suddenly found a trail and ran into the woods. For several hours the posse trampled through heavy brush in a burnt-over area only to lose the track when the trail ended in a marsh at the head of another dense clump of firs.

The manhunt remained at a standstill at that point until 2:45 when Eugene Fisher, a young man from Salem who had been with the posse since the first call was made from the penitentiary, spotted Tracy and Merrill in a field some distance from the main body of the group. By this time, the National Guard and local militias, which had been called out by Governor Geer, began arriving on the scene. When Fisher called out his find, the Woodburn militia had just arrived and they immediately surrounded the part of the field where Fisher thought he saw the men. Fisher wanted to go in after the convicts himself, but he was restrained by the leader of the militia. Word of the sighting was reported to Sheriff Durbin and he showed up in a few minutes in a wagon with Guard Carson and his dogs.

Together with a few of the more seasoned members of the posse, Durbin and Carson entered the field, led by the dogs, and picked up a trail. The bloodhounds excitedly followed the scent to a fence where they began barking and jumping up and down in a frenzy. Carson moved them to the other side of the fence where they once again took up the scent. The trail led to a shady lane which dipped into a small gulley. Before descending into the gulley, Sheriff Durbin peered through the fir branches and saw that a natural barricade of stones blocked the way. He feared an ambush in such a setting and he called a halt to the search. A large number of men in the posse wanted to continue to press forward in the search arguing that they should hurry while the trail was still warm. Sheriff Durbin did not listen to what he thought was an emotional and foolhardy plan, saying it was useless to sacrifice good lives for the worthless ones they were hunting. As the posse reluctantly turned back toward the edge of the field, a shot rang out behind them. It came for the rock barricade and clearly showed that Durbin had been wise in his assessment of the situation.

Knowing that he had the convicts trapped in the field, Durbin set up headquarters in a nearby orchard and called in his deputies to make plans for the night. While the discussion was taking place,

Oscar Gleason of Salem spotted what he thought were Tracy and Merrill in a patch of ferns a short distance from his post. Gleason fired a shot at the men, but they quickly disappeared back into the field. Before he could spread the word of his sighting, the convicts made their way into yet another clump of trees. Gleason fired four more shots at the distant fleeing figures but was too far away for his aim to be effective.

Night was falling and Sheriff Durbin once again ordered the wooded area to be surrounded with both his posse and the newly added contingent of guardsmen and militia. He had 250 men at his disposal and they made a tight circle around the wooded area. The cordon of men stretched for over five miles with a man placed at each interval of one hundred and fifty yards. In addition, all roads in the vicinity were lined with armed local citizens. The entire area was up in arms searching for the two escapees.

Just before dark, Governor Geer arrived in his private buggy to look over the situation. He was overwhelmingly pleased by the sight of so many men at arms in the search and after shaking a few hands in thanks, he left expressing great confidence that there was no route of escape for what he called, "the murderers."

Sheriff Durbin, having seen the daring and resourceful convicts elude capture for over two days, did not share the Governor's optimism. He ordered every member of the posse to remain awake all night. He hoped that the two men would try to make their break from the woods during the protection of dark as they had done the previous night. He felt like this was the moment to capture them. The wait stretched into the small hours of the morning with no sight of the convicts. Many of the posse, tired from an exhausting day's search, began to doze at their guard positions.

At 2:00 A.M. Charles Tuh decided to move from his place in the circle to what he thought was a more effective one several hundred yards away. The place he vacated was the place where Tracy and Merrill broke through the line. Tuh heard footsteps and saw darting shadows, but he was not sure of his aim and his four shots were fired without success.

Tracy and Merrill were again swallowed up by the dense undergrowth before any other posse members could come to Tuh's aid. Sheriff Durbin was disgusted, but he reconciled himself to the fact that once again his plan had been thwarted by the cunning of the convicts. Since none of the men in his posse had been able to sleep that night other than what they could snatch in quick cat naps, he called off the search until the morning. The sheriff understood that rest was necessary for an efficient effort at another anticipated hard day's chase.

The next news of Tracy and Merrill came at midmorning after the search resumed. The posse, having been rejuvenated by four hours sleep, was moving slowly toward the town of Monitor hoping to find the trail. Sheriff Durbin received a telephone message relayed by a runner who said the convicts had eaten breakfast at the nearby home of Barney Akers.

With renewed hope, the posse mounted horses, climbed into

buggies and jumped aboard wagons to rush off to the Akers' house.

Mrs. Akers was on the doorstep to meet the men and she told them that Tracy and Merrill had entered her home while she was preparing breakfast. A neighbor woman was visiting at the time and the two women had been locked in a store room while the food was cooking to stop them from trying to signal any posse members who might be in the area. Mrs. Akers said that Tracy had accompanied her out to the cooling house to get some milk. He had his rifle ready in his hands and his eyes were constantly surveying the horizon. She said that the two men had eaten the meal in a "nervous and agitated manner" and when the lumber mill whistle had blown calling workers to the job, they jumped out of their chairs, seized a loaf of bread and ran off into the woods.

Sheriff Durbin immediately set the posse to work. The trail left by the two men led up a meandering country road toward Monitor. After only a few hundred yards on the trail, the path ended in the brush.

Following the convicts through this kind of country was exceedingly difficult. A scraggily fir forest dominated the land and it was broken in only a few places by small clearings, low hills and deep gullies. At every point where the trees thinned, the land was covered with a thick growth of vines, bushes, blackberry brambles and ferns. Interspersed throughout were creek bottoms that sunk in an even thicker swarm of vegetation. The natural protection stretched for over five miles in every direction offering a seemingly infinite number of escape routes.

Even at this point, the posse was still growing in size. Groups were arriving from all over the state of Oregon, each banded together in semi-autonomy under some town marshal, city detective, deputy sheriff or militia officer. The cohesiveness of the past few days was completely lost because of each group's desire to be the one to make the capture. As rumors began to spread of the convict's possible whereabouts, various small numbers of men split off from the main body of the posse and began to search on their own. The search became unwieldy and chaotic.

The Woodburn Militia, under the leadership of a Major Leabo, decided to investigate a road that led toward the town of Springfield. At the Pudding River Bridge, they met another group of men led by Jack Luerman, a former prisoner at the Oregon State Penitentiary who had known the two escapees and was now in hot pursuit of both them and the large reward. Luerman took Major Leabo aside, led him up to a ridge on the east side of the river and pointed to a bend in the road. He explained that around the bend and beyond a few miles was a house in which lived Mrs. Koontz, a relative of Dave Merrill.

Leabo was so impressed with the information that he decided to move his men along with Luerman's to the Koontz house to guard the area. Their arrival only served to annoy poor Mrs. Koontz who had never heard of Dave Merrill or Harry Tracy and who did not appreciate all of the armed men surrounding her house.

With no actual sign of the convict's trail for the entire day, Durbin called in the widely dispersed posse. He stationed them at guard posts in such a way as to cut off the eastward and southward escape routes and telephoned Sheriff Cooke of Clackamas County to close in from the north. Durbin knew that their only chance was for Tracy and Merrill to surface again and leave another trail for them to follow.

******

While Tracy and Merrill were eluding the ineffective efforts of Sheriff Durbin's posse, Superintendent Lee was investigating the personal effects that the convicts had left behind in their cell. Hoping to find some clue that might suggest the direction of the convict's escape route, Lee discovered a letter that was apparently written by Tracy's mother, who, according to the other inmates, wrote regularly although her son had never written in reply.

The letter read like a painful lament:

"My Dear Boy,

My life is darkened with the sorrow that has come to me. Oh, why, why was it that my boy should ever do anything to be shut up in prison? It almost set me crazy. They thought in time I would not feel so bad, but oh, the pain is there just the same as it was in the first."

The few convicts who knew Tracy said that he had voiced some regard for his mother on several different occasions. But, it seemed that the pathos registered in the letter had no effect on his desire to escape from the prison.

Later, Lee received a letter from a woman claiming to be Harry Tracy's wife. She was living in Chicago and her name was

Mrs. Minnie Tracy. Her letter was dated June 13, 1902 and it had a return address of 2131 Wabash Avenue, Top Flat. The letter was addressed with a simple inscription on the envelope: "Police Judge, Salem Oregon."

It read:

"Warden,

I write you these few lines in regard to Harry Tracy. I saw in the Chicago American an item concerning Harry Tracy, which is of no use for me to mention, as you already know the details concerning it. The reason of my writing you is that I am nearly positive, by the picture that was sent, that he is the man I was united to in 1893 the 8th day of April.

Harry Tracy was in the 'pen' at Little Rock, Arkansas on August 14. He got out of there in about nine months. You will find inclosed (sic) a small picture of me, but, of course, I expect him to deny ever seeing me, but will wait patiently to see. I only hope there could be some mistake but I am afraid there is none. I will close at this time, hoping to hear from you soon. Don't be afraid to tell me all.

You will oblige me,

Mrs. Minnie Tracy

P.S.

In the letter which was sent to a gentleman, it was stated that Tracy married some other person. I hold my marriage certificate which can be referred to at any time."

The letter from "Mrs. Minnie Tracy" was intriguing to Oregon authorities. Its veracity was questioned due to the date, 1893, which she claimed to have married Harry Tracy. He was, according to Oregon State Penitentiary records (which were not overly reliable), supposed to be twenty seven years of age. Convicts remember Tracy telling them that he was thirty one. Most reliable records list his age as thirty one, making Tracy 20 years old when Mrs. Minnie Tracy said he had married her and making her claim plausible.

Some accounts of Harry Tracy's early life claim that he was a member of the notorious "Deer Creek Gang" in Chicago during the early 1890s. If this was the case, it adds proximity as well as age to her claim.

******

Sheriff Durbin and Sheriff Cooke spent the morning of Friday the thirteenth investigating rumors, which had begun to spread like wildfire throughout northern Oregon, concerning the whereabouts of Tracy and Merrill.

The posse, large and unmanageable, followed the two sheriffs like "lost pups in search of a home" in various conveyances: wagons, buggies and carryalls. Back and forth across the dusty and unseasonably dry Oregon country road system moved the posse - hoping for a positive clue that would once again put them on the trail of the elusive convicts. Many of the men had brought along whiskey flasks that were passed freely and frequently among them to both to wet parched throats and to ease the monotony.

Recent additions to the posse were the brothers of Frank

Ferrell, the slain penitentiary Shop Guard. James and George Ferrell had been waiting for their other brother, Charles, to arrive from his home in Reno, Nevada before joining the manhunt. Charles Ferrell arrived full of vengeance. He became, over the following weeks, one the most persistent of the hunters, joining whatever county posse happened to be closest to the action. He swore he would do whatever was necessary to bring his brother's killers to justice.

The vast armada of horse drawn vehicles trailing Sheriff Durbin and Sheriff Cooke around the countryside was reminiscent of the wagon trains which had brought many of the early settlers to the Oregon Territory. Due to a string of unusually hot early summer days, the wheels of the vehicles used in the search sent up large plumes of dust along the dusty dirt roads. Sheriff Durbin complained that all Tracy and Merrill would have to do to avoid the posse was to watch the horizon, spot the dust clouds and then walk the other way. His protestations did little to diminish the size of the group which had grown to nearly five hundred members.

After a full day of fruitless search, Durbin once again called the posse to a halt at a telephone station in the town of Needy. Cooke dismounted and walked into the station to check on yet another rumor of the convict's sighting near Barlow. After a short time, Cooke emerged and announced that the rumor had some basis of truth because of another confirmed report from New Era which claimed that two men matching the outlaw's descriptions were seen moving toward the Willamette River, the largest river in the valley, and toward New Era. A cheer went up from the posse members, many of whom were extremely intoxicated. Everyone supported the idea of moving to investigate the sightings with haste.

Sheriff Durbin, however, was suspicious of the reports. Thus far that day, the group had checked out at least a dozen such rumors with nothing but drunkenness among his posse to show for the effort. He announced that he did not want the entire procession of men and wagons racing over to Barlow, nearly ten miles away, without any sure evidence of the convict's presence. He suggested that the main body of the posse remain behind while he, Sheriff Cooke and six hand-picked men went on to investigate. Sheriff Cooke agreed. Groans and jeers of disappointment were shouted in response to the announcement. Posse members were not about to wait behind while a few men might get all the glory.

As Durbin, Cooke and the six chosen men set out for Barlow, they were disobediently followed, a few hundred yards behind, by the posse. If there was any possibility of action that day, no one wanted to be left out.

Two miles from Barlow, the buggy carrying Durbin and Cooke was stopped by a man on the road who warned that the rumor of Tracy and Merrill appearing in Barlow was a fake. When the army of followers joined them and heard the news, a disappointed hush rippled through the crowd; they all felt very silly about their latest wasted day of activity. The man on the street, a local farmer, said the rumor had begun in a saloon when two patrons who had seen two hobos near New Era that morning thought it would be a good joke if the countryside could be "terrorized" by such harmless men.

Sheriff Durbin was visibly disturbed by the farmer's story. Turning to the enormous gathering that followed despite his request that they stay behind, he again said to the men, this time in a sterner tone, to stay back and wait while he and Cooke along with two wagons of reporters proceeded into Barlow to investigate the story. This time he was obeyed. In Barlow, Durbin was told that no one knew anything about the rumor except the Dungan brothers who were known to have had company at breakfast. When questioned, Roy Dungan denied that he and his brother had started the rumor but Durbin was satisfied that the farmer had told him the truth about the origin of the report.

The sheriffs and the reporters drove back to the place where the posse was waiting. They told their respective men to return home since there was no use going back to where the day's activity had begun since the area had been left unguarded for most of the day.

Sheriff Cooke set out for Oregon City with a frustrated look firmly planted on his face. Sheriff Durbin made the long ride home to Salem with Guard Carson, the bloodhounds and two wagons of deputies. When he reached his office, he addressed another crowd of reporters who were awaiting news of the manhunt to dispatch stories to their respective newspapers.

"These reports and rumors are just what has done the mischief," he said bitterly. "My opinion is that the escapees are now headed for Portland with good prospects of making the city. I think they are as far in the mountains as they want to go, and as soon as they can do so safely, they will cross the railroad and the river south of Oregon City and make their way into Portland."

The massive Oregon posse, over five hundred strong at some points, disbanded in failure. It was too large to do any effective searching and was no match for the fleet-footed convicts and their cunning ways. In less than a week since their escape from the penitentiary, Tracy and Merrill had completely outmaneuvered the posse and were lost somewhere within the heavy timber. They had led the motley assembly of men in sheep fashion, over hills, down creek beds and through miles of dense forest without much chance of being captured. Tracy and Merrill were, for all intents and purposes, lost and at large; Oregon law officers could only hope for them to them to appear again and give some point of reference.

Chapter 7:

Through Southwest Washington

George Sunderland and Walter Burlingame were peacefully anchored in a slough of the Columbia River near Sunderland's home north of Portland fishing for catfish and an occasional trout. It was a warm Sunday, just the right kind of day to laze away at the end of a pole.

Suddenly, two armed men appeared on the bank. One of the men pointed a rifle at the boat and ordered the men ashore. Sunderland had an awful feeling at the pit of stomach that these were the escaped convicts, Tracy and Merrill.

"Good afternoon, gentlemen," said Tracy with a smile. "We're the convicts and we want you to row us across the Columbia."

"I'm sorry," replied the frightened Sunderland, "but this slough doesn't connect with the river. We can't go nowhere."

"Well," said Tracy, "I guess you'll just have to go with us 'till we find a boat for you to row us across."

Merrill asked where the two men lived and Sunderland replied that he had a small cabin about a mile down the slough. Tracy and Merrill climbed into the boat and had the fishermen row them to the cabin where they found another man, W.W. Paddock, waiting.

After the convicts had eaten their fill of Sunderland's food, the party of fugitives and hostages walked along the river bank until they found a large rowboat capable of carrying them across the wide Columbia River channel. Tracy was at the bow, Burlingame and Sunderland sat in the middle to work the oars and Merrill held a rifle on Paddock who held the rudder at the stern.

The trip across the river provided a spectacular view of the countryside. It was a fine Pacific Northwest summer day with bright blue sky in contrast to the light green brush and dark green Douglas firs which lined the horizon. To the east, the sharp peak of Mount Hood showed blue bare spots between the sheets of snow as a result of the spring melt. The pleasant temperature and calm water put the convicts in a good mood; they were sure that no posse was directly behind them for the first time since they had left the penitentiary walls.

Tracy entertained the group with the tale of their escape and flight across northern Oregon. He said that they had stolen a team of horses and a wagon from a farm fifteen miles south of Portland and had made their way, without being stopped or questioned, through Oregon City, Milwaukee and Sellwood. He recalled the second night after the breakout at the edge of a wheat field near Gervais. He said that one of the posse members was within an arm's length of him when the man had stopped and said, "This is far enough into the woods." A companion had agreed and said, "Yes, let's go back." Tracy bragged that the two posse members had been lucky men because he had been about to shoot them when they decided to turn back. Tracy also said that Sheriff Durbin owed him his life because he had restrained Merrill from shooting him when he made an easy target talking to the posse in the middle of the wheat field that same night.

Tracy was ebullient over their defeat of the posse. He kept up a constant stream of chatter as the boat made its way across the wide Columbia.

"I wasn't the least bit afraid of them, the bloodhounds," he said. "We fooled them. We didn't intend to kill those guards, though. I told Jones not to move, but he began to make signals after he had his hands up. Those guards were fools to allow us up the ladder and skin over the wall. We've got about all the money we need and plenty of ammunition."

"We're not bad men," said Merrill, "but we intend to get away, and if anyone stops us, they're sure going to get hurt. With us, it's a case of burned at the stake or get shot."

The three fishermen looked at each other with amazement. Why Merrill thought they would be burned at the stake was a mystery. The penalty for murder in both Oregon and Washington was hanging. Perhaps, since they had killed three prison guards, Merrill and Tracy believed that the population of the state of Oregon would not settle for an ordinary execution and would demand a more horrible retribution.

When the boat reached the Washington shore, Merrill turned to Sunderland and asked for his pocketbook.

"You have a $5.00 gold piece, I see," said Merrill examining the contents of the pocketbook, "but I won't take it. I'll just take $2.00. But I ain't a bad fellow, and to show you what I mean, I'll give you this Elk's badge that I got off a fellow the other day (Dr.

White of Gervais). Here's where you can join the Elks Club for only $2.00."

Merrill's wise crack was repeated the next day in the newspapers. It was quickly picked up by a group of touring vaudevillians and included in a skit in their act. So successful was the line, "Here's where you can join the Elks Club for only $2.00," that it became a vaudeville standard and was performed on stage for many years after the manhunt was forgotten.

The two convicts climbed out of the rowboat and Tracy exclaimed, "Thanks for rowing us across. I promise to send you $50.00 as soon as I get to Seattle. I've got friends there. I'd like to pay you fellows back for being so nice."

The spot where Tracy and Merrill had picked to land was a few miles upstream from the town of Vancouver, near Leiser Ranch. It was a broad, sandy beach strewn with driftwood.

Tracy ordered the hostages to row back to the Oregon side. He made sure they rowed at least half way back by pointing his rifle directly at the boat; he did not want the men to row to Vancouver and spread the alarm before he and Merrill had a chance to get a head start. Once they saw that their former hostages were definitely on their way back to the Oregon side, they set out into the flat, forested area of Southwest Washington.

The first home at which they stopped was the Ed Jones house located north of the Leiser Ranch from the river toward Mill Plain Road. Mrs. Jones was home alone and they told her they meant no harm and wanted only something to eat. Mrs. Jones suspected their identity but said nothing and provided them with two loaves of bread, some butter and a few pounds of bacon. They expressed their gratitude and continued their journey north.

Young Ralph Leiser was riding his bicycle near his parent's ranch, when he came upon the two men. With typical aplomb, Tracy announced to the boy, "We're the fugitives."

He asked directions to the road leading north and warned Leiser not to reveal any detail of the meeting until the next day under the threat of coming back to shoot him.

When the former hostages reached the Oregon side of the Columbia at the ferry slip, they immediately spread the word that the escapees had reached Washington. Sunderland went to Vancouver on the ferry, while Paddock and Burlingame traveled to Portland to notify officials there.

As soon as they received word of Tracy and Merrill, the Portland Police Department dispatched a posse to Vancouver. Since the two convicts had escaped from an Oregon prison and had killed Oregon men, authorities in the state felt a particular compulsion to hunt them down. The posse, which included Detectives Kerrigan, Day and Snow, Deputy Sheriff McMillan of Salem and Sheriff Cooke of Clackamas County, proceeded by trolley car and ferry to Vancouver.

The Portland posse, carrying rifles, pistols and cartridge belts, caused quite a commotion in the quiet streets of the small Washington town. Sheriff Marsh of Clark County in Washington met them at his office. He had received Sunderland's message and was waiting with a group of volunteers to join with the Oregon men to set out to search for Tracy and Merrill.

Detective Day, the nominal leader of the Portland posse, joined Sheriff Marsh in his buggy. The other men, Kerrigan, Snow, McMillan, Cooke, Fireman Castle, Emil Glutch and a Portland Oregonian reporter, all climbed into a large carryall wagon driven by Herbert Leiser, young Ralph's father. The wagon was pulled by two large black horses donated from the stable of Bud Smith and was so overloaded with men and guns that the springs almost touched the axel.

Sheriff Marsh whipped his buggy horse down the road which led east out of town and was followed slowly by the overburdened wagon. Herbert Leiser soon had the wagon moving at a good pace but he had to stop because of a loose harness which had snapped under the extra pressure. Leiser quickly spliced the harness with a strand of rope and hurried to catch up with Marsh's buggy which had not stopped for the delay.

Another stop had to be made by the wagon when it was found that one of the guns carried by the men would not fit the cartridges they had brought along. Leiser again had a solution. He stopped by a farm of a friend, Nicholas Goetshan, to borrow his Springfield rifle. Goetshan produced the rifle but wanted to test it before turning it over to the posse.

"Just wait until I see if this cartridge fits," Goetshan said, "I haven't had occasion to use this recently."

He slipped in a cartridge, raised the rifle above his head and pulled the trigger. A loud report proved the rifle's ability. He gave the Springfield to the posse saying, "It'll do," with a wide grin on his face. Goetshan was given the unusable repeater as a guarantee that his rifle would be returned.

Leiser then pushed the matched black horses to full speed and chased after Marsh and Day. A dozen or so Vancouver residents who had accompanied the posse from town on bicycles gave up one by one as the team gained stride. The last to fall behind was a young boy who struggled furiously at the pedals until his wind finally gave out and he had to abandon the chase.

At the Fourth Plain crossroads, Leiser caught up to Marsh's empty buggy parked at the side of the road underneath a tree. A man named Charles Stonehouse, a local blacksmith and a noted crack shot, was waiting for them with a message from Marsh to await his orders while he was scouting ahead with Detective Day. Leiser pulled the large wagon over next to the buggy and the eight posse members jumped down eager to begin the search.

After a few minutes, Day and Marsh returned and the Oregon men voiced an opinion to push on into the brush with the hope of surprising the fugitives before they realized anyone was chasing them.

Marsh disagreed with the plan but finally relented under pressure and said, "Very well, gentlemen, you go and I and Stonehouse will guard these four corners."

Sheriff Cooke went on a different mission. He set off on foot for the nearest telephone station to call Walla Walla to request assistance from the man who had helped the Oregon posse in Salem, Guard Carson, and his team of bloodhounds who had returned to Walla Walla after the Oregon posse had been disbanded.

The Oregon men, along with a few of their Washington helpers, tramped through the brush for hours without finding any evidence of the convicts.

At nightfall, Marsh positioned twenty men to guard Fourth Plain Road and assigned volunteers from Company G of the Washington National Guard who had appeared late in the day to watch Mill Plain Road from Burnt Bridge Creek to Fourth Plain.

The guards lay in wait throughout the night without hearing a sound. In the morning, they returned to Vancouver for refreshment and a little sleep. It was in that short time when most of the guards had left their positions, that Tracy and Merrill, in typical fashion, chose to move through the area. It was almost impossible for them to have moved through before or after that opportunity without someone noticing them.

Ironically enough, Sheriff Marsh knew Dave Merrill. He had been a schoolmate of his many years previously. Marsh knew that the job of hunting down Merrill and his partner, Tracy, would be difficult because of Merrill's familiarity with the area.

******

It was early on the next Sunday morning, when Tracy and Merrill emerged from the forest for their next contact with the residents of Southwest Washington. They walked to the door of a secluded cabin just off Fourth Plain Road at the edge of the area known as Brush Prairie. The owner of the cabin was an old German immigrant named Henry Tiede. He lived alone. Tiede was asleep when he heard a loud knocking at his door. Looking at his silver pocket watch which he kept on a table near his bed, he saw that it was only 6:30 A.M. He went to the door dressed in his nightgown wondering who could be bothering him at that hour. When he opened the door, he was met by Tracy and Merrill holding rifles. The men were dressed in tattered and torn clothing and a full week's growth of beard.

"Hurry up," said Merrill. "We want something to eat."

While Merrill followed the frightened and surprised Tiede into the cabin, Tracy inspected the surrounding woods for any sight of a posse. After a short search, Tracy entered the cabin an announced, "It's safe."

Merrill grunted his approval and seized a slab of bacon laying on the table which Tiede had recently purchased. He placed a large chunk of the bacon into a pan to fry.

"We're goddamned hungry," said Tracy apologetically. "Any of them guys around the place? Fellows hunting us?"

"No sir," said Tiede.

"Can you guess who we are?" asked Merrill.

"I guess you are the boys who escaped from Salem," ventured Tiede.

Tracy laughed. "You guessed right the first time."

When the bacon was cooked, Merrill served it on plates accompanied by some bread he found in Tiede's cupboard. The two men ate heartily and put the remaining bacon in a bag to take with them.

After the meal, Tracy and Merrill discarded their worn clothing on Tiede's floor and went to his closest to find replacements.

"You can have those rags," said Merrill pointing to the remnants of Dr. White's coat which still bore the imprint of the Elk's pin he had given away for $2.00. While rummaging through the closet, Tracy found an old copy of the Oregonian with pictures of them on the front page. He showed the paper to Merrill and joked about the bad likenesses. Merrill cut out the pictures with a pair of scissors and each man placed his respective picture in his pocket as a souvenir.

The fugitives were ready to leave after donning their new outfits. They were uncertain what to do with Tiede. Moving to a far corner of the cabin to discuss the matter, they held a whispered conference. Tiede, at this point more than any other, was frightened for his life. He knew it would be more convenient for the convicts to keep him from spreading a warning by killing him rather than tying him up. He strained to overhear the conversation that might determine his fate but could only make out Merrill saying "... follow my lay. I say to the British Columbia line."

Turning to Tiede, Merrill said in his normal voice, "Now we don't want to hurt you, old man, but we've got ourselves to look after and we don't want you to pipe us off. So we propose to make you keep quiet."

Tiede's heart almost stopped.

"We're going to tie you," said Merrill after a pause.

Instead of expressing his gratitude for sparing his life, Tiede retorted with an indignant, "And I may lie here helpless for four or five days and starve to death before anybody comes."

"Pooh, no fear," said Merrill.

Both men worked on the rope and tied Tiede's feet together. They carried him to the bed where his wrists were tied behind his back and a gag was stuffed in his mouth.

With their task completed, the fugitives picked up their rifles, sacks of ammunition and a bag of food and walked out the door.

It only took an hour for Tiede to free himself. He dressed in some of his remaining clothes and hurried to the telephone station at Orchards to notify Sheriff Marsh.

Marsh and Sheriff Cooke were only a few miles away from Tiede's cabin when the message arrived. A short search around the cabin showed no sign of a trail that Tracy and Merrill might have taken. Without the bloodhounds that had still not arrived, nothing could be done. Marsh called the posse into Vancouver for a rest.

******

There were reports that the Washington Nation Guard, members of the posse by their own voluntary offer, had not been as effective in their part of the search as they might have been had they limited their consumption of alcohol. Farmers complained of having their cows and horses used as target practice for the inebriated and itchy-fingered troops. When confronted on this subject by reporters, Sheriff Marsh explained that he could do nothing since the guard was not under his command.

Detective Day of Portland was one of the most vocal critics of the Guard's drunkenness.

"The whole damn country was full of militia and many of the boys were potted. They shot at everything in sight and Clark County sounded like the Spanish-American War all over again. It was the most dangerous place I was ever in."

Much to the Oregon man's dismay, however, alcoholic misuse did not limit itself to the Washington side of the Columbia. William Morris, a local painter who had decided to join the manhunt with his friend, L.D. Seal, was mistakenly shot by one of the Oregon party when the two men were sighted at a guard post near Salmon Creek. After wandering all day in the thick woods, Morris and Seal had stopped to rest on a hill overlooking the Salmon Creek Bridge. Below their vantage point, they saw a group of men swigging out of a pint. They did not imagine that the group would mistake them for the convicts.

It had been a long and frustrating day for the Oregon men stationed at the bridge. Some of them had been drinking all day to relieve their boredom. One of the drunkest, spotted Morris and Seal on the hillside and not wondering why there were sitting in plain view, yelled out that he had seen the convicts.

His disclosure sent off an instant reaction among the men. Walter Lyons, Governor Geer's private secretary and his liaison to the posse, quickly reached for his rifle and along with Deputy

Skipton of Marion County and Deputy Lou Wagner of Multnomah County, raced up the hill to make a capture.

Seal saw the commotion below and realized the posse was after them. He jumped behind a tree and yelled at Morris to do the same.

The simultaneous report of three rifles rang out before Morris could move. One of the bullets struck him in the leg.

"I'm hit," screamed Morris falling backwards in pain.

Seal waved a handkerchief and the three men realized their awful mistake.

Morris had been crouching and the bullet had entered his thigh, smashing the bone. He was taken to St. Joseph's Hospital in a buggy where he was operated on that night by Dr. Ebert and Dr. Gilchrist of the U.S. Army. He was first expected to lose his leg, but later he recovered enough to avoid having it amputated.

Deputy Wagner offered a hasty explanation of the incident to justify the Oregon posse's action.

"Though the shooting was unfortunate and a sad accident," he said, "it is lucky that the man was not killed. We were out there to do business and we were confident that we had the right men. I think the man who goes on this hunt with the intention of asking the convicts to hold up their hands is committing suicide."

******

Sheriff Marsh posted guards along Salmon Creek hoping to cut off the northerly direction of the fugitive's escape. He still did not have the services of the bloodhounds and thought that encirclement was his only chance until the dogs arrived.

Bert Biesecker and Lon Davidson took their position between the Tenny and Betts bridges on the evening of June, 15. Shortly before 11:00, Biesecker saw two men go down to the creek for a drink of water. The men were armed and answered, in a general way as far as he could see them in the murky shadows, to the general descriptions of Tracy and Merrill. Having heard of the earlier episode of Morris' shooting, the two men were reluctant to fire until they had a closer look. When the two unidentified men walked back to the road, Biesecker and Davidson stepped out from their concealed position and approached them.

At a distance of thirty yards, Biesecker was sure that these were the fugitives. He stopped, raised his rifle to his shoulder and pulled the trigger. The bullet missed. Davidson then joined in with each man firing three more shots. Their rifle fire was quickly answered by the opposing men, but it was so dark that no one could be sure of their aim. Both pairs of men jumped into the brush for cover.

Biesecker and Davidson waited for almost an hour before deciding to move up a quarter of a mile where they had left their horse and buggy. When they reached this position, they again took cover and stood motionless for another half an hour. With still no sign of the other two men, they cautiously boarded their buggy and started off down the road which led back to Vancouver.

After a few yards, they heard rifle fire behind them. Several bullets were on target and grazed their horse. The frightened animal broke into a gallop. Two more shots were fired from the brush behind them and one of the bullets caused a third superficial wound to the horse while the other penetrated Biesecker's coat under his right arm. Miraculously, the lead did not touch his flesh.

Biesecker and Davidson reached down about 3:00 A.M. and breathlessly reported to Sheriff Marsh the details of their harrowing encounter.

******

Guard M. E. Carson arrived in Vancouver from Walla Walla the next morning with his bloodhounds. He found the entire community talking excitedly about the previous night's sighting of Tracy and Merrill.

The combined Oregon and Washington posse, along with Captain Sparks and his much-maligned militia men from Company G of the Washington National Guard, proceeded to the point where the two posse members standing guard had seen the convicts. Together the posse numbered over fifty men - a rather large contingent of men for the dense brush which grew in profusion in the Salmon Creek area.

Guard Carson put the bloodhounds to the trail at the spot designated by Biesecker as the one he had last seen Tracy and Merrill. The two dogs followed the scent eagerly into the brush for about a mile, and, as had happened so many times before, it dissipated seemingly into thin air.

The remainder of the day was spent trying to locate another trail, but the effort was in vain.

Rumors began to surface in Vancouver, that the fugitives had doubled back on their trail and were hiding somewhere within the city limits. Mayor Eastham received a telephone message from a boy who swore that he saw Tracy and Merrill near Mill Plain Road. Mrs. Nellie Maitland, who lived near St. John's Church in the center of town, said she had seen the men run by her house early in the afternoon.

Sheriff Marsh set up headquarters for the night in the city of La Center because of another unconfirmed report that the fugitives had been seen passing Pioneer Church seven miles to the east. According to the report, two men had stolen horses from John Rathbun's farm after holding his father in law, A. Kauzler, and had galloped off in the direction of Lewisville.

Marsh had the posse try, late in the afternoon, to pick up the trail of the two unidentified horsemen several miles north of Pioneer, but the effort had to be abandoned when the dogs were unable to pick up a scent.

The sheriff assumed that Tracy and Merrill had taken the main road leading off Pioneer Road to La Center and then had proceeded north along a trail which followed the Lewis River to Lewisville. On the strength of that assumption, he assigned twenty men to guards' posts near Lewisville and other vantage points along the river. He and Sheriff Totten of Skamania Country commanded a guard position at the La Center Bridge.

At 6:00 that evening, Porter and Lansberry, two of the men stationed by Marsh, saw two men answering the fugitives' descriptions walking along the ridge of a hill above the home of Mrs. Titus south of La Center. The suspects dodged into the brush when the guards called to other members of the posse to assist them. Ten men, some of whom had been under fire in the Philippines during the Spanish-American War, plunged into the brush after the men, firing several shots into the area where they had last been seen. No sign of the two fugitives was found. The remainder of the posse was then summoned. However, Guard Carson's bloodhounds again would not take the scent, leaving Marsh with a feeling of doubt as to the identity of the men in question.

The next day, June 18, brought no encouraging news. Tracy and Merrill had kept under cover all day and there was no clue to their whereabouts. March declared that the search had developed into a "still hunt" and that nothing positive could be accomplished until the fugitives emerged to give away their position. Marsh stated that his posse would continue the search until "all hope has been abandoned of getting them."

Marsh's private opinion of the location of the elusive outlaws was that they were on the south side of the Lewis River somewhere in a secluded area where they could rest after the past four days of continuous movement. He reasoned that the men could have had little or no sleep during that period. He also thought that since they had not stopped at any farmhouses to replenish their supplies, the two men would have to stop somewhere for food in the near future.

Sheriff Huntington of Cowlitz County (the adjacent county to the north) joined the manhunt with his posse and was prepared to take up the chase as soon as it determined that Tracy and Merrill had crossed the Lewis River into his jurisdiction.

Guard Carson and the bloodhounds moved to the town of Woodland for a rest since the dogs could not manage to keep a scent for any length of time. Carson hoped that a day away from the dusty forest would increase their effectiveness.

Evidence that the convicts were in the area came from a man named Lindsley who ran a logging camp near Lewisville. He claimed that two men had appeared in his camp demanding a meal and had stayed only long enough to eat it and run out without paying. Lindsley was certain that the two men resembled the photographs of Tracy and Merrill he had seen in the newspapers.

At the same time, a disturbing message was received from a George Bloom, the owner of another logging operation on Anderson Island in Puget Sound. He stated that Benjamin Merrill, Dave Merrill's brother, had quit his job and had taken the steamer for Tacoma in order to join the two fugitives. Bloom said that Merrill had left a note behind which read, "I will help my brother or die with him."

The volunteers from the Washington National Guard returned home to Vancouver amid criticism from the Portland newspapers for their "general drunkenness" during the manhunt. They answered the charges with the statement that only one "depraved" youth had been drinking and he had not even been a actual member of the militia. The Vancouver Independent, a local newspaper, siding with the Washington men, announced in an editorial that the National Guard had been done an injustice.

******

A teenage boy was working hard in the field of his father's small farm - only recently cut from the sprawling forest for cultivation - when he was approached by two men on June, 19. One man wore a pair of jeans, a woolen shirt and a knit cap; the other man was dressed in striped trousers, a blue coat and a light brown campaign hat. Both men carried rifles and revolvers and appeared very menacing with their nearly two week's growth of scraggly beard.

The man in the campaign hat stepped forward and asked the boy, "Have you any bacon or flour? We're hungry."

The boy did not answer. He called to his mother and father inside the house.

Mrs. Torgeson explained that she had no flour or bacon to spare but that she was just about to send her husband into Vancouver for supplies.

"Where are you bound for?" asked Mr. Torgeson.

"We're out looking for the escaped convicts," said the older man. "What is the distance to Vancouver?"

"Around ten miles south of here," said Torgeson warily.

With that short exchange of conversation, the two men parted company with Torgesons and walked back into the woods.

As soon as Mr. Torgeson thought it was safe, he sent his son into Vancouver to report the meeting with the men the family was convinced were the fugitives, Tracy and Merrill.

Young Torgeson arrived in Vancouver at 11:00 A.M. and immediately went to see Sheriff Marsh who had returned to the city after no clues had turned up at La Center.

After hearing the report, Marsh telephoned Guard Carson at Woodland and told him to meet the posse at the Torgeson farm with his bloodhounds. He quickly rounded up four deputies and left Vancouver to meet Carson.

Of the number of men still scattered over Clark Country, no Oregon officials remained. They, with the exception of a few independent bounty hunters and Charles Ferrell who was on a one man vendetta, had abandoned the manhunt when it became obvious that they had very little to contribute to the effort other than their own physical presence because of their lack of knowledge of the countryside.

About a mile north of the Torgeson farm, Dave Merrill appeared at the door of Mrs. Martin. He asked her for some supplies and insisted on paying for them. Mrs. Martin gave him fifteen pounds of flour, part of a loaf of bread, a pound of butter and a quart of strawberries. She charged him $1.00.

Mrs. Martin had been in the process of preserving fresh strawberries when Merrill had knocked at her door; before leaving, Merrill turned, looked at a box of the red, ripe fruit and commented, "some strawberries and cream would be quite a treat." Although she guessed who the man might be, she offered him a bowl full. Merrill took what Mrs. Martin described as a "liberal portion" and ate it ravenously all the while cracking jokes about the chase between mouthfuls. As Merrill left the house, she noticed that another man, presumably Tracy, was standing guard on the road to be sure there were no members of the posse nearby. Merrill's last words to Mrs. Martin as he walked away were "When a posse catches up to us there's going to be a pretty warm fight."

A few miles down the road, Tracy and Merrill met a peddler. Thinking that the two men were part of the posse, the peddler walked up to them and asked, "Hunting the convicts, gentlemen?"

Tracy laughed at the question and replied, "No, but you came about as near as anyone, knowing where to find them."

Sheriff Marsh met Guard Carson at the Torgeson farm and put the bloodhounds to the trail. The dogs picked up the scent and followed it to Mrs. Martin's home, arriving at 3:00 in the afternoon. The scent was lost at this spot because of the dry and dusty conditions; no rain had fallen since the day Tracy and Merrill had escaped from the penitentiary and the dog's sensitive noses were constantly being irritated.

A previous report of the convicts' presence near La Center was found to be false when a farmer named Ayers rode into Vancouver to explain that the two men on horseback at Pioneer were not Tracy and Merrill, but his father in law, Mr. Shively, and a companion who had left Tuesday morning to take up timber claims farther up the river from Lewisville. Ayers did not know until the morning when Shively and his friend returned that they had been the men who had been fired upon near the Lewis River.

After searching for some clues late into the night, Marsh called off the pursuit once again and returned to Vancouver.

"It is the same old story," he said dejectedly, "the outlaws have disappeared. After diligent, though fruitless search for the past twenty four hours, we have again given up the search. At least until we get another clue."

The men who had been stationed at guard positions, thoroughly worn out and badly in need of sleep, were called in by Marsh for some rest. The other various posse members who had been tramping through the brush trying to follow the bloodhounds were even more exhausted. One by one, the tired and bedraggled men trickled into Vancouver and went back to their homes.

******

With no guards to block their progress, Tracy and Merrill took the road leading north the next morning.

They stopped at a farmhouse south of La Center for a meal and provisions. The farmer who gave them these essentials saw the fugitives as tired despite their brave façade. As they left his farm, Tracy firmly told the farmer that they "would never be taken alive."

That same day they were seen by a man named Dunlap who was out hunting with his wife. Dunlap saw them ranging through the brush not thirty feet away. One of the men (Merrill, from his description) fell over a log and got his foot caught in a cleft of a branch. Dunlap, guessing that these were the widely hunted fugitives, put his rifle to his shoulder was prepared to shoot when his wife intervened. She made such a fuss over their safety if he missed that he decided not to take a shot. Merrill removed his foot and scrambled back into the cover of the brush before Dunlap could think about changing his mind.

Sheriff Marsh was informed of the two sightings and he again formed a posse. The bloodhounds were put back to work but little hope was given for their success. They had continued to be a disappointment in Washington as they had in Oregon; no matter how hard Guard Carson tried to keep them on the trail, they were unable to keep the scent for more than a few miles. Tracy's methods of backtracking over heavily traveled trails and wading through creeks and swamps had thoroughly baffled the dogs at every turn. He was well schooled in how to cover a trail and how to fool the bloodhounds from his time in the "Hole in the Wall" in Colorado.

Carson and the bloodhounds, once again, found the fugitives trail at the point where Dunlap had seen Merrill, but, as usual, they were only able to follow the scent for about a mile. Marsh posted guards and sent the other posse members to La Center for the evening.

That night, three suspicious men were seen in La Center. They were immediately put under surveillance when Carson recognized them as former convicts at the Walla Walla Penitentiary. One of the men, after spending several hours in the brush on horseback near where Tracy and Merrill were last seen, started to leave La Center in a rowboat down the Lewis River but he was forced to return at gunpoint by the ever-vigilant Charles Ferrell.

After being questioned by Sheriff Marsh, the three men were escorted out of the area and told not to come back.

Sheriff Huntington of Cowlitz County moved his posse of twenty men to the northern bank of the Lewis River near La Center and set up a standing guard.

With no further clues to bolster his hopes, Sheriff Marsh turned over responsibility for the manhunt to Sheriff Huntington and again returned to Vancouver. Marsh, as tired as he was from his week of arduous search, took time to explain to reporters and sightseers in Vancouver why Tracy and Merrill had not been caught. He said that he thought the work done by the posse in Clark County was superior to that done in Oregon because the convicts had been kept in a radius of eight miles while in Oregon they had covered three counties in the same amount of time. The reason that Tracy and Merrill were still at large, according to Marsh, was because of the dusty conditions which reduced the effectiveness of the bloodhounds. Rain had fallen that day for the first time since the breakout from the Oregon State Penitentiary and Marsh hoped that it would settle the dust enough for the dogs to follow a trail for longer than a mile.

******

As the alarm spread northward through Cowlitz and Lewis Counties, the excitement among the population spread with it. Several men were seen in northern Lewis County supposedly carrying rifles through the forest. A small posse went to investigate. The men were so anxious about the possibility of a confrontation with Tracy and Merrill, that they almost opened fire on a group of men camped in a clearing without an investigation. However, cooler heads prevailed and further inspection proved the trigger-happy men wrong: the campers were Professor Van Winkle of the United States Geological Survey and his three assistants on a field trip. They were armed only with axes and geological equipment.

June 25 brought no new clues. A few die-hard volunteers, including Charles Ferrell, still watched the Lewis River but the number was not sufficient to prevent an unnoticed crossing.

In Vancouver, Guard Carson expressed his disappointment over the performance of his bloodhounds. Even the rain had not improved their ability to keep a scent. He reasoned that perhaps the dog's delicate noses had been damaged through prolonged exposure to the dust.

Sheriff Marsh left his office and went to his home. He said that he would not go out after the convicts again unless he was summoned by some "extraordinary clue."

William Taft, an owner of a farm near Kelso (forty miles down the Columbia from Vancouver in a northwesterly direction) had the first news of Tracy and Merrill outside of Clark County. He had seen the two men eating a meal out of sacks near his woodshed.

Another farmer named Alberni corroborated the story when he said that he had talked to the fugitives near his land in Cowlitz County. According to Alberni, Tracy and Merrill were making off with two of his horses, but when he pleaded that he was a poor man and needed the horses for farm work, they dismounted and ran off on foot.

Only these two sightings offered any hope. The convicts appeared to have been lost somewhere in Cowlitz County. They were slowly making their way north, hidden by the forest and dense undergrowth. It was becoming painfully obvious that due to the landscape, the fugitives were unstoppable. Only a chance meeting with an armed posse would offer any chance for their death or capture.

Stories began to drift in from other parts of the state that Tracy and Merrill had somehow escaped by leapfrogging huge amounts of territory. These proved untrue but did not help in the general confusion surrounding the search.

There were many rumors. There was a story from a Tacoma man, who wished to remain anonymous for obvious reasons, who stated that he had gone to school with Harry Tracy in that city and that his real name was Cosgrove, not Tracy. Cosgrove, the man said, had always been a bad character and was no doubt located in Tacoma at that moment in the home of one his unscrupulous friends.

In Salt Lake City, Utah, two men applied for work at the Bingham Copper and Gold Smelting Company at Bingham Junction. Superintendent Nuttings of Bingham sent the men to the smelter office but was suspicious of their actions and followed them. While he was on the telephone reporting their descriptions to the local authorities, the two men fled from the building. The foreman of the smelter said that he had known one of the men in Leadville, Colorado several years before and that his name was Merrill. The sheriff formed a posse to search for the men but they were never found.

Word of the manhunt was reaching throughout the Northwest and across the country. Two deputy sheriffs from Shoshone County in Idaho, Williams and Idelman, arrived in Portland by train to join the chase and to claim the swelling reward (over five thousand dollars). Both men were experienced in hunting criminals with dogs and were friends of Guard Carson. They planned to wait in Portland for another solid clue before heading north.

******

Tracy and Merrill were positively sighted on June 28 on the upper Ostrander River. They were headed for Silver Lake. Sheriff Maxie of Ellensburg and his newly acquired team of dogs accompanied a posse to follow up the trail while Guard Carson and his well-rested bloodhounds scouted the land surrounding the lake.

The next day the young son of James Ferrier of Little Falls (near Silver Lake) met two men walking along the railroad tracks. He walked with them for over a mile. The men said they were soldiers looking for the escaped convicts. One man claimed his name was Ira Johnson from Neewaukum, just south of Chehalis. The boy reported that they were very nervous and raised their rifles to a hobo who was lying beside the tracks at a crossroads. The two men left the boy and the railroad track at Ainslie and started down a dirt road that led toward Winlock. The boy was positive that the men were Tracy and Merrill by the disheveled clothing and unshaven beards. Shortly afterwards the same two men were seen by railroad section hands. One of the men asked for directions to Toledo and then they proceeded down a military road leading north.

A farmer named Porter reported that his house had been broken into while no one was at home. Clothing and food had been stolen. Sheriff Deggeiler of Lewis County, now in charge of the manhunt, hurried to the Porter home to search the surrounding area. He discovered a campfire where a meal had been made with eggs stolen from Porter's farm.

Guard Carson arrived at the scene at 5:30 PM and put his bloodhounds to a trail which led to a pile of clothing discarded by the fugitives. The trail ended there.

Ed Sanford of Bucoda was awakened the next morning by a stranger asking for eggs. The man looked like Harry Tracy and carried a revolver; Sanford said that he appeared very worn and tired. Only fifteen minutes after the stranger had left the Sanford property, Guard Carson arrived with his wildly barking dogs. When the bloodhounds were put to the trail, they refused the scent. A disgusted Carson sat down and waited for the posse; Tracy had foiled him again. He had been closer to his quarry than at any time since the wheat field outside of Gervais, Oregon, but his dogs had failed again.

The posse found Carson waiting in dejection. The group included Sheriff Deggeiler of Lewis County, Policeman Taylor of

Olympia, the two Idaho Deputy Sheriffs who were friends of Carson (Williams and Idelman), J. C. Bush of Chehalis, the tireless Charles Ferrell and a few other local volunteers. After little success searching the area during the day, they split into two groups and patrolled the roads at night.

Tracy and Merrill were again lost to their pursuers. They had left three Washington counties as well as three Oregon counties in their wake. Posses were simply incapable of matching the escape techniques applied by the fugitives. Charles Ferrell and Guard Carson were the only constant factors during the chase. Although disheartened by the lack of success, Ferrell summed up the determination of lawmen throughout the state of Washington to eventually kill or capture Tracy and Merrill when he said, "As long as these men are alive, I will be on their trail and will not be satisfied until I see them pay the penalty for their crimes."

Chapter 8:

On Puget Sound

After a month of eating, sleeping and fighting on the run, Harry Tracy was exhausted even though his determination to escape the clutches of the law was undiminished.

Squinting through his olive-shaped steel blue eyes and covered with a month's growth of matted beard, he was a frightening sight standing on the porch of Alexander Laird's cabin outside of Olympia. He was worn and haggard and his usually perfect posture was beginning to slump. His face mirrored the struggle; his high cheek bones and prominent chin became more dominating as his flesh tightened due to lack of nutrition.

"I'm Tracy," he announced to a terrified Laird answering the knock on his door.

Without wasting time, Tracy tied Laird with his own rope and proceeded to fix himself something to eat. Laird asked Tracy where Merrill was. He received a reply that "Merrill was guarding the road, one mile away."

In midst of Tracy's meal, a chimney fire sprang up and Tracy released Laird from his bonds long enough for the two to squelch it. When the fire was out, Tracy rebound his captive and left the home promising to leave a note pinned on a gatepost at Rancher Johnson's place which would tell of Laird's situation.

Laird managed to free himself in few hours. He went directly to Johnson's ranch and found that a saddle and bridle had been stolen.

Tracy moved quickly to the home John McCloud of Olympia and stole two horses. He was on the southern shore of Puget Sound by morning.

Puget Sound was one of the largest natural harbors on the Pacific coast. It stretched from its southern tip in Olympia one hundred and fifty miles north past the cities of Tacoma, Seattle, Everett and Bellingham. Besides being a beautiful scenic marvel of blue water, emerald islands and gentle beaches, the Sound offered a natural highway for commerce at the turn of the century when roads were in scarce supply. Even when there was a road leading from city to city, it was generally in rough repair due to the constant rain and rugged terrain. From his previous visits to the Pacific Northwest, Tracy was familiar with this waterway and figured it would be easier to ride into Seattle on a motor launch than tramp through sixty miles of timber and brush.

As the sun broke through the mist of the morning of July 2, Tracy walked up to Horatio Alling, the manager of the Capitol City Oyster Company and former Deputy Secretary of State, W.D. Jenkins, and confronted the two with his identity.

"I'm Tracy, the convict," he said. "I want something to eat right away. Be quiet and raise no fuss and I'll not harm you."

They offered no argument. They took Tracy to the cook tent where William Adair, the company cook, was preparing breakfast for the men who had been fishing on an oyster boat all night. Two other company employees, John Hessegee and Frank Scott were already sitting down at a table and were startled by the sight of the armed and menacing stranger. Tracy ordered the men to stand at one end of the kitchen tent while he drank coffee and ate a hearty breakfast of bacon and fried potatoes.

Noticing the launch *N & S* sitting at anchor in the harbor, he ordered the cook to call in the master of the ship for his morning meal.

There were three men aboard the *N & S*, Captain Clarke, his young son, Edwin, and a deck hand, J. Munro. They entered the tent and Tracy, without identifying himself, ordered the three to stand with the others at the opposite end of the tent from where he was eating his meal.

Not guessing the identity of the man who was carrying a rife and issuing harsh orders, Captain Clarke - a man used to giving orders himself - fidgeted uncomfortably in the corner, stuffed his hands into his large wool coat and made grumbling noises of discontent.

Tracy looked up from his plate and said, "Take your hands out of your pockets, Captain, you have a gun in there. It's no use for you to pull it."

Clarke stared at Tracy and refused to remove his hands.

"Are you ready to shoot, then?" asked Tracy. "If you are, so am I."

The air was charged with tension. Clarke was a stubborn man and he did not like being pushed around. Finally, the captain realized that the man eating his breakfast was deadly serious. He laughed half out of fear and half out of the absurdity of the situation and removed his hands from his coat pockets.

"Who are you?" asked the Captain.

"Tracy," said the outlaw in a matter of fact tone.

One mention of the name was enough to cause Clarke to stiffen. He knew he had been a lucky man not to have been shot. He did not have a pistol in his pocket and had only been testing the will of the man unknown to him at the time.

The assembled group of company men breathed a sigh of relief when the confrontation between the captain and Tracy was over.

After finishing his breakfast, Tracy asked to see a newspaper. He said that he had not had time to read one since Clark County because of the chase. A paper was not to be found, however, and his face mirrored his disappointment.

Someone in the group asked about where Dave Merrill was located and Tracy shocked everyone with his answer.

"Oh, I killed that son-of-a-bitch three days ago. I heard that he had written a letter to the authorities telling them to arrest me in Portland. I shot him three times with my rifle and threw his dead body under a clump of trees."

No one dared probe the incident any further. There was nothing but silence in the room as the men tried to comprehend Tracy's matter of fact mention of Merrill's killing.

At 8:00 AM Tracy decided to move. He ordered Munro to tie Alling and Adair securely with rope. He then marched Munro,

Clarke, young Edwin Clarke and Frank Scott down to the beach to board the launch, *N & S.* Tracy helped Clarke start the engines. While the motors rumbled below in warm-up mode, Tracy ordered Munro to return to the cook tent for some clothes and a pair of shoes. He was wearing shoes made for a man who was crippled with one sole two inches thicker than the other. He wanted a pair that would allow him to walk unimpeded. Munro returned to the launch quickly with a coat and vest from Alling and Adair's trousers and shoes. As soon as Munro boarded the launch, Tracy flew into a rage. He was upset at his own stupidity. He had let Munro return to the cook tent without a warning to him not to untie the bound men. Pushing Munro into a corner, Tracy demanded to know if he had released the two men. Munro pleaded that he had not done so, but Tracy did not fully believe him and swore to kill him if someone attempted to affect a capture on the journey across Puget Sound. He explained to the crew that he had a deadly fear that if he was caught that he would be hanged or burned at the stake. He said that he did not mind being hung but he could not stand the thought of feeling his flesh catch fire. In a hushed voice, he told the bewildered crew that it was because he had believed he was going to be burned at the stake that he had made a solemn oath never to be taken alive. Where he got this notion, no one could understand.

Once the launch was underway, Tracy's good spirits returned and he became an amiable captor. He sat at one end of the little cabin on the bow of the launch with his rifle on his lap and surveyed the green shoreline of Puget Sound as they glided through the calm blue waters. Captain Clarke was anxious to cover the distance between Olympia and Seattle as soon as possible; he pushed his engines to the maximum. Twice the engines overheated, causing the launch to float free in the water until they cooled, but the launch continued onward and made good progress as it headed north up the Sound.

"Don't push her too hard, Captain," warned Tracy after the second overheating. "I don't want to get to Seattle before it gets dark."

As the journey progressed, Tracy took a liking to Frank Scott, the deckhand, and joked about his red hair being as bright as flames in a campfire. It was to "Scottie" as Scott was nicknamed, that Harry Tracy told the complete story of what had happened with Dave Merrill.

"I shot him in the woods," confirmed Tracy without a trace of shame or remorse, 'but he was going to shoot me. We quarreled. Some days before the quarrel we found a newspaper which contained an account of our escape and the pursuit. That account gave Merrill equal credit with myself for the deeds which I alone committed. The newspapers since we have escaped have all along persisted in giving him equal credit for the escape and getaway with me. The fact of the case is that he didn't have the nerve of a rabbit. He always wanted to sneak through the country keeping under cover and he preferred to go hungry rather than show himself for the purpose of getting food."

"That isn't my style. No man can take me alone. And if I had proper traveling companion, a man of nerve, I couldn't be taken by a regiment of deputies. If I am shot it will be from behind. And with another man to guard the opposite direction, a man of some nerve who knew how to handle a gun, we could go wherever we wanted to and not be compelled to keep under cover a portion of the time as I am when traveling alone."

"But Merrill was N. G. (no good)", Tracy continued. He was never anything but an impediment to me and I am glad that he's out of the way. I never could trust him on guard except in places where there was no danger anyway and then he was so frightened that at times he would wake me needlessly for fear that we were being surrounded. So, when I got the newspaper and saw that the reporters and the people thought he had some nerve, it just made me hot. I thought at first I would shake him and travel alone, but before we agreed to separate, I taunted him with his cowardice and he got huffy. Then we agreed to fight a duel. This was in the woods in Lewis County not far from Chehalis."

"How did it happen?" asked the amazed Scott.

"Well," continued Tracy as if he were weaving a yarn, "we agreed to stand together from a line and walk ten steps each, in opposite directions from each other, then turn simultaneously and begin firing. From his haggling in arranging the terms I was convinced he was intending to turn before he had taken the ten steps and I was determined not to let him get the drop on me like that. So, when I had taken eight steps, I turned around and took a shot at him. It hit him in the back. The first shot didn't finish him and I shot again. That finished him. I then hid the body in the brush and continued on my way."

"Merrill only got what he deserved. He intended to turn and shoot me in the back, then he would have sneaked out of the country through the big timber and would not have been heard of for months. I would not only have been dead, but would never have been found, because he would have been afraid to tell where my body was."

Harry Tracy's account of his "duel" with his former partner, Dave Merrill, seemed plausible only because of the strait forward nature of his telling of it. It would not occur to him to tell a lie about his shooting of Merrill for the simple reason that it would have violated his own particular code of self-serving justice. His exploits and his reputation as a brave man were always on his mind; he wanted to be remembered, strangely, as something more than just a criminal. Whatever negative qualities there were that made Harry Tracy a murderer and an outlaw, in his own mind it was more important that people knew that he was honest in his meetings with people and bold in his actions. Telling the truth relating his exploits was somehow tied together with "not being taken from the front" and "not sneaking around." Evidently, Tracy was caught up in his emerging legend as it steadily increased in stature with the growing number of newspapers featuring his story on the front pages nearly every day of the chase. He seemed determined to show people that he was even more bold and intrepid than in the newspaper reports.

******

As the *N & S* passed by McNeil Island, the foreboding walls of the federal penitentiary could be clearly seen from the boat. Tracy riveted his gaze on the prison and was seen to be filled with a reactionary dread. He recounted his violent dealings with prison guards in past harsh times at the Oregon and Utah penitentiaries.

"I'm going to take a crack at one of those guards," said Tracy lifting his rifle to his shoulder. "Just so long as it was a man who tried to keep a gun pointed at the heads of prisoners."

Captain Clarke tried to talk Tracy out of carrying out his threat. He pointed out the fact that it would only cause an alarm to be spread over the Puget Sound region and might lead to his capture.

Tracy agreed with the captain's reasoning and instead amused the crew by taking a "potshot" at a seal swimming near the shoreline of McNeil Island. If it had not been for the roll of the boat, he would have shot the seal; the bullet landed in a wave just a few yards in front of its head.

The launch continued pressing north. Passing Point Defiance near Tacoma, the tug boat *Sea Foam* - whose captain was a personal friend of Captain Clarke - was sighted on a collision course with the *N & S*.

"I guess I'll take a crack at that fellow," said Tracy thinking that there was a threat from the *Sea Foam*.

Captain Clarke begged him not to shoot explaining that it was only a good natured seaman's josh and that no good could come from harming an innocent man. Once again, Tracy accepted Clarke's plea, although he watched intently to make sure the tug turned off course. The *Sea Foam's* captain could be seen inside the cabin giving everyone a hearty wave as the two boats passed by each other.

******

Shortly after 5:00 PM the *N & S* reached Seattle.

Tracy sat at the bow of the boat leaning back on an old wooden chair, rifle across his lap, with his eyes scanning the shore of Elliot Bay as he searched for a good place to land. The launch chugged slowly through Smith Cove and Tracy remarked at the beauty of Seattle with its magnificent backdrop of water, mountains and blue sky. Seeing no adequate landing area, he ordered Clarke to continue north to Meadow Point.

The *N & S* began to sputter at the West Point lighthouse but recovered and limped up to Meadow Point, two and a half miles north of the northern suburb of Seattle, Ballard. It was 6:00 PM when they dropped anchor.

Tracy ordered Frank Scott to bind the crew. As Scott tied the men's hands and feet behind their backs, Tracy noticed that Edwin Clarke had a sore wrist. He told Scott to tie the boy only at the elbows.

Before disembarking, the outlaw turned to Captain Clarke and said, "Goodbye Captain, you've been kind to me and I'll reward you. I'll send you a lot of money to make up for kidnapping you and the launch. I'll have plenty of dough pretty soon now and I

won't forget you fellows. Well, so long for now." Tracy climbed
into a rowboat and Frank Scott accompanied him as a hostage.

On the shore of the broad dirty sand beach of Meadow Point,
Tracy immediately voiced his need for a pistol. He told Scott that
he had lost all three of the ones he had with him as he left the state
of Oregon. He had had to discard them as excess weight during the
frantic chase through Southwest Washington.

"But I'll soon fix that," he told Scott as the two men walked
toward Ballard. "I'm going to search for a policeman first and get
his gun before I do any real business here."

Tracy had Scott walk in front of him about five paces ahead.
When they passed the Globe Navigation Company in Ballard and
saw a man coming toward them, he told Scott to step aside so he
could take a shot.

"That man has some money," said Tracy. "I guess I'll wing
him and get it. I might need it someday."

"Don't shoot him here," pleaded Scott. "Can't you see that if
you do, it will implicate me?"

"Well, damn it," said Tracy. "I don't want to get you into
trouble, so I'll wait until you leave me."

The two men continued walking west as they followed the
railroad track which ran through Ballard. After they had walked
several miles from the beach, Tracy remarked that he was tired and
wanted to rest for a while. The two men sat down alongside the
rails a few blocks from the center of Ballard. At this time, Tracy
revealed to Scott the exact location of Dave Merrill's body outside

of Chehalis, hoping that his description would lead him to receive the reward money offered by the state of Oregon for the fugitive's return, dead or alive.

They walked a block farther down the tracks and Tracy turned and faced his hostage.

"You can go back now," he told Scott.

"What are you going to do?" asked Scott.

"First I have to get a six-shooter. I need one badly. I must have it. I'll first hold up a policeman and get his gun. Then I'll go out to Lake Washington and come down Pike Street."

"What then?" asked Scott.

"Oh, I'm going down to hold up Clancey's Saloon and Gambling House," said Tracy. "I hear they've got some dough down there. But in Seattle I am among friends. This is the only place I can make my getaway. They can't catch me in Seattle. If they do take me, they'll have to shoot me from behind for no man can take me from the front."

Tracy shook hands with Scott and said goodbye. The last Scott saw of him, he was walking down the train track which led to Seattle with his rifle in one hand and a sack of ammunition and food slung over the other.

Frank Scott said later:

"While I was mortally afraid of the man, still he made a fellow feel at home."

It was obvious from his knowledge of Puget Sound shoreline and from his conversation with Frank Scott that Harry Tracy was well-acquainted with the city of Seattle and that he knew people there. His short stint as a student fireman on the Northern Pacific Railroad six years before would serve him well in the following days.

Frank Scott, armed with Tracy's description of the location of Dave Merrill's body, quit his job with the Capitol City Oyster Company and set out to find both the body and his fortune.

"No more fishing for Scottie," he said. "After this week, I will be living in luxury at the expense of the taxpayers of Oregon."

Chapter 9:

Deadly Confrontations

As soon as King County Sheriff Cudihee learned that the escaped convict, Harry Tracy, had landed in his jurisdiction, he set a plan in motion which he hoped would succeed where other attempts had failed. He knew that he was in for a difficult task, having followed the manhunt with growing interest in every step taken by Tracy and his now missing partner toward Seattle.

Edward Cudihee was beginning his second term as King County Sheriff in that summer of 1902. A Democrat, he was one of the few members of his party who ran for office to be either elected or reelected, due to the political influence held by the Republican pillars of the community, the business establishment and the so-called "Pioneer Families" (descendents of the original settlers of the city). During his first term, he had been involved in another large-scale manhunt: the search for the notorious murderer, Tom Blanck. He had been nearly killed in the process of that investigation and, but for the intervention of one of his deputies, undoubtedly would have been. The courageous and dogged work he performed during the Blanck manhunt, helped fix his reputation deep enough in the minds of the King Country voters to cause his reelection by a two thousand vote majority in the 1901 campaign.

Until Harry Tracy escaped from the Oregon State Penitentiary, the most infamous outlaw in the Seattle area was Thomas Blanck. Blanck's trail of outlaw activity ranged from British Columbia through Montana, Washington, Oregon to California. He was purported to have robbed stage coaches, banks, saloons, hotels and many private citizens without regard to anyone's safety. He had admitted to killing more than five people and wounding over 20 more. He was dubbed the "Jesse James of the Pacific Northwest" by the press for the scope and ruthlessness of the violence he perpetrated during his crimes.

Edward Cudihee, at that time a detective in the Seattle Police Department, along with Officer John Corbett, had managed to corner Blanck at the Bay View House in Belltown after he had shot and killed a bartender named Charles Bridwell. The capture was a close call for Cudihee who was nearly shot himself during the process. The event effectively raised Cudihee's profile as a lawman and was responsible for his subsequent election as King County Sheriff.

In late 1894, Blanck was convicted of the murder of Charles Bridwell and was sentenced to be hanged on Dec. 7, 1895. The case was under appeal and the execution stayed pending review by the Washington State Supreme Court.

While being housed at the King County Jail, Blanck, a notorious blowhard and a man who was not shy about telling tales of his previous crimes, told anyone who would listen – jailers, fellow inmates and reporters - of the many crimes he had supposedly committed. These stories were subsequently published in the Seattle Post Intelligencer.

While in Weiser, Idaho in March of 1890, Blanck said that he had mistakenly shot and killed his friend "Doc" Sweeney during a poker game. He said that he had meant to shoot another player, Judge Hanthorn, but his aim was off target and the bullet fatally struck Sweeney.

Blanck related that in 1890 he had shot and wounded a police officer in Fairhaven, Washington after committing a burglary. He had been captured in Port Townsend and brought back to the Whatcom County. Before trial, he said that he had escaped and fled across the British Columbia border into Canada. He had held up a stagecoach near Nelson, British Columbia and made off with over $4,000 in silver and gold, killing the driver in the process. He then had headed back across the border and in early 1891 he had robbed a safe at the Bingham and Holbrook Bank at Woolley, Washington in Skagit County. Blanck had moved on to California and according to his own account, stole enough money and gold to facilitate a trip to New York City where he celebrated until his ill-gotten money ran dry.

Back in the West by 1894, Blanck said that he had attempted to break into a safe at the Northern Pacific Railroad Depot in Helena, Montana but ended up killing a station agent and had to make a quick escape.

On August 17, 1894, he said that he had shot and killed Northern Pacific Station Agent William Ogle in Belgrade, Montana while attempting another safe cracking. He then had robbed the bar at the Hotel Broadwater in Helena, Montana in late August without managing to shoot or kill any of the employees or patrons. On

September 7, 1894, Blanck said that he had killed a saloon keeper in Meaderville, Montana during an attempted robbery and on September 13, he had robbed the Club Saloon in Marysville, Montana. By this time, Montana authorities had raised a posse and were pursuing him closely. He said that he had successfully evaded capture by boarding a train to Tacoma.

After his execution was put on hold, Blanck was moved from the isolation cell into the main cell block. For the next few weeks, Blanck was quiet and seemed to behave like a model prisoner. He was secretly planning his escape, telling his cellmate, a condemned murderer named Henry Creamer, that he was either going to escape or die in the attempt.

Reporters, who often spoke with Blanck trying to get the story of his sordid criminal career, knew, given his history, that he would try at some point to affect an escape.

Blanck bided his time by observing the daily patterns of the jailers, making friends with fellow prisoners while scavenging pieces of wood and other items that might be useful in attempting an escape. While the other prisoners were asleep, he fashioned a replica of a .44 caliber revolver using a knife made from a steel shank in his shoe. He whittled and fashioned the pieces, glued them together with gum and soap, smoothed them with bits of broken glass and then blackened the finished replica by applying a mixture of soot and grease. To add an even more authentic flavor to the fake gun, he made reasonable facsimiles of bullets from pieces of tobacco wrap tinfoil and inserted them into the ends of the revolver cylinder. It took him nearly three months to create the artificial revolver but when he was finished, it might have fooled anyone due to its intricacy.

On Sunday March 17, 1895, the night jailer, Jeremiah Yerbury, left the jailer's office and made his way to the pass-through window of the main cell block (nicknamed the "steel tank") to deliver a nightly dose of medicine to a prisoner. When he arrived at the window, Blanck was waiting for him. He pulled the fake weapon from his shirt, pushed it through the bars and ordered the night jailer to surrender or be killed immediately. Blanck told Yerbury to approach the bars and turn his back. Reaching through the bars, Blanck tied Yerbury's arm to a bar and told him to unlock the cell doors. With help from a fellow prospective escapee, Frank Hart, he searched the jailer and relieved him of his .38 caliber Colt Model 1889 Revolver, the keys to the cells, his money ($.30) and his gray fedora.

Blanck finished tying Yerbury and locked him in the nearest cell. He invited any prisoners who desired their freedom to follow him out of the prison. There were 21 prisoners in the King County Jail at the time and 10 of them chose to accompany Blanck on his breakout. Two of the ten immediately ran to the Seattle Police Headquarters in Seattle City Hall at 3rd Avenue and Jefferson Street and gave the alarm.

Policemen rushed to the King County Jail and took a prisoner headcount. Newly elected King County Sheriff, Aaron Van de Vanter, sent word to all of the towns surrounding Seattle of the breakout and wired a list of the escapees and their descriptions to all authorities in the state. Deputies were dispatched in every direction to form posses and commence the search. James Woolery, a former sheriff, was directed to head search operations around and east of Lake Washington while Seattle Police Chief Bolton Rogers sent groups of officers to guard in key areas of the city. Since Blanck had spent some time in Tacoma, it was presumed that he might head for the area, so every trail, bridge, railroad track or road south of Seattle was blocked by guards.

Just after midnight, Deputy Sheriffs Kelly and Burkman who were guarding the Northern Pacific Railroad crossing one half mile south of the Black River Junction saw two men approaching them. When ordered to raise their hands, one man threw his arms while the other one disappeared into the brush. They captured one escapee, Servius Rutan, who named Blanck as the other man. Sheriff Van de Vanter immediately concentrated his efforts on guarding the area between Seattle and Tacoma. A special train was sent out with deputies to man stations at Renton, Black River, Orillia, Kent and Auburn. By 4:00 PM three additional escapees had been captured but Blanck continued to be at large.

No contact with Blanck was made for three days. He doubled back on his trail and did not challenge the guard posts. He hid in the dense woods and begged food at farmhouses where he was sure that people had not heard the news of his escape. Over one hundred men were in the posse and they drew an ever tighter circle with each sighting or discovery of a visit. Sheriffs Van de Vanter and

Woolery, who were on horseback, tracked down leads and repositioned guards as the situation changed.

Late in the afternoon on March, 21, Blanck appeared at the James Nelson farmhouse just east of Orillia and asked for food. Nelson recognized him from a picture he had been given by the posse. After providing the fugitive with his meal, Nelson made his way to the Orillia train station and wired the Kent station that Blanck was in the area and was undoubtedly moving south. Two special deputies, John Shepich and Robert Crow, took their specially issued 44-40 caliber Winchester lever action rifles (each holding 10 cartridges) and began walking north along the railroad tracks toward O'Brien Junction.

A mile north of Kent, they saw a stranger walking south toward them. When the man was about 30 yards from them, the deputies recognized that the man was Blanck and Shepich ordered him to raise his hands. Blanck ignored the order, drew the revolver he had stolen from the jailer Yerbury and fired. Shepich tried to raise his rifle to meet the challenge but was struck in the left forearm by a glancing bullet which continued on and broke his shoulder. Shepich returned fire not realizing that he was badly wounded. When Blanck moved off the tracks to the east embankment, Crow also began firing. Blanck fired his last round from the revolver and dove down the steep embankment of the railroad bed toward a marsh where he hoped to find a good place to hide.

Shepich finally realized that he had been shot and shouted out to Crow, "My God, Bob, I'm done for!" At that point, Special Deputy Charles Newell arrived at the scene carrying a shotgun. Shepich pointed out the area where Blanck was concealed and told Newell to fire in that direction in order to force him from his hiding place.

Shepich then ordered Blanck to surrender. Realizing that he was cornered, Blanck reluctantly emerged from the marsh and walked toward the railroad embankment with his arms in the air. Shepich warned the other deputies to watch out for Blanck trying to draw another weapon. Mistakenly thinking that Blanck was going for his gun, Crow and Newell immediately started firing at the fugitive. Blanck dropped to the ground and began crawling back to cover.

Crow fired two more shots into Blanck's retreating form. Hearing the gunfire, other deputies in the area rushed to join in and Thomas Crow, Robert's brother, climbed down the embankment and found the lifeless body of Blanck at the base.

Shepich was taken by handcar to Kent for medical attention. Blanck's body was loaded onto another handcar and was taken to the Kent railroad station where many of the townsfolk, hearing of the killing of the escaped prisoner, were waiting. The body was transferred to a baggage car of a special train and was taken by Sheriff Van de Vanter to Seattle where thousands more were gathered.

Underestimating the size of the crowd of morbid curiosity-seekers, Seattle Police Chief Rogers sent a patrol wagon with only

12 officers to manage crowd control. When Van de Vanter opened the sliding door to the baggage car, the crowd which had by that point become an unruly mob shouted, cheered and surged forward for a closer view.

With some difficulty, the sheriff and his deputies were able to drop the body into an awaiting coffin, shut the lid and load it onto a wagon that moved quickly to the Butterworth and Sons mortuary at 1425 2nd Avenue. Awaiting the wagon was another crowd of hundreds of men. In the crowd were Detective Cudihee and Officer Corbett, the two men who had originally captured Blanck prior to his escape.

The coroners assigned to the case, Dr. Oliver Askam and Dr. William Gibson, were able to determine that Blanck had died from seven gunshot wounds, three of which would have been fatal. They also found that Blanck was suffering from pneumonia, undoubtedly contracted during his four days on the run in the wet and cold Pacific Northwest weather. If he had not been shot, the coroners determined that he would probably have died from the disease.

A coroner's inquest into Blanck's death was held on March 22. Despite the fact that Blanck had been shot while trying to surrender, the six-man jury quickly returned a unanimous verdict that the deputies were acting in accordance with the law and were justified in killing the fugitive. No one was about to defend a convicted murderer, no matter what the circumstances.

Blanck's body was embalmed and displayed for three days at the viewing salon of the Butterworth and Sons Mortuary. People filed in from morning until night to see the body of the Pacific Northwest's most infamous criminal. As many women came as men, some brought flowers to place in the open coffin. One woman was reported to have kissed the corpse on the cheek.

People continued to hold a great curiosity about all things associated with the outlaw, Tom Blanck. Hyams, Paulson and Company, a purveyor of men's clothing, dressed a mannequin in the outfit that Blanck was wearing when was shot and killed. The display contained a large portrait of Blanck and also included the revolver that Blanck had stolen from Jailer Yerbury under the inscription, "T. B. from Yerbury, March 17, 1895."

The replica revolver that Blanck had fashioned in his cell and had used to escape from the King County Jail was auctioned off in Port Townsend, a town in which he had once been arrested, to raise money for a church charity netting the tidy sum of $6.50.

The memory of Tom Blank, only seven years in advance of the manhunt for Harry Tracy, was fresh in everyone's mind. Citizens expected a similar outcome with a short chase and the killing of the outlaw. Harry Tracy proved to be a much more intrepid fugitive than Tom Blank. This manhunt would take on more dreadful consequences for the posse and a frustrating series of events for the then King County Sheriff Cudihee.

Edward Cudihee was forty nine years old and a veteran of over two decades of police experience. Before coming to Seattle, he had served in Leadville, Colorado, a mining town noted for its wide-open atmosphere and frequent violence. He had spent four years in that city as a policeman and two years as Chief of Police. In 1889 he left Leadville and made his way to Seattle. He promptly joined the Seattle Police Department and remained with the department until his subsequent election as King County Sheriff.

With his experience, common sense and woodsman's instinctive practical nature, Cudihee was a man eminently suited to his job. A sheriff at the turn of the century in the West had to be a combination of frontier lawman and city constable. He had to have both the citified qualities of an administrator and politician and the country savvy to move quickly into the wild sections of the county to track down violent criminals.

As much as America was in transition from an agriculturally oriented economy to a more industrialized world power, so too was a citizen's outlook on crime changing; no longer was robbery and gunplay considered a harsh but necessary part of life. However, despite the changes happening throughout what had been known previously as untamed frontier, there was still a hangover of romantic nostalgia for the "wild west" and the life of an outlaw. A sheriff had to bridge the gap between both romantic and realistic points of view that often times emerged from the general population in an outpouring of love vs. hate and fear vs. admiration. Edward Cudihee had the unenviable job of hunting down dangerous men who were, at once, considered to be both folk heroes and bloodthirsty fiends.

The countryside that the sheriff had to police, King County, was unique in its difficulties. In the center was the boomtown of

Seattle with all of its attendant hotbeds for metropolitan crime: saloons, brothels, gambling houses and the surrounding shops and businesses. Outside of the city limits, the land quickly became wilderness as civilization was quickly swallowed up in thick undergrowth and primeval forest. Tracking a man through the inhospitable jungle was no easy matter, as the sheriffs of Northern Oregon and Southwest Washington could attest. It required a complete knowledge of all the natural advantages and disadvantages a hunted man might encounter in his quest for freedom. In addition to this information, a general's ability for planning maneuvers and tactics was needed in order to make sure the landscape would work in favor of the posse instead of the man being chased. With Puget Sound to the west and the Cascade Mountains to the east, King County was a funnel which only had to be blocked from the north and south to ensnare a victim. Cudihee was confidently aware of his jurisdiction and familiar enough with its character to be an effective leader of a posse. However, the manhunt for Harry Tracy was not to be an ordinary chase. The outlaw sought by Sheriff Cudihee had the experience and the intelligence to match any opponent and the two men, though never meeting face to face, would come to know each other with equal enmity and respect.

Edward Cudihee was one of ten children born to Irish immigrants who came to the United States in 1826. His father was a stone mason - a trade which young Edward both learned and learned to dislike. In his early adulthood, he worked for some time on a farm and as a clerk in a store. He grew tired of a mundane life in the east and, like so many others of the time - like Harry Tracy - he came west to find a new life in a new land.

His election to the office of King County Sheriff was a duty and honor which he did not take lightly. He used all of his energy and skill to pursue his job to the utmost. At this time, he was still a bachelor and he gave almost all of his time to being a sheriff. Because of his dedication, he held the respect of his fellow officers and of the community at large. One of the reasons for his universal popularity was his quality of passionate humanity which tempered his single-minded pursuit of justice. According to book *Memories And Genealogy Of Representative Citizens Of The City Of Seattle and King County, Washington*, Edward Cudihee was a "kind-hearted man and no prisoner in his charge had reason to complain of ill treatment."

In physical appearance, Cudihee was not particularly imposing. He was of medium height and tended toward being overweight. Despite his bulk, he was in good shape for a man of his age, having spent many arduous days tramping through the rough country of his county. A fashionable handle-bar moustache drooped luxuriously over his wide mouth helping to distinguish his rotund face. A thinning hairline promised baldness in old age. He had warm, dark eyes which held both compassion and resolve. A working sheriff, he never asked his deputies to do anything he would not do himself; consequently he always dressed simply and practically, never knowing when he would be required to direct a search for a criminal in the backwoods of King County.

******

Sheriff Cudihee was in Issaquah, a small town about twenty miles east of Seattle, on regular police business when he received a call that Harry Tracy had arrived in King County. John Freeman, a watchman at the University of Washington - located on a hill north of Seattle just above Lake Washington, had seen Tracy with a rifle and a sack slung over his shoulders making his way along the Northern Pacific Railway tracks that led around the lake toward the town of Bothell. Freeman said he had made eye contact with the man and had stared at him until he disappeared around the bend in the tracks. Freeman reported that even at a long distance, he had almost been "mesmerized" by Tracy's hypnotic eyes.

Cudihee assigned the leadership of a posse he ordered to Bothell to the one lawman in Seattle who knew anything about Harry Tracy, Deputy Sheriff Jack Williams, the man who had conducted the investigation of Harry Tracy-Severns-Bliss six years previously.

Deputy Williams was anxious to get to Bothell. He knew that Tracy had been a formidable opponent before, and now, with his maturity and experience, the outlaw would have to be captured quickly if the posse was to have a chance at success. The posse was hurriedly formed; it included Williams, Deputy Nelson and two newspaper reporters, one from each of the daily papers, The Seattle Times and the Seattle Post-Intelligencer. Williams planned to add a few Bothell men with knowledge of the local topography as soon as they arrived in that city. The four men took a streetcar to the foot of Madison Street where they boarded a motor launch to take them across Lake Washington to Kirkland. From Kirkland, they rode on horseback to Bothell. Sheriff Cudihee made haste from Issaquah toward Bothell where he planned to direct the search.

******

July 3 was to become the most infamous day in the manhunt since the day Harry Tracy broke out of prison. It was the kind of day which held portent of disastrous things to come: a dark and dreary sky draped low over Lake Washington as it hung like a shroud over the deep and dripping forest on the shoreline. Rain, that constant determinant of Pacific Northwest land and life, was falling in drizzling regularity. It was so cold that it seemed more like one of those awful dark winter days in January rather than an early day in summer. To the west, clouds billowed out of the Olympic Mountains like black streams of volcanic ash. It was the kind of day most local residents would prefer not to venture out, but would rather stay home to build a nice cheery fire out of alder logs to lounge beside.

But on this damp morning, Deputy Williams and Deputy Nelson set out with the accompanying reporters, Bothell residents Snohomish County Deputy Sheriff Raymond and a volunteer named Brewer, to try to find some evidence of Harry Tracy's presence in the area.

The small group proceeded down the railroad track in an easterly direction toward Woodinville. After only a mile or so, they met a man walking toward them. He was stopped and questioned. He proved to be a local citizen, not the outlaw they were seeking. The man informed the posse that he had not seen any sign of another man on the tracks all morning. Taking the citizen's word, the men turned and began searching the tracks leading back toward Seattle.

About a quarter mile west of the community of Wayne, the posse came upon a small cabin below the tracks. A short discussion followed between Williams and Raymond about the possibility that Tracy might be in the cabin. When all agreed that due to the inclemency of the weather the cabin might be a likely place of shelter, Williams decided not to force the issue with a direct assault that might give away the element of surprise. Instead, the posse doubled back on the railroad tracks to Wayne. There they borrowed a large canoe and proceeded along the shore of Lake Washington as quietly as they could dipping the oars softly into the choppy waters.

The landed on a spit of land just below the cabin and gingerly climbed out of the canoe onto the shore. Louis Sefrit, one of the reporters, found a path which led from the railroad tracks to the cabin. In the thick mud caused by the steadily falling rain, he discovered a fresh boot print.

"This is our place," said Deputy Williams in a tone of hushed excitement.

He decided to divide the posse. He, Nelson and Brewer were going to approach the cabin from the east side of the path while Raymond, Sefrit and Anderson were to flank them on the west side.

With side-long looks of anticipation, the men slowly moved forward as stealthily as they could with rifles and revolvers drawn for immediate action.

The rain chose that time to increase its flow of large, soaking drops. It was so wet and cold that the posse members' fingers began to numb against the cold metal of their weapons. It continued to fall in torrents across their field of vision.

The spit of land on which the cabin was located was choked with overgrown brush and slag. The cabin was nearly obscured by thick, overhanging tree branches.

As the men began to close in from their two positions, Tracy's head suddenly popped up from behind a large alder stump thirty feet in front of the cabin. The posse was taken completely by surprise. They had been focusing on the cabin.

Sighting down the barrel of his infamous Winchester, Tracy aimed for the first target he saw: Anderson's head at point blank range. Seeing movement out of the corner of his eye, Anderson jerked his face away just as the shot was fired. Miraculously, Anderson suffered only a graze on the cheek. However, he was dazed from the force of the bullet against his cheekbone and he stumbled on rubbery legs and fell into a ditch filled with a rivulet of rain water.

It took Anderson only a few seconds to be revived by the cold stream of water. As he rose, Tracy fired two more shots, this time at Deputy Raymond who had taken a crouching position in front of the stricken reporter in order to protect him from further fire.

Raymond's lifeless body fell back against Anderson as Tracy's deadly bullets smashed into his forehead.

Realizing that Tracy had an overwhelmingly superior position, Anderson plunged into the surrounding brush hoping to sneak around the outlaw's left flank. In the undergrowth, he met Nelson and Brewer who had the same idea. Hurrying to reach their new position, the men heard three more rifle shots. A few seconds later, the saw Deputy Williams crawl out of the brush on the opposite side of the path on his hands and knees. The three men watched helplessly as Williams, obviously wounded and in pain, snaked his way along the ground toward the safety of the cabin.

Williams reached the cabin and dragged himself through the front door. The other three men emerged from their concealment and rushed after him to render assistance. They found him groaning on the wood floor of the cabin with three bullet wounds just under his heart. Blood was flowing down his clasped hands into pools on the floor. Anderson tried to stop the bleeding with his handkerchief but in the process, Williams lurched to the side, muttered some unintelligible words and lapsed into unconsciousness.

Louis Sefrit then joined the group in the cabin. He remarked that Tracy had escaped into the woods behind the railroad tracks.

Anderson later filed this report on the gun battle:

"The fight occurred about 3:15 in the afternoon and was over in an incredibly short time. We were prepared to meet Tracy and while his appearance was rather sudden, we got into action at once. His head had hardly appeared before he fired. We were caught in an ambush and while Tracy was practically under cover, we were exposed almost entirely."

"The rain was falling so heavy that we were somewhat hampered in keeping a lookout. We were surrounded by dripping branches. He had the advantage. He was able to watch us approach while we had to move toward him not knowing if he was left or right. Not a syllable was uttered from the time we started down the path until we went to Williams' assistance. Williams was about 100 feet away and separated from our crowd when the fighting opened. He was still some distance away when Tracy saw him and turned his Winchester on him."

The gun battle was over almost before it began. Tracy had completely thwarted his opposition with only a few well-aimed shots. The diminished and disheartened posse took the lifeless body of Deputy Raymond and grievously wounded Deputy Williams back to the town of Bothell. Williams was immediately treated in Bothell by Dr. Lyle but he never fully recovered from his wounds and died a few years later as a result of complications from them.

******

Tracy moved quickly to distance himself from the confrontation with the posse. He stole a horse from a nearby barn and rode to the farm of Louis Johnson.

"I'm a deputy sheriff and one of the men on Tracy's trail," he said approaching the farmer. "I must get to Seattle at once and need your wagon. There's no time for delay."

When Johnson protested, Tracy changed his story. "Hitch it

up and do it quickly. I'm Tracy. I only have a few moments. Hurry."

Johnson obeyed the command. He hitched up his horses to the wagon which was in the process of repair, missing both sides and the bottom. Both men had to ride on the frame.

He whipped the horses into a run and started down the road which led to Seattle. Tracy sat behind Johnson with his deadly Winchester gripped tightly in his hands.

At one point on the road, a man emerged from the woods alongside the road and casually tried to climb on the wagon for a free ride. Tracy yelled down to him, "Stay off," and the wagon rushed by as the man fell back from the road.

About two miles from Green Lake, Tracy and Johnson came upon two deputies who were supposed to be guarding the road. However, at that time, they were preoccupied with their dinner.

"Drive slow," Tracy told Johnson. "They're deputies. I know by their guns."

Johnson pulled back on the reins and slowed his horses to a normal pace. The wagon passed by without so much as a look from the hungry deputies. When they were safely out of the guards' view, Tracy ordered Johnson to push the horses back to full speed.

The wagon continued down the road toward Fremont at a fast pace until the two men reached the Van Horn farmhouse, a two story home on the Fremont-Richmond Beach Road at the point where the thoroughfare skirted the southwest corner of Woodland Park. It was 8:00 in the evening. The large frame house was on the border of a wheat field which sloped down the hill toward Ballard. From the upper story of the house, a panoramic view of the suburbs north of Seattle could be seen as they encroached on the thick fir forests. Beyond Ballard, was Puget Sound framed at the horizon by the darkly pointed peaks of the Olympic Mountains.

Tracy and Johnson left the wagon at the side of the road and walked to the door of the house. There they were met by Mrs. Van Horn who had noticed their hasty approach. Tracy wasted no time in identifying himself and ordering a meal.

While waiting for Mrs. Van Horn to prepare dinner, Tracy sat at the dining room table with his back to a large picture window which offered a broad view of the well-traveled road. Mrs. Van Horn won Tracy's confidence by explaining the danger he was putting himself into by exposing himself so overtly.

"Do you know that we are right on a public road," she said, "and that the men who are hunting you are liable to pass at any moment and see you through the window? Anybody would recognize you from the pictures that have been printed in the papers."

Tracy thanked Mrs. Van Horn for the warning and asked her to draw the curtains over the window. While she was doing this, he went into the living room and pulled the curtains over the other exposed windows. He returned to his seat at the table and began talking to Johnson while Mrs. Van Horn finished her preparations in the kitchen.

"Why are you going back to Seattle?" asked Johnson. "Don't

you know that Sheriff Cudihee is close on your track?"

"Sheriff Cudihee is crowding me too closely," said Tracy. "Things have been different since I reached King County. I'm tired. I want to get to Seattle. This isn't a bluff. I'd feel safer there. I want to get into the city before daylight if possible. I'm going to take you downtown with me."

"But say, Tracy," said Johnson, "have you any hope of escaping?"

"I've had success so far," he said with a tone that was as much humorous as boastful.

Tracy told Johnson the details of the gun battle near Bothell. Johnson sat listening in morbid fascination as the deadly story was told by Tracy in a matter of fact manner.

According to Johnson, Tracy talked easily and acted "like a gentleman."

Mrs. Van Horn served the outlaw a large dinner which he ate ravenously. The excellent quality of the meal put Tracy in an agreeable mood.

"Give me your name and address," he said to Johnson.

"Why?" asked Johnson in surprise.

"Because I've troubled you a lot and if I ever do get a big wad again, I'm going to make things square with you. See?"

At 9:00 the grocery boy made his way up the slow rise of the hill which led up from Fremont to the Van Horn house. He was met at the gate by Mrs. Van Horn who had seen him coming down the road and had slipped out of the house through the kitchen door without Tracy noticing her. She cautioned the grocery boy to keep quiet and whispered that the outlaw, Harry Tracy, was in her house eating dinner. Without waiting another moment, the boy ran down to his box-shaped delivery wagon and whipped his horse into a full gallop back down the hill toward the town of Fremont.

At a main corner of the major street running through Fremont, he stopped and began screaming at the top of his lungs, trying to spread the alarm. He was so excited that his words spewed forth as unintelligible mumblings.

As luck would have it, at that very moment, Sheriff Cudihee, who had secured a buggy in Bothell and enlisted its owner, John Rogers, to drive him south in pursuit of Tracy, arrived in Fremont. He noticed the commotion at the center of town and told Rogers to head for it. It took the sheriff several minutes to extract the whole story from the excited grocery boy and for him to explain the outlaw's current location. A soon as the boy mentioned the Van Horn house, other local citizens explained to Cudihee how to reach it.

The news that the escaped convict, Harry Tracy, was in the immediate area, coupled with Sheriff Cudihee's information that he had killed at least one and possibly two men several hours earlier in Bothell, struck terror into the hearts of the innocent people on the Fremont streets. When the sheriff asked for volunteers for a posse to surround the Van Horn house, most men understandably declined. A few men including Constable Breece, Neil Rawley, a coal miner from Oregon visiting his family in town, and J. I.

Knight, a local insurance salesman, offered to join the posse as soon as they could get their weapons from their homes.

The sheriff set off immediately for the Van Horn house with the grocery boy showing the way. The other members of the posse were told to follow as soon as they could after retrieving their guns.

Cudihee was pleased to find that Johnson's wagon was still parked at the side of the Richmond Beach Road. As night was beginning to fall, he decided to surround the house and wait for Tracy to appear. He took a position directly in front of the wagon thinking that his most opportune time for a shot would be when Tracy mounted it. The other men, joining the sheriff, took positions in a semi-circle around the road side of the house.

They did not have to wait long. Tracy, after taking two pistols form the bureau drawer in the dining room, forced Johnson and an old man named Butterfield who boarded at the Van Horn house to walk on either side of him as he emerged from the house and walked toward the wagon. Although he had not seen the posse approach, Tracy was wary of taking any chances after staying such a long time in one place along the well traveled area.

Cudihee did not trust the makeshift posse to give him much help. He did not like working with unprofessional deputies, but, in this dangerous situation, he had to make do with what was available. To have waited for regular deputies, would surely have meant losing Harry Tracy to woods again; the sheriff did not want to risk having the outlaw on the loose another day. In his commanding position near the wagon, he hoped to get a shot at

Tracy without endangering any of his posse's lives. With no mishaps, he thought he could either wound or kill his adversary without additional help.

In the gathering darkness, Tracy pushed his hostages toward the wagon. At one point the three men passed by Cudihee's position, but the sheriff chose not to take a shot for fear of hitting one of the hostages. He decided to wait until Tracy climbed aboard the wagon. To his horror, he saw two men, Constable Breece and Neil Rawley who had just arrived on the scene and who had not seen any other members of the posse in their concealed positions, approach Tracy and his hostages.

The two men had no idea of the identity of the three men walking across the road and Rawley casually walked up and asked them if they had seen the sheriff.

"No," said Butterfield, his voice choked with fear.

Tracy carefully placed Johnson between him and the two posse members.

"Whose rig is that?" asked Rawley.

"I don't know," said Butterfield.

"Why, it's Tracy's," exclaimed Rawley.

Constable Breece stepped forward and ordered, 'Drop that rifle, Tracy," seeing the outlaw trying to hide his weapon behind his leg.

Tracy flipped the butt of his rifle, which was partially concealed under his coat, into the crotch of his elbow and fired a shot at Breece with his right hand (his left hand held Butterfield in position as a shield). The bullet struck the dumbfounded Breece squarely in the forehead, killing him instantly.

Letting go of his grip on Butterfield, Tracy swung his rifle to his shoulder and fired another shot into Breece's head as he fell.

Rawley saw Breece fall and was close enough to grab Tracy's shooting arm while drawing his own pistol. Tracy would not relinquish his grip on his rifle although it was of no use in a close fight with Rawley. He pulled one of the two pistols he had obtained from the Van Horn bureau only minutes before and fired two shots at point blank range into Rawley's stomach.

Seeing the gunplay, J. I. Knight jumped up from his concealed position and fired his .38 caliber revolver in the dim light at what he thought was the fleeing figure of Tracy. Cudihee also rose, realizing that his plan had been completely ruined by the blundering of Breece and Rawley and fired a shot in the direction of another man, who was in reality, Butterfield.

The gun battle, as was the previous one in Bothell, was short, deadly and confused. All shots were fired in almost total darkness, causing no one to see exactly what was happening. Tracy disappeared again into the protection of the forest.

Constable Breece lay dead in a pool of brains and blood. Next to him, only feet away, lay the mortally wounded form of Neil Rawley, moaning and writhing in pain. It was a shocking and gruesome sight to the Fremont men who only an hour before had been peacefully going about their evening business.

This was J. I. Knight's account of the gun battle:

"I was hiding within six feet of the team. Tracy and the two men came out, the desperado walking between the two. They approached the horses from the opposite side where I was concealed and passed within six feet of where I was crouching."

"It had grown so dark that it was a matter of conjecture as to the exact locations occupied by the men. Breece arose and called out, 'Drop that gun, Tracy,' just as the middle man passed around where I was concealed. No sooner had the words left his lips than two shots rang out in quick succession and by the finish of the last one I saw Breece reel and fall to the ground. I did not know at that time that one of the bullets had also found a target in Rawley, whom I could see by the flash, stood a few feet from Breece. I am certain that Breece also fired before he fell to the ground."

"Here, I arose from my place of concealment and fired two shots with a revolver at the retreating murderer."

Although Knight's account was fairly accurate considering the darkness and confusion, some facts remained unclear as to who shot whom and how long the actual firing took place. A later inspection of the bodies was to reveal that Breece was killed with two .30 caliber rifle slugs and that Brawley was killed with bullets from a .38 caliber revolver.

A controversy raged over the next few days about the possibility that Knight may have killed Rawley by accident before it was finally determined that it was Tracy who had killed him with the Van Horn revolvers.

Tracy had again emerged victorious from a gun battle and a

confrontation with a posse. He was still no closer to being captured than the day he escaped. He was simply just too wily and experienced to be captured by ordinary citizens. He was a dead shot who hit his target with every round he fired. He was bold and resourceful and seemed unconcerned about facing any armed posse. He had escaped once again by breaking the posse's spirit with quick action and immediate disappearance. He appeared to be invincible. Sheriff Cudihee was forced to reorganize the search as if it were just beginning.

Photograph of Seattle in 1902 (Courtesy of Museum of History and Industry).

Seattle Waterfront as it appeared in 1902 (Image courtesy of
Library of Congress Prints and Photographs Division).

Photograph of Seattle streetcars - the main form of transportation
for the posse chasing Tracy (from The Seattle Times).

Pier 3/54 (where Ivar's Acres of Clams is now located) in 1902
(from The Seattle Times).

Seattle street scene in 1902 (from Seattle Municipal Archives),

Harry Tracy in Utah in 1897 (photo from Utah State Historical
Soc.).

Mug shot of Harry Tracy (Oregon State Penitentiary).

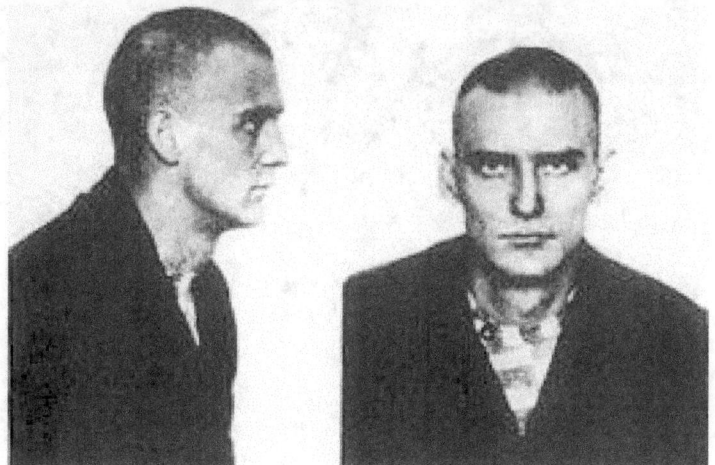

Mug shot of Dave Merrill (Oregon State Penitentiary).

Photograph of the Oregon State Penitentiary in 1902.

A posse searching for Tracy and Merrill after they escaped from the Oregon State Penitentiary in Salem in 1902.

Guard Carson (in his rolled up Stetson) and his bloodhounds (photograph from a newspaper article in the Daily Oregon Statesman in Salem).

Newspaper photographic rendering of the Oregon Posse during the
early days of the manhunt.

Composite image of Harry Tracy dressed in black during the King
County manhunt (from Seattle Times).

EDWARD CUDIHEE

Photograph of King County Sheriff Edward Cudihee.

THOMAS BLANCK.

The murderer Thomas Black first captured by Detective Edward Cudihee in 1894.

Newspaper drawing of Deputy Sheriff Jack Williams severely wounded in Bothell on July 3, 1902.

Newspaper drawing of Deputy Sheriff Williams killed by Tracy in Bothell on July 3, 1902.

Newspaper drawing of Policeman Breece shot and killed by Harry
Tracy near Fremont on July 3, 1902.

Newspaper Drawing of Posse member Neil Rowley shot and killed by Harry Tracy near Fremont on July 3, 1902.

Photograph of the keel laying ceremony of the Battleship Nebraska on July 4, 1902.

The USS Battleship Nebraska (US Naval Service Archives).

Photo illustration by Charles George in the New York City Daily News.

Newspaper illustration of John Anderson, the hired hand
captured by Tracy on Bainbridge Island.

Newspaper illustration of Harry Tracy forcing Anderson
to row him across Puget Sound.

The "Plucky" Miss May Baker (from The Seattle Times).

Newspaper illustration of the E. M. Johnson farm near Auburn, WA.

Photograph of the E. M. Johnson family held captive by Harry Tracy (photograph by Asahel Curtis Seattle P I).

Photograph of posse members inspecting a cabin where Tracy was thought to hidden.

The Johnson (Olson) farm near Auburn, Washington where Tracy sent Mr. Johnson to Tacoma for a pistol that he would later use to commit suicide rather than be captured.

The Eddy Ranch, where Tracy made his final stand in 1902.
(Courtesy Jim Dullenty, Hamilton, Montana)

Photo from Clayton Deer Park Historical Society.

The Creston Posse - the expanded version - after Harry Tracy's body had been recovered.(photograph courtesy of Creston Historical Society).

Tracy's body in the Eddy's field after the final gunfight with the Creston posse (from a postcard).

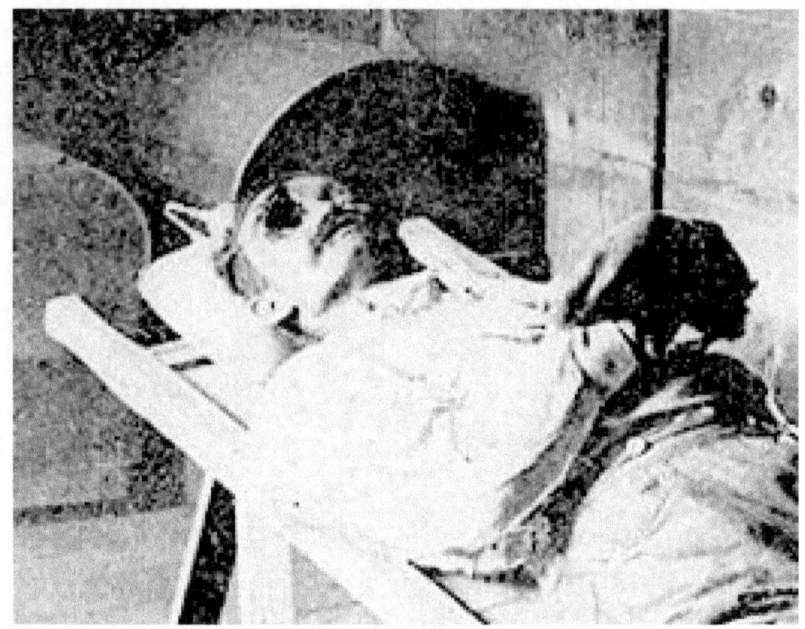

Harry Tracy's body showing the self-inflicted bullet wound in his right eye (photograph from Spokane Gazette).

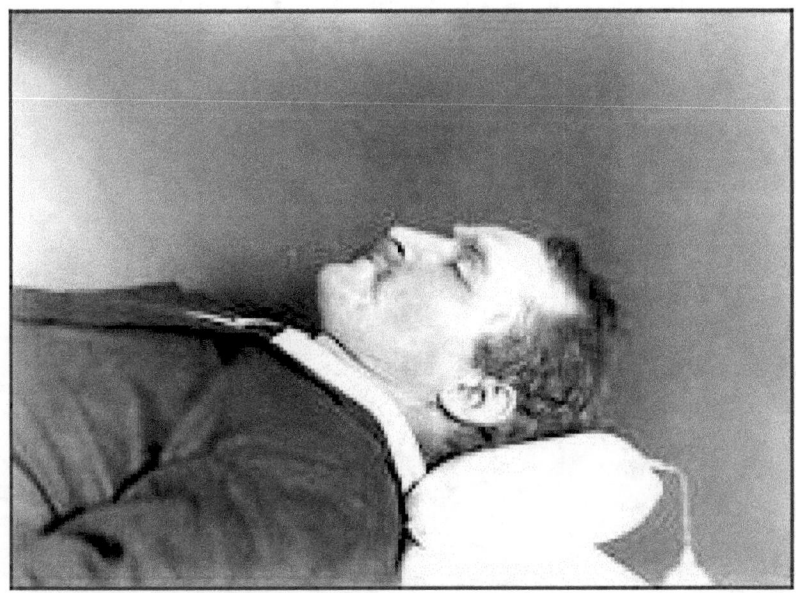

The lifeless Body of Harry Tracy after embalming
(photograph from Spokane Gazette).

Chapter 10:

Excitement in the City

July 3 was a hectic day in Seattle. Hundreds of people left their homes and jobs to mill around the streets near the newspaper buildings hoping to catch the latest news on the manhunt posted on bulletin sheets in the windows. As the grisly details of the first gun battle were placed into position, men, women and children "pushed and hauled each other around" to get a good view.

Groups of men gathered in the saloons and on street corners to discuss, as amateur lawmen, what should be done to capture the fugitive, Harry Tracy. Many men, carried away by their bold talk and liquid courage, rushed to the hardware stores to buy guns and ammunition and planned to either join the official posse or go out on their own.

The focal point of activity in the city was at the Union Station Depot, a large brick building recently constructed in the prevailing style of the day - a semi-elegant, somewhat gothic, somewhat early twentieth century utilitarian edifice with a large clock spire. Undersheriff Corcoran was the man in charge at the depot. He was forming a posse to assist Sheriff Cudihee in the field. Word of the outlaw's presence in the area north of the city had spread as fast as a bad rumor could in a small town and wave after wave of volunteers had reported to the depot ready for action, dressed in assorted hunting outfits with boots laced half way to the knee, and armed with every kind of rifle, bird gun and pistol imaginable.

Most of the volunteers wanted nothing to do with any official posse and only asked to be let off somewhere near the scene of the Bothell gun battle so they could have a chance to ambush Tracy in the woods.

An almost circus atmosphere prevailed at the depot with little groups of men standing around the yards impatiently talking and laughing about what they would do when they came face to face with the notorious outlaw. It was as if the men welcomed the chance to leave their mundane occupations as clerks, farmers, office workers and laborers to take part in the strange adventure which was unfolding in their county. The added zest of possible danger made the call to adventure all the more attractive.

As the day wore on, the crowd at the Union Station continued to grow until it reached around 5,000 people.

Undersheriff Corcoran decided to send out the first train of deputies and volunteers (the more serious ones including Jim Wilson who was a friend of Deputy Sheriff Raymond and Dick Burkman who had participated in the manhunt for Tom Blanck eight years previously) without the request of Sheriff Cudihee. Before the train reached the Interbay Station, it had to be called back when the sheriff phoned and said he was not ready for any more men.

While the impatient deputies waited for a second start, the regularly scheduled train from the north pulled into the yard with the blood-soaked body of Deputy Sheriff Raymond. The laughter and gaiety hushed at the sight.

Mrs. Williams, the wife of the wounded Deputy Sheriff Williams, made her way through the crowd to board a special train which was to take her to Bothell and to the side of her ailing husband. Her tears aroused the crowd from lethargic pity for the plight of Raymond to mood of vengeful determination.

The trainload of deputies and volunteers finally left the station at 8:00 PM when a telephoned message from Cudihee to Corcoran told him to send the men to the Ravenna area rather than Bothell because he thought Tracy was on the move south.

After seeing off the train, Corcoran proceeded to the Hardy and Wells Hardware Store. There, he gave out rifles to those who volunteered to travel to Ravenna by streetcars. Many more men offered their services than were allowed to go since most had never handled a firearm in their life. Corcoran only gave rifles to those men he knew he could recognize; he did not want the volunteers to walk off with the borrowed weapons.

That evening, people were still arriving from the small towns and communities around Lake Washington with more news of the second gun battle and with the hope of joining a posse. One man, Constable Hubbard of Green Lake, had walked all day from that town with an armload of firewood for his children. When he reached home and found that Harry Tracy was in the area, he filled his pockets with cartridges, got his rifle, borrowed a rig from a nearby farm and hurried to join the posse.

Undersheriff Corcoran returned to the sheriff's office and tried feverishly to contact all of the marshals of the small towns north of

Seattle. However, many of them had already left their offices and were unreachable until morning.

Every outbound streetcar on Third Avenue carried a full load of heavily armed men hoping to participate in the manhunt. Each man was determined to shoot the outlaw on sight. As one of the streetcars pulled away from the loading area, a man from the crowd who was caught up in the excitement of the moment yelled, "No one is safe until that wild beast is shot to death." His exhortation was met with exuberant agreement from the departing man hunters; they waved their rifles in the air and shouted back with whoops and yells.

Corcoran was still on the move; he was a man possessed. Seeing that the armed men were moving in a steady flow to the north, he gave up his organizational position and rushed over to the hotel where he knew Governor McBride and Adjutant General Drain were staying for the night. Both men were in town for a special occasion to be held the next day.

It was the evening before the Fourth of July ceremony at the Moran Shipyards to lay the keel of the battleship *Nebraska*. Governor McBride was about to pay a formal call on Governor Savage of Nebraska when Corcoran approached him in the lobby of the hotel to discuss the details of the manhunt. The governor did not like being interrupted on his mission of furthering the reputation of the state of Washington as an up and coming industrial center by talk of an outlaw gone berserk. On the eve of such a propitious event as the laying of the keel of a battleship, the uncivilized goings-on reflected badly upon the supposedly modern city that Seattle was trying to become. When Corcoran requested that the Washington National Guard be called out to assist the posse, McBride dismissed him with the excuse that he would need Sheriff Cudihee's personal request in order to move forward. Corcoran grudgingly but loyally accepted the governor's refusal and went to the Western Union offices to send a message to Cudihee.

The telegram read:

"Governor McBride in town. Have requested him to order out a company of militia to go to Bothell. He says the sheriff himself must make the request. Can only send you about fifteen men. If you think that number insufficient, wire the governor direct. Corcoran."

Sheriff Cudihee did not receive the message.

Governor McBride, after making his call on Nebraska Governor Savage, gave this statement to reporters about his refusal to order out the Guard.

"I will be in Seattle until two o'clock tomorrow afternoon and by that time something may develop. We will give any assistance in our power. As I understand it, Tracy is in full flight so it would be a hard matter to know where to send troops even if they were called to help."

The contingent of VIPs from Nebraska expressed a strong interest in what one man called "the game of hide and seek going on for a desperate man with nothing to lose and everything to gain, and law abiding citizens who want to crush his life out because it is a menace to people at large." Many of the Nebraska men were old Indian fighters, veterans of the wars with the Sioux and Cheyenne on the Midwestern plains, and their martial spirit had been stirred by the newspaper accounts of the deeds of Harry Tracy. They announced to all who would listen that they would like nothing better than to join the manhunt which "must end in death if the outlaw is encountered."

******

Undersheriff Corcoran remained in the city late into the night talking with various men eager to join the search. He said the reason for the large turnout of men was partially because of the reward incentive but also because there were many "solid, substantial citizens who want Tracy killed as a measure of safety and protection to the community at large."

Sheriff Cudihee returned to Seattle at 1:00 AM. He was covered with a coating of dark King County mud, his trousers were torn and his left hand was gashed by a run-in with a barbed wire fence. He had come into the city to change his wet and soiled clothes and try to get a few hours sleep. As soon as he reached his office, he was besieged by reporters eager to know the details of the gun battles that had occurred that day.

"There are too many men after Tracy," he announced with a look of exhaustion and disgust. "Twice today we had him dead to rights, when other men butted in and we lost him. I had him just as certain as fate had not Breece and Rawley come up at Van Horn's house. I told Breece not to come up there as I wanted to ambush him myself and make sure. I made up my mind to shoot the man who carried a gun out of that house. I did not propose to take any chances and wanted to make sure of my man. I had a perfect view from three sides and he could not get to his horse without my seeing him. Then this shooting began and the next thing I know Tracy came jumping over the fence and I began to pump lead at him. I don't suppose I was closer than a hundred yards from him when I shot and it was quite dark. Had those men jumped away I would have had a beautiful chance to bring him down. The same thing was true at Bothell when that old man came crowding in with his horse which Tracy took from him."

"It is my opinion," continued Cudihee, "that Tracy is crazy and that he will shoot any man on sight. For that reason, it is dangerous to have so many men after him. It will not do at all to beat the brush for a man like him. The only thing to do is patrol the roads and have men stay where they are ordered and shoot Tracy down from ambush. There are a lot of young fellows beating around the timber up there by Woodland Park that I knew nothing about. If one of them gets a shot at him it will be purely by accident."

At the Union Street Depot, the crowd of several thousand which had been waiting throughout the day for more news, stayed late in to the night hoping that they might see Tracy's dead body come in on the train. Most of the people, however, had left the station for the Second Avenue newspaper bulletin boards when the Bonney and Stewart dead wagon took the body of Deputy Raymond to the undertaker parlors at the corner of Third and Columbia. Several hundred people followed the dead wagon. A few men clamored for admittance to view the body and inspect the wounds, but they were refused until a postmortem could be performed.

Deputy Raymond had been a member of the Seattle Police Department from 1889 to 1890 before he had moved to the Snohomish County Sheriff's Department. He had left the Seattle force when he had a disagreement with Police Chief Charles Munroe. Raymond left a widow and five children along with many Seattle friends from the days when he had walked a beat south of Yesler Way.

Wounded Deputy Sheriff Williams arrived at the depot at 11:30 PM on a special train from Bothell. It had been discovered that he had been struck by only one bullet; however, the bullet had split into four pieces when it hit the barrel of his rifle. Three pieces of lead had pierced his chest under his heart; the fourth went into his right wrist. Williams was taken to Providence Hospital in a patrol wagon where it was determined that he would live. Years later, he would die as a result of complications associated with his wounds making a total of four men to die under the expert and deadly marksmanship of Harry Tracy in that single day.

Citizens of King County went to bed that night with a feeling of dread. The escaped convict and killer, Harry Tracy, had murdered their sleep. Bolts and latches which had never before been used were placed into position with the hope that they would hold back the one man terror. In the northern suburbs of Seattle, where the outlaw remained at large, children cried themselves to sleep, women prayed and men sat up all night with guns across their laps.

Chapter 11:

Keel Laying Ceremonies: July 4, 1902

The gates to the Moran Brothers shipyards were opened to the public at 10:00 on the morning of the Fourth of July holiday. Despite the rain which fell in a light drizzle all morning long, the spirits of the crowd, which numbered up to twenty thousand people, were not dampened.

It was a showcase day for the city of Seattle and the state of Washington. The laying of the keel of the battleship *Nebraska* was symbolic of the region's desire to break out of its "pioneer" image into the mainstream of twentieth century technological life. The fact that most of the city was in the grips of virtual siege created by the fugitive killer, Harry Tracy, was an embarrassing reminder that the Pacific Northwest still had some way to go before it shed its frontier trappings.

The Moran Brothers shipyard had prospered during the Klondike Gold Rush of 1897, perhaps the single most important event in the history of Seattle. The discovery of gold in the Klondike region of the Yukon Territory in Canada turned the city from a backwater logging community into a thriving economic center of the Pacific Northwest. In so doing it helped bring to an end, at least in the Pacific Northwest, to the terrible effects of the Panic of 1893, one of America's worst economic depressions. It also enriched, in a non-monetary way, the lives of many of the men and women who participated in the Klondike Gold Rush and who returned home with scarcely a nugget or ounce of precious dust. Many "Klondikers" told stories to their families and friends of the "Great Adventure" they had experienced and the wonderful country they had seen both in Alaska and in the Pacific Northwest.

On July 17th, the steamship *Portland* docked in Seattle from St Michael, Alaska, carrying returning prospectors and what newspapers said was "a ton of gold." Two days earlier a similarly laden ship had arrived in San Francisco from Alaska. The "Klondike Gold Rush" was on as newspapers spread the word through telegraph messages from Seattle that gold had been found along a remote river in the Yukon Territory of Canada.

Fearing mass starvation in the rugged, trackless area, Canada's Northwest Mounted Police soon required each person headed there to bring a year's supply of food and equipment. This requirement fueled an economic boom as Seattle merchants quickly exploited the ruling, advertising the city as the "Gateway to the Gold Fields" - the place where all one's gold prospecting needs, from food and warm clothing to tents and transportation could be supplied. Roughly 70% of the estimated 100,000 people who ultimately attempted to reach the Klondike bought their required ton of provisions in Seattle. The city prospered economically and the population doubled to encompass 80,000 citizens by 1900.

During the Gold Rush, the Moran Brothers stayed home and struck it rich refitting old boats and supplying them with new machinery. The brothers also constructed a Yukon River fleet of 14 stern wheel river steamers and four freight barges.

Most of the prospectors made their way north by boat to the Alaskan towns of Skagway and Dyea, located at the head of the Lynn Canal. From these towns they traveled up the Chilkoot trail and crossed the Chilkoot Pass, or they hiked up and over to White Pass and then proceeded to Lake Bennett at the headwaters of the Yukon River. Prospectors then built rafts and boats that would take them the final 500-plus miles down the Yukon to Dawson City, the nearest town to the gold fields At the top of the passes, the prospectors encountered Canada's North West Mounted Police Post that enforced that regulation requiring the "ton of supplies" as well as customs and duties. It was put in place to avert shortages like those that had occurred previously in Dawson City, and also to restrict the entry of guns, particularly handguns, into British territory. Another reason the "Mounties," as they came to be called, were stationed at the border was to keep out of Canadian territory the criminal element under the leadership of the notorious Soapy Smith which had established itself in Skagway and the other Yukon Ports. There was also a fear among both Canadians and the British alike that there might be a possible armed takeover of the gold fields by the United States military.

Among the many people to take part in the gold rush was the writer Jack London. His books *The Call of he Wild*, *White Fang* and *Burning Daylight* were influenced by his experiences in Alaska and at the gold fields. London was inspired to write his stories by the interesting people he met along the way. Another literary luminary connected with the rush, and whose cabin still stands in Dawson

City, was the legendary song lyricist and folk poet, Robert W. Service. The opening lines of Robert W. Service's most famous poem set the tone for the incredible excitement and inherent danger of the gold rush adventure.

"The Cremation of Sam Magee by Robert Service
There are strange things done in the midnight sun
    By the men who moil for gold;
The Arctic trails have their secret tales
    That would make your blood run cold;
The Northern Lights have seen queer sights,
    But the queerest they ever did see
Was that night on the marge of Lake Lebarge
    I cremated Sam McGee."

Dawson City was also the setting for the beginning of the career of theatric "impresario" Alexander Pantages. He opened a small theater in the city that catered for the needs of the miners. He also became a partner and lover with the legendary "Kondike Kate." Rockwell. Kate was a tap dancer and vaudeville performer with the Savoy Theatrical Company whose act was very popular among the gold rush prospectors in Dawson City. When she joined forces with Pantages, they both became very successful. However, they had legendary arguments that eventually led to an end to their relationship. When the gold rush died down, Pantages activities expanded and he went on to become one of America's greatest theater and movie tycoons. Pantages' theatres still dot the west as a reminder of his success. The "Klondike Gold Rush" helped many Seattle businesses make money quickly.

By 1900, the Moran Brothers Company was known nationwide as a premier shipbuilder. In 1901, they won the contract to build the battleship *Nebraska*. The keel of the battleship was laid on July 4, 1902, and over the next two years more than 1,000 workmen were employed in the making of the battleship.

The *Nebraska* was launched on October 7, 1904. Over the next two years the battleship was in the shipyards, undergoing many changes in armaments. It was commissioned on July 1, 1907, the last battleship in the *Virginia Class*, and was regarded as the flagship of the United States Navy. The *Nebraska* was part of the "Great White Fleet" in 1908 and also saw action off Veracruz in 1914 and 1916. During the First World War, the *Nebraska* served as a training ship and as an escort of mercantile convoys. In 1923, the old battleship was dismantled and sold for $37,100 to a California scrap metal dealer.

The strain of building the *Nebraska* took its toll on Robert Moran. He was told by his doctor in 1905 that he had one year to live. He moved to Orcas Island in the San Juan Islands of Puget Sound where he built the Moran Mansion which was surrounded at that time by 7,800 acres of land. The mansion later became the Rosario Resort, a signature luxury property of the region. Moran outlived his doctor's prediction, sold his shipbuilding enterprise and went on to live another 38 years secluded on Orcas Island in his mansion.

The people who had come to attend the keel-laying ceremony for the *Nebraska* were dressed in the best attire. The men wore conservative suits with starched collars and cravats. To protect themselves from the inclement weather, they were covered with long overcoats that were a bit too heavy for the summer season. The women tried to appear sophisticated in the long, fashionable summer pastel dresses, but they had to huddle underneath parasols to protect their carefully coiffed hairstyles.

The shipyards were festively decorated in red, white and blue bunting and banners. They were hung in profusion under the direction of A. B. Bullion, the chief draftsman of Moran Brothers.

The main shed, where the battleship *Nebraska* was under construction, was the center of the activities. The machines were put in operation for the visitors to see; lathes, shaping machines and steel and iron cutters were whirring with impressive precision. The shed was an enormous building nearly one thousand feet long and one hundred feet wide, large enough to accommodate most of the crowd under its broad roof.

The grandstand was set up on one side under the looping drapes of bunting with "Nebraska" spelled out on the right and "Washington" on the left. In the center of the display were the flags of the two states flanking a large American flag gilded with gold fringe and topped with a brass eagle. Facing the grandstand on the opposite side of the shed was the bandstand; it was also covered in bunting. The marine band, largely brass and percussion, fidgeted in their chairs waiting to for their chance to perform. Above the band were the words, "Equality Before The Law."

Giant traveling cranes that were to lift the massive keel and place it into position were decorated with incandescent bulbs running along their sides with *Nebraska* spelled out in letters of more lights. When the cranes began to move, the letters flashed on and off adding glitter to the show.

At the entrance to the shed, the lighthouse tender, *Columbia*, had her signal flags flying for the occasion. The transport ship, *Sevard*, was lying in dry dock and also had her colors on display.

The procession of speakers and dignitaries began at 12:00 noon accompanied by the sound of pistol shots, tooting horns, shrieking whistles and blare of the marine band playing "a lively air." The canons which were supposed to mark the opening of the ceremonies with a tremendous boom failed to fire: they had been spiked by what the newspapers later called "a handful of mischievous and malicious persons."

There were those among the crowd who objected to the keel-laying ceremonies as evidence of "creeping imperialism in America." But, according to the Seattle Times whose owner, Colonel Alden J. Blethen, was part of the procession, these people were only a "puny opposition" who "undertook to interpose against the laying of the keel of the battleship." Due to the enthusiastic reception of the large crowd, the Daily Times concluded that "no juster a rebuke could be given the puerile and un-American attempt to prevent a successful laying."

The advance guard of the procession was a squad of Marines under the command of Lieutenant D. P. Hall. They marched up sharply to the stairway leading to the grandstand and stood at attention.

Two policemen dressed in the best blues with long coats and high hats lead the main body of VIPS. Chairman Josiah Collins and ex-Governor McGraw of the reception committee walked abreast of each other immediately in front of the guest of honor, Governor Savage of Nebraska, who was on the arm of President Clise of the Chamber of Commerce. They were followed by Governor McBride of Washington leaning on the arm of Judge Thomas Burke who was to serve as Master Of Ceremonies. Next in the procession was Governor McBride's wife escorted by Colonel Blethen (a fact conveniently omitted by the rival Post Intelligencer in its account of the proceedings). Behind the civilian officials, were representatives of the two states' militias: General Colby of Nebraska (famous for his bloody campaigns against the Indians of the Midwestern plains) and Adjutant General Drain of Washington. Following the generals were their respective contingents in order of rank.

The Washington National Guard was noticeably uncomfortable because their plain uniforms of faded blue and soft campaign hats were in stark contrast to the Nebraska National Guard who wore the full dress uniforms of U.S. Army staff officers with gold lace trim and gold braid looped over the rich, blue coats. On their heads the Nebraska men proudly wore cockade hats with long, golden plumes floating magnificently in the breeze.

Major Mills, the engineer in charge of government fortifications in the district, walked quietly to his place on the grandstand dressed in his fatigue uniform as the only representative of the regular United States Army. His face bore the marks of displeasure at witnessing the spectacle of "Sunday Soldiers" on parade.

Governor Savage walked in large striding steps. He was a "tall, courtly gentleman" and he was adorned in a lush goatee and moustache with long flowing hair that fell across his shoulders in silver-gold profusion. He wore a long western style jacket and soft wide-brimmed hat which he swept frequently off his head to acknowledge the cheers of the crowd.

Governor McBride was not as tall at his counterpart but he had a massive bull physique that made him appear taller than he was. He walked with the "quiet air of a jurist" and seemed a fitting representative of his growing state.

When at last all members of the procession were in their appointed positions on the grandstand, Chairman Collins stepped up to the podium and led the assembly in the Pledge Of Allegiance.

He then addressed the crowd:

"Ladies and Gentlemen, Nebraska has never built a battleship. Nor, for that matter has Washington. But Washington is going to build one and it is to be named *Nebraska*. We have invited the chief executive of Nebraska to come to the state of Washington to see us begin the construction of the battleship which is to be built in this state and named in honor of the state of Nebraska. And allow me, on this occasion, to predict that when the battleship is constructed and goes forth upon the seas to join the others of this nation that she will be one of the best fighting machines, not only in the navy of the United States, but in the navies of the world. I take pleasure in introducing the honorable Thomas Burke who will act as the Master Of Ceremonies on this occasion."

Judge Burke took the stand to the cheers and applause of the crowd. Despite a reputation for a few questionable business dealings, he was well liked by the ordinary people of Seattle and was widely recognized as being the best orator in the state. He was a short, stocky man with a flat, jowly face, but when his voice thundered out of his small visage it resounded like that of a giant. He took his speaking time to expound on the future of Washington in the United States which was just beginning to feel the potential of its destiny.

"This is one of the most interesting occasions in the history of Seattle. It is not too much to say that the laying of the keel of a first class battleship in a Puget Sound shipyard is today an event of national importance. It emphasizes, as nothing else could do, the wonderful advances made in the last few years in this part of the country. Not only has this great seaport state increased in population at an astonishing rate, but its seagoing commerce and its shipbuilding interests have outstripped in rapidity of growth the great advance made in population. Two facts briefly stated will illustrate the wonderful development of these two interests."

"In the building of sailing vessels the state of Washington

today is second only to the state of Maine both in number of vessels built and their tonnage capacity - while as a builder of steam vessels our state ranks seventh among maritime states of the Union."

"The admiralty cases brought and disposed of in this state's district court for the state of Washington exceed in number and amounts involved those of any other district court in the United States except the district of New York. These two facts tell the story of the marvelous rise of shipbuilding interests and sea-going commerce on Puget Sound more impressively than mere volumes of statistics. And we have only just begun."

"It was the great mission of the pioneers of Washington to blaze a way across the continent in order to make room for an expanding national commerce and to lay foundations of a great seaport state. In the days when this was undertaken, it was a bold and daring enterprise carried to success with a courage, fortitude, skill and judgment worthy of all praise. Their successors are now engaged in a still more stupendous task - the men of Washington today propose no less than commercial conquest of the mighty ocean hat stretches from our doors for 6,000 miles away to strange lands and strange peoples. The great merchant fleets that this enterprise will call forth must not be left without protection. The vast commerce of the United States upon land is abundantly protected both from foreign and domestic foes; the same cannot, or at least not until very recently, be said of commerce and property of our citizens upon the high seas. In an old address to both houses of Congress in 1790, Washington declared that 'to be prepared for war is one of the most effective ways of preserving the peace.' The experience of all ages has vindicated the wisdom of that sentiment. The building of great battleships and such warlike preparations are really in the interests of peace. Competition in trade and commerce is bound to give rise to sharp disputes and where, as now, there are earnest, sometimes intense, international contests for new markets, disputes may at anytime flame out into quarrels and the nation whose flag is without support or protection of an adequate navy is likely in such controversies to suffer defeat or humiliation or even worse. Therefore, in making ample provision for the protection of our great and growing interests upon every sea in every part of the world, we are but following the advice of the father of our country as a well as the lesson of universal history."

"On the other hand, it is undeniable that the possession of great powers is apt to foster a bullying spirit, which, in a great and powerful nation is to be deplored. It is excellent to have a giant's strength, but it is tyrannical to use it like a giant. Between two dangers, as between two evils, we should choose the lesser one and the past experience of this country warrants us, I hope, in the belief that intelligence, forbearance and sense of justice of the people of the United States will always be sufficient to deter them from acting the part of a bully toward other nations."

"At the close of the Civil War, our statesmen were apparently so indifferent to the necessity for making provisions for the protection of the nation's rights at sea that in the language of Spears, the historian, 'our warships were sold off in job lots as a merchant would dispose of his shopworn goods and no thought was given, or measures taken, to replace them with superior vessels.' The country was left without a navy. It is a singular and interesting fact - interesting because it shows at once the great change in the sentiment of the people of the United States towards the navy and the marvelous strides which have been made in shipbuilding and commerce on Puget Sound - that no less than twenty years ago there was not a shipyard in the United States able to produce a battleship of the type of the 'Nebraska.' And yet, as a recent historian of the Navy has said, 'the foundation of all sea power is the shipyard.' But two decades ago we had neither a shipyard where a navy could be built, nor a navy. What we all see before us which has so recently added luster and renown to American arms and such a glorious page to American history has come into existence since 1885."

"The courage and patriotism of the sailors of this new navy, guided and inspired by the by the genius and daring of a Dewey, have given us an island continent in the middle of the far eastern seas. For weal or woe, our flag is planted in the Philippines to stay. No one will deny that our position there has elements of weakness as well as strength. But whatever else it may bring to us, it certainly brings the necessity of a powerful navy capable of defending and protecting our commercial interests in every sea. Hitherto, our domination has been on land, henceforth, it must be on sea."

"The bold and adventurous spirit of our people will not rest or halt until our supremacy in commerce upon the high seas is as complete and as universally acknowledged as it now is upon land. The field, the theatre of this impending commercial contest for this coveted prize, will be the Pacific Ocean and our rivals will be all the nations of the earth."

"Already from the four quarters of the globe our competitors are preparing for this absorbing race for commercial supremacy. The natural advantages are with us. Our magnificent coastline on the Pacific, our matchless harbors and commanding position we now hold in the Orient must prove powerful factors in the contest. And Seattle, so admirably situated on that unrivaled inland sea at our door, is destined to play an important part in this great international movement. It is the place where the great currents of trade by land and by water meet and unite."

"With a continent of boundless riches at its back, a noble harbor and the broad ocean at its door, no seaport of ancient or modern times was ever more favorably situated for trade and commerce. But natural advantages alone never made a great city or a great state. Men of the right mold and stamp, men of energy, of resolution, of enterprise, of broad intelligence - men like the creator of the splendid industrial plant before us - are necessary to utilize the gifts of nature. Such men are at work today here and elsewhere upon the lines that will give as signal advisotory (sic) to American commerce on the Pacific as the new navy gave the country in the late war. Chief among these workers and far-seeing men, is that eminent private citizen of the U. S. who, having been without government aid or bounty, by the sheer force of his genius, spanned the American continent with a system of land and water transportation which as an economical and effective carrying and distributing agency is unsurpassed in all the world, is now engaged in construction of great steamships, veritable leviathans of the sea, which, when once in commission, will speedily revolutionize the water transportation of the world.   Within ten years, yes probably within five years from the day those giants of the deep shall sail from the port of Seattle for ports of Yokohama and Hong Kong, the commerce and primacy of the United States upon sea and land will be firmly established forever.   Our country will then be easily the mistress of the sea; and within that ancient watery park, within that pathless trace of ocean, America will take her pleasure as huntress through the winter and summer from the rising to the setting of the sun."

After waiting a decent period of time for the applause to continue, the Marine band began to play.

Judge Burke then introduced Governor McBride who offered his address of welcome to the visiting governor from Nebraska.

"Governor Savage," Burke announced, "it affords me great pleasure to extend to you and those with you, the hand of friendly greeting and in the name of the people of this commonwealth to bid you a hearty welcome to the state of Washington."

"We believe out here we have a great state, a state destined to become one of the greatest in the Union.   Were the occasion appropriate, I would delight in telling you something of its glories.

But you are here, and we prefer that you should see and judge for yourselves."

"Our people are a cosmopolitan people. Each state in the Union, as well as many a foreign land, has sent us of its best. Nebraska, your own state, has dealt generously with us. She has parted, as you doubtless discovered since your arrival, with many of sons to assist in our up building - her loss is our gain. And now she has placed us under additional obligation and added to our debt of gratitude by sending her chief magistrate."

"Again permit me in the name of the people of the state of Washington, to bid you a cordial welcome hoping that your stay within our borders may prove a pleasant one and trusting that when, in response to the call of duty, your faces are turned homeward, you may join with us in regretting your departure."

Governor Savage stepped up to the podium and shook hands with Governor McBride. After a few sweeps of his broad-brimmed hat, he addressed the cheering crowd.

"To be with you and witness the laying of the keel of the battleship which is to bear the honored name of the great state of Nebraska affords me more pleasure than words can express."

"While every act looking to the perpetuation of this method of settling disputes is a bold reflection on our civilization, and while the genius of our statesmanship should be enlisted in the interest of peaceful arbitration, still, until all nations agree on a peaceful form of adjudication, our own nation would be pursuing a perilous course should it neglect to bring its naval strength up to a proper standard."

"For irrespective of the lessons of history, it must be apparent to every student of military and naval affairs that arena of conquest is surely changing from land to water and that in the future the principle and decisive arrangements must be fought out on the high seas."

"This being logically true, the burden of responsibility is shifted away from the Army to the Navy, and if we are to remain in our position at the head of the nations of the earth, we must give scrupulous attention to the development of our naval resources."

"We can safely boast of the best seamen because those of other nations can in no way compare with our seamen from a standpoint of intelligence, courage, valor and patriotism, but to be in a position to reap the benefits of those superior mental and physical endowments, we must have war vessels equally as formidable as those of our rivals."

"I do not mean to convey the impression that I am in favor of military or naval judicature as means of settling disputes. I am voicing my own, and I believe the opinion of American citizens generally, when I say that war should be resorted to only when all means of a peaceful settlement have been exhausted."

"War is not an institution of civilization. It is not American. Ours is a nation of peace and our appeals are directed not to baser but to the nobler passions and instincts of mankind. Intelligence, honesty and statesmanship are our preferred weapons."

"With these I am sure we shall ultimately subjugate the barbarism of the world. America is, by scholars of all nations, accorded first place in point of intelligence and since intelligence exercises potent influence on and over all affairs of mankind, it is apparent at once that time alone will suffice to spread our social dominion and sovereignty over and throughout both hemispheres."

"Wherever civilization reigns, our morals, our manners and our customs are impressing themselves on human character. Being the lamp which lights up the pathway of civilization throughout the land, we are admonished by the highest sense of duty to avoid throwing light on pathways which lead to social iniquity and ruin. Every example set by us should, above all things, bear evidence of honesty, intelligence and social purity."

"It may be difficult to reconcile this philosophy with our present policy in regard to development of our Army and Navy. Advocates of peaceful arbitration contend, and with some force, that the development of our maritime commerce and the care of our insular possessions afford poor excuse for the creation of a strong naval fleet. They forget, however, that the time has come and come again when our nation may stand in need of naval equipment to protect its commerce, the interests of its citizens abroad and in exacting obedience to the demands on the part of other powers."

"The goal of our ambition should be to blot out this barbarous method of settling disputes from the face of civilization, but until the world shall learn of more humane methods of adjudicating international questions, we shall be required for our own safety and protection to stand prepared to defend our rights on sea and land in courts of war no less than in those of peace, and failure on our part to measure up to military or naval standards of other powers would be a grave misconception and miscalculation of our nation's duty."

"I for one have abiding faith in the ability of American statesmen to master our great responsibilities. We have already achieved financial and commercial supremacy on land and the construction of the isthmian canal coupled with a reasonable subsidization of our merchant marine, would soon give us supremacy on the seas."

"Just so sure as you have witnessed the great orb of day kiss at twilight the billows of yonder deep, just so sure will be the time when the rank and subtle monarchy will give way to popular government and that type of intelligence and morals which today distinguishes Americans, will reign throughout the world."

"If this vessel shall render unto our government as valuable and efficient service as that rendered by the citizens of the state whose honored name it is to bear, then the day will never come when its construction and naval competence will give occasion for regret on the part of anyone."

"For if you would know more of loyalty, valor and patriotism of the citizens of Nebraska, examine the master roll, examine military history and look at the graves of the known and unknown in our national cemeteries."

"Look anywhere where there is a record of patriotic sacrifice and military achievements and you will conclude, I am sure, that, so far as upholding the strong arm of this republic is concerned, Nebraska has done her share."

"No state has done more to maintain the honor of the flag, no state has done more to stimulate the public morals, no state has contributed more generously to the manhood and statesmanship or to the welfare of the American people and no state is more willing to perform whatever task the parent government may assign it in the future than dear old Nebraska - always true, always loyal, always patriotic."

While Governor Savage was acknowledging the applause for his speech, young Malcomb Moran, the seven year old son of the shipyard owner, trotted down the gangway in full dress naval uniform to the speaker's stand and came to a salute before the audience. The governor was taken by surprise by this show of impromptu dramatics. He was even more taken aback when the boy spoke.

"Governor Savage," said the boy, "I want to present you with first piece of steel punched from the keel of the battleship "Nebraska" as a souvenir of this occasion and I hope Nebraska will have a good corn crop this year."

The governor stammered his thanks as the boy opened his little sailor's coat and presented him with further souvenirs: gold buttons commemorating the date and occasion. After receiving the mementos, Savage held up the piece of steel mounted on wood form the famous old battleship, *Hartford*. It had the dimensions of the *Nebraska* engraved in gold plate. The crowd roared their approval.

Governor McBride stepped up and gestured for Governor

Savage to proceed first down the plank to the platform where the silver spike would be driven home in the new keel. Impressed by his politeness, the Nebraska governor bowed out of the way and offered the privilege to McBride. Finally, the two men compromised, like the true politicians they were, and they walked down side by side as the band played a rousing version of "Dixie."

When the two governors reached the platform, they carefully removed their coats and rolled up their sleeves to prepare for swinging hammers. Both men looked with mock disdain at the small hammers they were given for their task.

"Oh, they're toys," said Savage.

"Mere tack hammers," retorted McBride.

"I use that size with my left hand," boasted Savage in friendly bravado.

"We use those things to crack nuts with in Skagit County," returned McBride.

Both men laughed in bold tones that the crowd was sure to hear. Workmen then placed the red-hot rivet into position and the governors took their positions on either side of the keel. The first blow was struck lustily by Savage with McBride right behind. The band took the cue to play the "Star Spangled Banner" and the officers on the platform began to sing along. Soon the thousands in the crowd joined in the singing. The fast swinging governors kept time by beating a "tattoo" on the rivet which was quickly turning black as it cooled.

After the governors had finished their task and were putting on their coats, Robert Moran stepped up to the platform and presented the men with individual paychecks made out for $.03. Governor Savage reached into his vest pocket and pulled out his nose glasses to read the check.

"It is not enough," he wisecracked.

With a wink, Governor McBride added, "We strike right here."

The exchange between the governors, spoken in just a loud enough voice so it could be heard by the audience, was a sly attack on the labor unions which were just beginning to wield some power in the Pacific Northwest as the boom economy picked up momentum.

The Moran Brothers Shipyard was beginning to experience protests as Robert Moran refused to hire union workers. Later, the building of the battleship *Nebraska* was to be postponed many times because of union pressure. It was not until two years had passed that the ship was launched.

The two governors accompanied by Robert Moran walked back up to the grandstand and began the recession to yet another tune from the Marine band.

With the formal ceremonies concluded, the crowd began milling back to their waiting carriages, buggies and carryalls which would take them on to a picnic or to home. They had come to witness the first keel laying on the Fourth Of July holiday in the history of the United States and they had not been disappointed by the show.

Some men carried weapons with them in their buggies and wagons in the chance that they would meet Harry Tracy along the way. Other men purposely left their weapons at behind, thinking that an unarmed family would offer no threat to the outlaw. In any event, the previous day's gun battles were set firmly in every citizen's mind. No promise of the future could erase their immediate concern.

Chapter 12:
Fruitless Search

While the majority of Seattle residents were enjoying the holiday, Sheriff Cudihee and a posse of fifty men resumed the search in the same heavily forested region between Bothell and Seattle where the activity of the past few days had been concentrated. It was thought that Tracy would still try to make his way though this part of King County in order to cross the Cascade Mountains into the open high desert plains country of Eastern Washington.

Cudihee set in motion the plans of an ambush. Men were positioned in strategic intervals at crossroads and along the railroad tracks which led to the eastern shore of Lake Washington. Although the heavy rains of the past week had lessened somewhat, it was still drizzling and there was an almost wintry chill in the air. To the men having to stand for long hours in the open, there was nothing more miserable than guard duty in the rain.

The sheriff returned to Seattle at 5:30 PM on July 4 when no new clues were uncovered. He was driven in a buggy owned by the relentless Charles Ferrell who had refused to give up the chase and who was encouraged by the near-misses of the previous day.

"We can't state positively where Tracy is," said Cudihee to reporters. "We are watching closely for his next appearance. We are not sure if he is near Bothell. The reports received, however, make it imperative that we should patrol this part of the county with increasing vigilance. We can take no chances. Nearly fifty men are tonight watching from Woodinville to Woodland Park. We should get some trace of the convict tomorrow. If we do, the posse will be hard on the track. The chase has been a hard one but we are not beaten yet. Tracy must be exhausted by his last flight across the country and we must keep hard after him."

John Rogers, the man who had driven Cudihee to Fremont in the pursuit of Tracy on the day of the Bothell and Woodland Park gun battle and who was also the proprietor of the American Hotel in Bothell, told reporters that he had seen a man answering Tracy's description on a county road leading from Seattle to Bothell earlier in the day. Since Rogers had seen Tracy at Van Horn's, Cudihee put great credence in his report and stationed most of the men in the area of the sighting.

******

During the day of the holiday, several incidents occurred in the posse-crowded woods north of the Seattle which gave the manhunt both comic and near-tragic dimensions.

Near Ravenna, two posse members came upon a strange man carrying a rifle near the railroad tracks. The two guards were positioned behind a shelter and they remained hidden because of the chance that he might be Tracy. When one of the guards saw the man aim his rifle at Harry Schumacher, another posse member who was flagging down an oncoming train, he fired a shot in the stranger's direction. The train stopped to take the posse members on board and when it started up again and drew abreast of the position where the man had been seen, twelve men pointed their rifles out of the car windows hoping to get a shot. Before any of the men on the train could see to get a good shot, the stranger rose from his hiding place and jumped over a dike made from landfill. By the time that the train had slowed to a speed where the posse members could disembark, the stranger had disappeared leaving only his footprints leading into the thick brush. The stranger was never identified.

Jean Buhlert, the Ballad pound master, claimed that Tracy had held him up with the help of a tramp he had forced into his service. Buhlert said that Tracy had cursed when nothing of value had been found in his pockets and that he walked away on the tracks leading north from Ballard.

The same man passed a sixteen year old boy named Owen Baker at Fourth Avenue and Broadway in Ballard. The boy ran into a store and informed Deputy Town Marshall Ledger of his sighting. A short time later, two posses led respectively by Ledger and Marshal Hunt set out to find the man they thought might be Tracy. Hunt notified Cudihee of the possible location of the outlaw and Cudihee sent word to the other town marshals in area to be ready.

Hunt's posse proceeded to Edmonds to cut off any northerly escape route, while Ledger's men worked their way up the shoreline of Puget Sound. An old man was found on the beach by Ledger and the discovery caused momentary excitement within the posse. The old man explained that he was not Harry Tracy and that he had already been mistaken for the outlaw earlier that day when he had been shot at from the tracks. Ledger thought he was lying and one of the posse members suggested that he might be an accomplice of Tracy. Some men wanted to beat the old man until he told the truth, but Ledger calmed the overzealous suggestion and let the old man go on his way.

A Japanese man, hardly resembling Tracy, was nearly shot as he was trying to flag a train from the brush and had his flag mistaken for a rifle by a special car-load of deputies. Trembling with fright, the man walked from the brush with his hands raised and quickly identified himself.

******

While the search was reaching immense proportions north of Seattle, in the city Coroner Hoye was examining the bodies of Neil Rawley and Constable Breece, the two men who had been killed at the Van Horn house the night previously.

Hoye found that the bullet which had caused Rawley's death was a .38 caliber slug from a revolver. At that time, no one yet knew that Tracy had taken the weapon from the Van Horn house and speculation still persisted that a fellow posse member, J. I. Knight, was responsible because it was widely known that he carried a .38 pistol.

Knight was questioned by eager reporters trying to discover if he was, indeed, the killer of Rawley.

"It was very dark when the shooting took place," said Knight not knowing himself exactly what had happened. "When the firing commenced, I clearly remember seeing a man raise his gun and fire directly at Breece. At that instant, I leveled my .38 caliber revolver and fired in that direction. By that time other members of the posse had discharged their weapons at the convict. After a few seconds we discovered that Rawley had been shot. I do not remember seeing the dead man in our party."

Knight's statement did nothing to remove him from suspicion. Some people, after reading his account, were ready to blame him for the entire sorry outcome of the event.

In Knight's defense, Coroner Hoye said, "A man takes his life into his hands when he goes gunning for another man in the dark. It is impossible to hold anyone responsible."

After viewing Breece's body, several Civil War veterans were certain that he had been shot with a .44 caliber Civil War pistol because the wounds were similar to ones they had seen during that war.

Knight was adamant, however, in his view that Tracy had shot Breece with a .30 caliber Winchester; Coroner Hoye verified his report, regardless of the opinions of the Civil War veterans.

A large crowd gathered at the Bonney-Stewart Funeral Parlor. Many people had come over after the keel-laying ceremony at the Moran shipyards. The sight of the bullet-riddled bodies aroused the anger of a number of men who swore they would join the manhunt as soon as possible.

Neil Rawley had lived at 916 Ewing Avenue. He left a widow, three children, his mother and his father, three brothers and four sisters. He had been on vacation at the time of his death from his quartz mining job in Oregon. He had moved to Oregon after losing his mining job in Seattle.

Constable Breece had lived at 4034 14th Avenue North. He had been a policeman for four years and had left a widow, three children and his mother.

******

The northern suburbs of Seattle had literally become infested with official posse members and unofficial bounty hunters. Almost every turn in the roads leading north out of the city had a small group of men lying in ambush hoping to get a shot at Harry Tracy. A reporter who had ventured into the dangerous area north of Ballard on horseback to get an eyewitness account of the chaos and disorganization was stopped, searched and threatened twice by two motley groups of shotgun toting men.

Rumors were sweeping King County as fast as Harry Tracy's reputation was spreading across the country. Sheriff Cudihee had so many possible sightings and clues to investigate that he could scarcely sift the hysteria from the truth.

One of the wildest conjectures originated in Fremont where citizens were convinced that there had been another gun battle in which two more deputies had been killed. The story was quickly repudiated by Deputy Marshal Ledger of the Meadow Point posse who were standing guard in the area where the supposed altercation was thought to have taken place.

Near Bothell, an episode (called a "howling farce" by one of the newspapers) occurred when one of the passengers on the

Steamer Acme thought they had seen a man answering Tracy's description crossing Blythe's bridge (one mile from Bothell). The steamer had been proceeding down the Sammamish Slough to Lake Washington when it had stopped momentarily for a log jam. It was during this stop when the man had been seen disappearing behind the Blythe barn.

When the Acme reached Bothell, J. W. Morehead, a passenger on the steamer, reported immediately to posse headquarters at the American Hotel. He told the few men stationed there at the time that he had seen Harry Tracy with his pack over his back and his rifle in his hand.

Sheriff Cudihee was out on a tour of inspection of the posse at the time and no one else seemed too anxious to proceed to Blythe barn where it was speculated that Tracy had taken refuge. Deputy McClellen from Thurston County returned from a scouting patrol in the middle of Morehead's report and he immediately asked to hear the entire report from the beginning. Without a minute to rest, McClellen headed to the Blythe farm by himself. Four other men hurriedly went to their homes, armed themselves with rifles and followed McClellen.

The makeshift posse surrounded the barn and waited while the deputy went inside the barn to investigate. McClellen found nothing in the barn that might arouse suspicion. Farmer Blythe then appeared and got a good laugh out of the commotion he had caused by carrying a pig home from market in a sack. He said that he had been carrying a rifle because of the possibility that Tracy might be in the area. It was another of the many cases of mistaken identity.

With conjecture running rampant, the question on everyone's mind was, "Where is Tracy?"

At 7:00 on the morning of July 4, a German farmer named Fisher was out working on his small vegetable garden with his young son. His home was located near Green Lake about three miles north of Ravenna.

A man appeared from the brush and said to Fisher, "I'm Tracy and I want you to get me something to eat, and do it quick. I'm as hungry as a bear. Both of you come inside with me and if you make a move that looks like you mean any injury, I'll kill you."

Fisher was so frightened that he could scarcely remain standing. Tracy herded the frightened man and his son into the house and found Mrs. Fisher and a three year old daughter still finishing their cleaning chores after breakfast. He discovered that Mrs. Fisher could not speak English, so he told Mr. Fisher to ask her to fix him something to eat.

While bacon and eggs were being prepared by the woman, Tracy asked for some clean and dry socks. Fisher said that the only ones he had other than the ones he was wearing were wet and hanging on the line. Tracy took off his damp socks and hung them on the back of a chair to dry.

Taking Fisher into the bedroom off the kitchen, Tracy asked for a change of clothing. When Fisher started to search slowly through his closet, Tracy pushed him aside and chose a brown suit and black shirt with white stripes. He also took a cap with flaps that he could let down over his ears.

"I would prefer that black hat you have there," he said pointing to the wide-brimmed hat hanging on the wall near the end of the bed. "But I guess it's a Sunday article and as you appear to be a poor man, I'll leave it."

"Fisher," he said, "go into the kitchen and tell your wife that if anybody appears down the road, or from any direction, she and the girls must stand in the doorway. Nobody must come into this house while I'm here."

In short time the meal was ready and Tracy, newly outfitted in Fisher's clothes, sat down to eat heartily.

After the meal, he put on his almost-dry socks and called for a pair of boots. Fisher brought him a series of shoes and boots but none suited him until a pair of logging boots that lace up to the knees. They were the boy's size nine work boots.

"Well, young fellow," said Tracy trying on the boots, "you're a husky lad for your age, but those shoes are big enough for most men. You must come from Maine. The best I've done is to wear a number eight. However, these will do. I've got to have a new pair anyhow, because these cursed man hunters are all the time following me with dogs and I must throw them off the track. I'm not afraid of the men - I can stand them off a bit - but I don't like dogs a little bit."

As Tracy finished putting on the boots, a dog owned by a neighbor of the Fishers barked. He rose to his feet with a look of mixed fear and hatred, but Fisher told him not to worry, that he knew the dog and it was harmless.

Taking a seat at the corner of the house, Tracy told Fisher to tell his wife to start making sandwiches that he could take along with him. Mrs. Fisher obediently began slicing and buttering two loaves of bread and boiling some bacon to put between the halves. She also boiled some eggs, cut off the top of a gunny sack to use as a container and found a piece of bailing wire to close it. While she was going about this task, Tracy chatted with Fisher. He kept close watch on Mrs. Fisher out of the corner of his eye. He seemed to find something in her manner that made him suspicious.

"I shot and killed two men near Bothell yesterday," he said matter-of-factly, "and last night killed two men near Fremont. One of them I killed with my revolver and the other with my rifle. The man I killed with my revolver I shot twice."

Tracy rambled on. He told the farmer the story of how he had shot Merrill, repeating many of the same facts that he had related to Frank Scott on the *N & S.* He said that Merrill had been the reason for his having to spend three years in the Oregon State Penitentiary and that "I never had any love for him, anyway."

While he talked, he lovingly displayed for the entire Fisher family to admire with dread, the rifle that he had used to spread such a wake of fear and death across Oregon and Washington.

Tracy held their attention. He stroked the barrel and said that it was the only thing that had delivered him from trouble. He pointed to the bead on the front sight which had been filed to a fine point and said, "The man who did it knew his business; because it's accurate and quick aim can be taken." He explained that aiming made little difference except at a distance. He always shot from the hip without aim at close quarters. Dipping into his ammunition bag, Tracy displayed a few of the cartridges he carried in ample supply.

"I have one hundred and fifty cartridges here and before they get me I'll have a good many less."

Before leaving, Tracy decided to tie the family up. He told them he regretted having to do so, especially Mrs. Fisher and the girls, but that it was necessary to insure his escape. But when the eighteen month old baby toddled into her mother's arms, he relented.

"No, I'll not tie you people up, because somebody will have to tend to that baby and if I left its mother loose to look after it she could release the others. But one thing I want you to do, and that is to give me a solemn promise that you will not tell anybody I've been here for the next forty-eight hours."

Fisher assented to Tracy's request for an oath and the outlaw further cautioned him against letting anyone in the family leave.

Taking out a note pad, Tracy took down Fisher's name and address telling the farmer that he had no money at the moment but would remember him if he succeeded in making his escape. He promised that the food and clothing he had taken would be repaid in full.

"I'm not trying to hurt anybody," Tracy told the Fishers, "except those that are after me and I'm not going to forget those people that have done me favors."

He said goodbye and then climbed the back yard fence and walked down the road in a northwesterly direction toward George and Charlie Baker's house three hundred yards away from the Fisher house.

It was not until the next morning when a friend of the Fisher family named Taylor walked into the yard, that anyone heard of Tracy's appearance. Taylor was told of Tracy's visit by Fisher and warned not to say anything to betray the promise of silence that he had given under the threat of peril. But Taylor could not contain the information. As soon as he could reach a telephone, he called Undersheriff Corcoran at the sheriff's office.

Corcoran sent out Deputy Oscar Springer, who spoke fluent German, to join Deputy Zimmerman of Snohomish County in the investigation of Taylor's report.

When the two deputies arrived at the Fisher farm, Mr. Fisher was not at home; however, Mrs. Fisher told the entire story in German and identified a reward poster of Harry Tracy.

She also gave an account (translated) of almost poisoning the outlaw:

"I would have poisoned Tracy but he watched me too closely. I had the poison in the house but could not get a chance to put it in the sandwiches. I would have been afraid to put it in the food he ate because he might have killed us all when it began to work on his system, but if I had got a chance I would have put it in the sandwiches and then he would have died after taking it before he could have gotten back to the house. Once I started to the cupboard where the poison is in the little bottle on the shelf, but he kept his eyes on me and I had to get and cup and saucer instead."

With the knowledge that Tracy was still in the area north of Seattle, Sheriff Cudihee realized that his ambush plans were not working and sent for Guard Carson and his bloodhounds back in Walla Walla.

Cudihee talked to reporters at the end of another day of fruitless search:

"From the report, it looks like Tracy is between Bothell and Maple Leaf. At the later place, Tracy held up a man named Fisher Friday morning and secured a new suit of clothes. In my opinion, judging from his movements up to this time, Tracy's main objective point is the Cascades. Tracy, however, does the unexpected. The escaped convict is undoubtedly the most audacious and luckiest criminal I ever heard of. By taking everything into consideration, I am inclined to believe that since his departure from Thurston County he has been heading for the mountains."

"The Cascades form a good hiding place on account of the number of mining shacks. He could also be concealed in a mining camp more easily than perhaps any other place."

"I am not positive as to the reports we are receiving. We are running each one down, however, and finding out what is fact and what is only rumor. Since the fight at the Van Horn home we have been searching for clues. Today's reports indicate that the convict has not passed through Bothell. Every place is guarded tonight. Nothing within our power can be overlooked. He can hardly escape by the roads or the railroad track."

In Bothell that day the investigation of a "mysterious buggy" was being carried out. According to several members of the posse stationed near Wayne, a buggy with three eerie lights had stopped at the same cabin where the gun battle had taken place on July 3 - where Deputy Raymond had been killed and Deputy Williams gravely wounded.

Deputies Woolery and Brewer had been assigned to guard the cabin and late on the night of July 3 they witnessed a buggy approaching. The two deputies were not overly suspicious since the area was a known lover's lane. They overheard a discussion between and man and a woman.

"This is the town of Wayne," they heard the man say. The woman had offered a reply but the words did not carry to where the deputies stood. The buggy had parked at the entrance to the trail which led down to the cabin (the same trail taken by the ill-fated posse). After only waiting a few minutes, the buggy had pulled away passing by the deputies on the way. "What time is it?" the man in the buggy yelled at Brewer. "12:30," answered Brewer. It was only later that the two deputies wondered if the mysterious buggy might have contained confederates of Tracy.

"I couldn't see how many people were in the buggy," said Brewer. "It was pitch dark and the vehicle went past very quickly."

The next morning Brewer and Woolery returned to the cabin to search the cabin to see if anything had been left inside by the people in the buggy. They found an outfit: a blanket, bread, fresh veal, bacon, butter, a frying pan and a can of salmon. Whether or not this was left by Tracy on July 3 was not known, but it was thought that the cabin had been thoroughly gone over after the shooting and that the collection of supplies could not have been overlooked. If some person had occupied the cabin that night, was that person Tracy and were the people in the buggy trying to hide food for him? There was no real answer. Harry Tracy was still on the loose.

Chapter 13:

The Unpredictable Outlaw

On the afternoon of July 5, Mrs. Johnson answered a hard knock at the door of her home located near Port Madison - the only town of any size on Bainbridge Island (a large island in Puget Sound located directly to the west of Meadow Point north of Seattle). When she opened her door, she was confronted by a rough-looking man who appeared to have been living in the open for some time. The man was holding her husband's hired hand, John Anderson, by the collar.

The stranger told her that he did not want any trouble but because he was being followed around the country by "a lot of men," he was hungry and would like something to eat.

"My God," Mrs. Johnson gasped, "are you Tracy?"

"Yes, I'm Tracy," the man said, "but you have nothing to fear. I'm not going to hurt you. All I want now is something to eat and if I get that and you make no fuss, you'll not be harmed."

Mrs. Johnson was too frightened to listen to Tracy's words of reassurance. She broke away from the doorway and ran down the beach screaming. Tracy told the hired hand to call her back or he would be forced to shoot.

Hearing Anderson's plea to come back, Mrs. Johnson ceased her flight and returned to the house.

"That was a foolish thing to do," Tracy scolded. "If you'd kept on running, I would've shot you. There's no use for you to be scared. I told you that so long as you acted sensibly you would not get hurt and I mean it. Now, come into the house and get me something to eat."

While Mrs. Johnson fixed his meal, Tracy sat in the corner of the kitchen with the rifle across his knee and began talking about Mrs. Van Horn, the woman whose house he visited two days previously. He told Mrs. Johnson how much he admired her spunk and courage.

Yes," said Mrs. Johnson, "but she told you were there when the grocery boy appeared."

"No, she didn't," said Tracy. "She simply nodded her head; but that was enough. However, that only proves her nerve. She is not the kind of woman who wants my life. She told on me because she thought she was doing right. I have a whole lot of respect for that woman. It's you people that appear scared that want to kill me. You're after the reward. You people are afraid to do it when I'm looking. Now, Mrs. Van Horn is the kind of woman that would risk a shot while I was looking if she felt satisfied she could hit me. That is the difference between you."

Tracy explained that he felt bad about the fact that Breece had a family, but he said that a man with a family had no business looking for people whom he knew would have to shoot back.

"Why, if I were the bloodthirsty villain the papers make me out, I could have killed twenty more men than I have. Many times I've been in the brush while parties of three or four men passed along the road, talking so loud you could hear them a quarter mile.

Some of them carried guns over their shoulders and none of them was ready to shoot. I've had them in places where I could've shot from cover and they were situated so I could've killed every one of them before they got away. I let them go because I don't care to kill anybody unless it's to save my own life. I guess by this time that most people understand that when I do shoot something, it is going to happen."

Tracy ate his meal and shortly afterwards, Mrs. Johnson's husband came in from the fields. With all of the family at that time under the roof and under his control, Tracy gathered them all together in the living room - Mr. and Mrs. Johnson, their small son and the hired hand, Anderson.

"I want you to all understand that I'm a desperate man," he announced. "My name is Tracy and I would kill you all were it not for that pretty little child. I want all I can get to eat and good clothes in place of the ones I have on. If you give me these things, you will not be harmed."

In broken English, Johnson, who had emigrated from Sweden, told Tracy he had read all about him in the newspapers and that he would do anything he asked of him. Tracy told Johnson to first lock the doors and bring him the keys. The outlaw talked sporadically to the family; a worried, haggard look was imprinted on his face. He was very tired and worn-out from the exhausting events of the last few days on the run. Anderson asked him why he had come to Bainbridge Island.

"This is none of your business," said Tracy. "But I'll tell you all about it after I've had some more to eat."

Turning to Mrs. Johnson he said, "Madam, I dislike to order a woman about. But I want you to hurry up and get me a big dinner. I want lots of coffee."

As she started off to do his bidding, Tracy said to the two men, "Come on you fellows, bring the kid and we'll all go in the kitchen."

Mrs. Johnson set only one place at the counter. This prompted Tracy to say, "You're forgetting the rest of the company. Move the table up here by me and then we'll all dine together."

Anderson followed the order and Johnson drew up the chairs which were spread out against the wall. When the meal was ready, the family sat down and Tracy threw his blue coat on the floor beside the chair, laid his revolver out on the table and began to eat. The others only watched as he devoured four fried eggs, some ham, potatoes, brown beans warmed-over stew, bread, butter and some strawberry preserves Mrs. Johnson had finished canning the day before. He also drank four cups of coffee to wash down the meal. When he had had enough, he asked Mrs. Johnson if she had some bacon. She rose to cook it for the seemingly still ravenous outlaw but he stopped her and said, "No, no, you have given me all I can eat here; I mean a piece of bacon I can carry with me. It's the best thing in the world for a man to eat who is knocking about these cold, rainy nights, as I am."

As he sipped his last cup of coffee, Tracy sat back from the table and asked for some newspapers. The Johnsons had several copies of the Seattle Post-Intelligencer in the house, one of which gave the full account of his gun battle near Fremont on July 3.

"That was a useless waste of life," he said sadly. "But Ed Cudihee was pursuing me too close and I had to do what I did. I didn't know, however, until now that the sheriff was so close on my heels. I thought he was up near Bothell."

Tracy continued his rambling conversation throughout the evening, finally coming to the story of his trip over to Bainbridge Island. After spending the night in a cemetery near Van Horn's, he had made his visit to the Fishers. When he left them he had taken a cross country path back to Meadow Point. There, he said he had held up a Japanese fisherman and forced him to take him across Puget Sound to Port Madison. Once on the island, he said that he had slept in the brush until Saturday afternoon and then walked to their farm. He had waited an hour or so before going to their door in order to see how many people lived on the farm and how many men there were that he might have to deal with.

Taking off his too-large logging boots, he asked Mrs. Johnson to bring him some water in a basin so he could bathe his feet. Mrs. Johnson brought the basin and soaked his feet for over a half an hour. He savored the soak like it was the best luxury civilization could offer.

Tracy selected a pair of Johnson's trousers, a new black coat and vest, clean socks and two colored shirts from his wardrobe as replacements for his worn clothes which he tied his into a bundle and left them on the floor.

Tracy spent the rest of the day talking to the family in order to waste time until was dark.

At about 9:00 PM he said, "It's plenty late enough. I guess I'll go."

He had Anderson tie up the family with a coil of rope and then told the man that he was taking him along as a hostage.

It only took Mrs. Johnson a few hours to free herself from her bonds and free her husband. Mr. Johnson went immediately to Deputy Sheriff McKay at Port Madison and told of Tracy's appearance.

Port Madison was immediately plunged into a fever of excitement as a large posse was formed to search the beach where the tracks of Tracy and Anderson led. The search was short-lived, however, when it was discovered that a boat had been taken from the beach onto the Sound.

******

The number of men officially counted in the manhunt on July 5 in King County was estimated at around one hundred. Unofficially, hundreds more were roaming the woods in search of the fugitive. The cordon of men set up by Sheriff Cudihee stretched over fifteen miles of road and railroad. He was sure that the day would bring success.

Undersheriff Corcoran, again in charge at the Seattle office, received the news by telephone of Tracy's sighting on Bainbridge Island. He quickly notified other law enforcement officers in the area by filing notices to be sent in a fifty mile radius at the Western

Union office with Tracy's description in his new clothing. He sent Deputy Sheriff Cook to Bainbridge Island on a launch as an official investigator. He telephoned Cudihee in Bothell to let him know the news.

The alarm spread quickly throughout every county that touched Puget Sound. An unidentified boat was seen outside Deception Pass between Fidalgo and Whidbey Islands and the news was passed on to Sheriff Brisbane of Whatcom County. Scouts were sent out to patrol the shorelines of Chuckanut Bay below the town of Fairhaven. Sheriff Brisbane theorized that Tracy might be coming to the area to join a relative of Dave Merrill, Cub Merrill, whom Brisbane said lived near Whatcom. On the previous Saturday night while drunk, Cub Merrill had bragged that Harry Tracy was on his way to his place to carry out some arrangements that had been made earlier. Why Tracy would ever consider teaming up with a relative of the man he had murdered only days before, seemed not to be a question to consider for the local authorities.

Sheriff Cudihee returned to Seattle from Bothell on the morning train to organize a new posse. The tugboat, *Sea Lion*, was chartered for voyage to Port Madison.

Harry Tracy's appearance on Bainbridge Island brought new rumors. Reported sightings were made from one side of Puget Sound to the other. Sheriff Hammond of Jefferson County took a group of men on the revenue cutter, *Grant*, and began a search off Port Townsend (on the northwestern shore of Puget Sound).

A wild conjecture sprang up about a desperate encounter between two members of the *Grant* posse and the fugitive in vicinity of Apple Tree Cove. The story was the first credited to men on the tug, *Dolphin*, but when they were questioned, they emphatically denied that it had come from them. A special dispatch reached Seattle from Washington D. C. stating that the *Grant* had not been ordered by the Treasury Department into the manhunt and that the commander of the ship was acting under his own authority or the authority of the Collector of Customs at Port Townsend. However, the entire story of the confrontation between the posse on the *Grant* and Harry Tracy proved totally false.

Marshall Hunt of Ballard refused to believe the story that Tracy had told to the Johnsons about forcing a Japanese fisherman to ferry him to Bainbridge Island. He said it could not be true because he and group of reliable deputies had been closely watching the Meadow Point area for the past three days and no such event could have occurred without their knowledge. Hunt made a careful inquiry of the boats moored at the docks near Ballard and Meadow Point and found that none were missing. He said that no Japanese fisherman were known to frequent those waters and since no one had come forward to report a commandeering of a vessel, he ventured that a "willing assistant" had accomplished the ferrying of Tracy with perhaps a plan to meet the fugitive later when the search had slackened on the mainland.

Hunt's conjecture again brought up the question of whether or not Tracy had confederates helping him to elude the posses. In the opinion of most Bothell residents, where the manhunt had been concentrated in the last few days, Tracy must have had some help. There was a report that another of Dave Merrill's relatives who lived in the area fifteen miles north of Bothell was Tracy's main objective. The "mysterious buggy" that had been seen near Wayne stopping at the cabin where the Thursday gun battle had taken place was thought to have been occupied by a woman who was also a relative of Merrill's. Since there was a road which left the main road north of Bothell and headed directly to Meadow Point, many people thought that Tracy may have spent the night at the cabin before moving to the Fisher farm.

The possibility of a relative of Dave Merrill living the area was remote; it seemed that everyone who had the last name Merrill was assumed to be somehow related to him. Benjamin Merrill, the same man who had left the logging camp on Anderson Island swearing to join his brother and Tracy, had worked for some time in a logging camp located between Ravenna and Bothell some years previously, but he had moved south when a better job had come his way. L. R. Roper, a store keeper in the Ravenna area, claimed he had known Benjamin Merrill at the time he had been working at the camp, but Roper had not seen the man since his departure. Roper was known to be a bit of a storyteller and he undoubtedly could not resist the temptation to come up with a "fantastic" story; he related that although he had not talked with Benjamin Merrill, he did have a conversation with Dave Merrill. According to Roper's tale, Dave Merrill had approached him and had asked for directions to the

Bothell lumber mill - the place where he said that Benjamin had once worked. He related to the man that he did not know the way and that Merrill had continued on his way. The man had a scar on his head behind the right ear, similar to the one Merrill was supposed to have, and this fact had convinced Roper of his identity.

A "queer-looking" man had volunteered his services to the posse at Bothell on Friday, July 4. Several of the posse members noticed that the man's actions and manners were suspicious as he walked among the members of the crowd at posse headquarters in the American Hotel. He had remained at the hotel until the plans for the following day's search had been distributed and then had disappeared.

On the Greenleaf Bridge outside of Bothell, four men were seen at the east side of the creek. They crossed the bridge three nights in succession. When they discovered that they were being watched, they left the area and were not seen again. The Greenleaf Bridge was located on the road which led from Bothell to Meadow Point landing, giving further credence to the theory that confederates might have helped Tracy avoid the posse.

******

In the absence of any real news, there was much discussion of how Harry Tracy had been able to escape the King County posse. Whatever the reason, he had slipped through the guard posts and the search in that area was over.

While conjecture and rumor dominated the discussions about the search for the outlaw, J. T. Knight was trying to clear himself of the accusation that he had shot Neil Rawley. Tracy's statement to the Fishers about his shooting Rawley with a pistol strengthened Knight's story. He was not, however, content with just the outlaw's admission; he wanted to prove beyond a doubt that he had no culpability.

"Thursday night when Tracy and two other men appeared, it was very dark.' he told the newspaper reporters. "Tracy fired because he heard Breece's command of 'Drop that rifle, Tracy.' I fired at the man with the rifle, naturally believing him to be Tracy because he had the weapon aimed in that direction. I must have fired at the wrong man because Mr. Butterfield tells me Tracy had the butt of his rifle concealed under his coat and operated it with his right hand while holding Butterfield with the left. The man I shot at had the stock of his weapon pressed against his face. Cudihee fired at a man because he saw him running away. This man proved to be Butterfield according to the latter's statement."

"The fact that my shot was the last one fired further convinces me that I did not kill Rawley. According to the latter's statement at the drug store immediately after the affray, he was falling wounded when he saw Breece fall. According to this, Rawley shot first. My shot being the last one, could not have hit him."

Knight also stated that Butterfield had told him that he had examined one of the bullets from the pistol stolen from the Van Horn house and that it clearly had .38 written on the butt of the shell.

As to Sheriff Cudihee's comments concerning the inefficiency of the Fremont posse, Knight added:

"I think Mr. Cudihee was unfair in making an assertion of this kind - saying he would have shot Tracy if the others had not interfered. - if he did so for the reason that he was the first man on the scene. He had his choice of positions and before Tracy and his escorts were near any of the rest of us, the trio passed slowly down the path covered by the sheriff, just as he calculated they would. Now I feel that Mr. Cudihee had his chance for that particular fight and it passed him and that criticisms of other's actions after that were entirely out of order coming from him."

In anticipation of Tracy's landing, the entire shoreline of Puget Sound was being watched. Wherever he might land, deputies were ready to take up the search. The northern end of Hood Canal was closely watched because Tracy had asked Johnson, the Bainbridge Island farmer he had visited, for directions to the area. Forty Native Americans patrolled the beach area ready to report any sightings. The lower Sound was being guarded by volunteer posses of private citizens who lived in the area.

A boat that bore a strong resemblance to the one stolen by Tracy on Bainbridge Island was found in a secluded cove near Port Gamble, but it proved to be one owned by a local man, Sam Horsey.

An elderly Native American woman thought she had sighted Tracy on the beach near Port Madison, however, that man was found to be a limping beach-comber, out making his daily rounds.

In Seattle, the tug, *Sea Lion*, was standing by under a full head of steam. It was ready to take Sheriff Cudihee and King County deputies to any point where a sure sighting was made.

Guard Carson, who had participated in the search in Oregon and Southwest Washington, arrived at the Union Depot to rejoin the manhunt. He was met by Walter Lyons, the private secretary of Governor Geer, and who had been involved in the search from the start, along with Deputy Sheriffs Springer and Pennington and a small group of local residents.

Carson had become a minor celebrity in the state because of his contribution to the manhunt. Dressed in his tan uniform and his familiar tightly rolled white Stetson, Carson proudly displayed his bloodhounds for the crowd. He brought two young dogs, Don and Bell - both about eighteen months old, from his kennel of twenty one animals. Don was the larger of the two, of English bloodhound stock, liver colored and sporting a well-shaped head and the conspicuous veins that were prominent characteristics of his breed. Bell was of Georgia Redbone stock. Black and tan in color, she was chosen from a litter of pups because of her liveliness and potential. Don had been in the chase on both sides of the Columbia River with his half-brother, Hunter. Because of the difficult conditions (hot sun, thick dust, long tiring chases and the thick swarm of brush), both Don and Hunter had given out completely and had refused to do anymore tracking. Don had recovered from the ordeal but Hunter had snagged his foot and had to be left behind. Carson had wanted to replace Hunter with Old Bess, the keenest nose in the pack, but she was in poor condition and was expected to die as a result of poor treatment in Oregon (she had been run until overheated and plunged into an icy-cold creek by an inexperienced handler).

Guard Carson said of his bloodhounds:

"They are first rate hounds and I believe good work may be expected of them. They are given regular training and should take the trail without much trouble. Bell has never been engaged in an actual manhunt, but her training has been as good as Don. Many difficulties are experienced by dogs in trailing in the woods. The odor of the timber is likely to confuse them and other obstacles may arise. Too much should not be expected of the animals, but I feel confident that they will make a good showing if they are given the proper opportunity."

While the various posse groups were waiting for some kind of clue to begin the search, John Anderson - the Johnson's hired hand - was undergoing an arduous ordeal as Tracy's hostage. He was being used as a virtual slave. Anderson first had to row the boat the entire distance from Bainbridge Island to Alki Point, the peninsula south and west of downtown Seattle, and upon arrival, he was forced to carry Tracy's bundles of food and ammunition once on dry land.

The two men first touched shore in the area known as West Seattle on Sunday morning - long before the posses had a chance to get organized. Anderson, of Swedish descent like his employer, was a simple, uneducated man used to the daily toil of farm work but not to life on the run. He was nearly broken by the fast pace and constant physical demands of his captor. Although he was tall and muscular, Anderson could scarcely keep up with Tracy's strength and energy - recently renewed by several days without a posse on his trail.

Speaking with a thick Swedish accent, Anderson gave his account of the days he spent with the outlaw after his release:

"We left Port Madison Saturday night 9:00 and arrived at West Seattle at daylight. I pulled the boat and Tracy held a gun on me all the way. We landed south of the West Seattle elevator (grain) under the trestle and immediately went into the woods near West Seattle and when night came we came across the bay in our boat and landed at the sawmill in South Seattle. We then started on the track (railroad) at Black River. We turned off the track to the left. Shortly before we reached Black River, we crossed a large hay field and went into the woods again."

"He ordered me to cook breakfast Monday morning in the timber after which we rested until after noon. About 3:00 Monday afternoon, we started through the timber towards Renton, but just before we reached the railroad track over the Black River, we met four men. Tracy said, 'Hello Fred,' and jumped down to meet them."

Anderson's story was particularly surprising. If he was telling the truth, and there was no reason to suspect that he wasn't, then it was the first confirmation of the fact that Tracy had been receiving some help from friends or "confederates" while he was in King County. Just who they were and how much help they gave him would never be known, since none of the men were heard from again. However, the stories in Bothell of the "mysterious buggy" and the four strange men at Greenleaf Bridge were given more credence and became more important in retrospect. If Tracy had been able to meet with men who had knowledge of the posse's plans and positions, it would have been much easier for him to avoid those areas. However, if Tracy indeed had confederates, then why would he stop at farmhouses for food and clothing, when it would seem far easier for his accomplices to supply it? If Harry Tracy had friends in Seattle who were aiding him, then the facts seem to support the contention that he could only have met with them a few times. The addition of possible confederates complicated the manhunt. If Tracy knew where the posses were located and had ongoing information about their plans, then he would be that much more difficult to capture.

"Tracy talked to the men for a few minutes," said Anderson, "and when the talk was finished, Tracy blindfolded me and left one of the men to guard me while he and the others went away. They were gone about an hour and when they came back they had a bottle of whiskey."

"When we started again, Tracy forced me to walk in front and the four men followed behind. We arrived at Renton about 11:00 and walked up the railroad track through town about one mile and a half. Here he tied me up again and he and the four men left. They returned at daylight and we went further into the brush where Tracy told me he was going away for a while but would be back in an hour. When he returned he brought with him a little boy from the Gerrells house and we walked down (to the house)."

"Tracy never got tired. He was always walking fast and watching both sides. He got cross at me when I was forced to slow up sometimes. His health is good and he hasn't a scratch. He has been eating heartily and regularly and has built up his strength and told me he was now in better condition to fight and travel than at any time since he left the penitentiary at Salem. He said, 'I'm getting stronger all the time. I never felt better in my life.'"

Chapter 14:
Like Robin Hood

From a concealed position in the brush, Harry Tracy watched two young women picking blackberries - the ubiquitous berried weed that plaques the Pacific Northwest countryside with its invasive tendrils of thorny greenery. They came so close to his hiding place that he could have reached out and touched them. He remained motionless and stared; forgotten memories stirred from within. It had been over three years since had talked with any women near his own age. In his sight, at that moment, were two pretty, young women, one of whom seemed so bright and spirited that he was moved to admiration.

The young women finished their picking and started back toward a house one half mile up the railroad track. Tracy moved and snapped a branch. Charles Gerrells, the oldest boy in the family that lived in the house, was walking alongside the tracks above Tracy's position and stopped when he heard the telltale signs of someone moving in the brush. The boy peered into the brush, walked a few more steps and looked again. Realizing that he had been discovered, Tracy called out, "Hey, stop a moment, boy." He rose from his cover and approached the frightened young man.

"Well, I guess you've heard of me," said Tracy smiling pleasantly at the boy and the two women accompanying him. They had stopped and turned around when the strange man had emerged from cover. "Well, I'm Tracy."

The three young people were extremely frightened and Tracy sensed their fear.

"Now don't be afraid," he said. "I won't hurt you."

Awkwardly, Mrs. McKinney, the older of the two young women, said, "Well, Mr. Tracy, I'm glad to see you."

"I would never have known you from your picture," said the younger and prettier of the two, eighteen year old Miss May Baker. Her remark was delivered in a sarcastic tone and it impressed Tracy that such a young woman would stand up to him despite his reputation. He took an immediate special liking to people who did not seem to be afraid of him.

"Ah, now, you're jollying me, but don't be afraid," he said returning the mocking tone, "I never harmed a woman in my life." Taking off his hat respectfully like the knight errant he fancied himself to be, he suggested that everyone continue on to the Gerrells house where Miss Baker and Mrs. McKinney said that they staying as guests for the day. Tracy sent Charles ahead to warn his mother not to be afraid. "Tell her I mean no harm."

The two women and the fugitive entered the house and Tracy once again doffed his hat.

"Excuse me, lady," he said politely to Mrs. Gerrells, "for entering your home, but you have nothing to fear."

Tracy appeared to the women to be in excellent physical condition. They had read in the newspapers that he was supposed to be painfully thin and totally exhausted, but they saw him as wiry and well-muscled. His face, which was described as being drawn and gaunt by the crew of the *N & S*, appeared to be full and healthy. With his growing interest in Miss Baker - which was becoming obvious - his eyes took on a warmer, almost deep blue color. He was mentally alert and sharp; so much so that the women commented later that he had one of the keenest minds they had ever met. Dressed in the clothes he had taken from the Johnsons, all dark shades and black, he fit the dime novel image of a courtly bad man. His pants, however, were far too short and they became a subject about which he kidded himself throughout his stay with the Gerrrells.

When one of the small Gerrells girls first saw the outlaw in her home, she broke out in tears. Tracy walked over to her and as he comforted her with the gentle motion of his hand stroking her head, he said, "Don't cry." "I wouldn't let anyone harm an innocent thing like you." His voice evoked both strength and tenderness and the girl warmed to his attention. She was so totally won over that when the posse later surrounded the home, she moved to Tracy's side for protection.

Remembering his traveling partner, Tracy left the house taking Charles with him to insure that no one would try to give an alarm and went to retrieve John Anderson, the hostage he had taken on Bainbridge Island. The big farm hand came along quietly and Tracy bound him to a tree in the Gerrells' back yard where his movements could be watched.

Tracy then sent Charles into downtown Seattle with two watches he had stolen from the Johnsons and told the boy to sell them and to use the money to purchase two revolvers.

One of the watches was a gold-encased hunting timepiece and the other was an open silver-encased pocket watch. These items were well worth the price of two pistols.

"I want two Colt .45s with six inch barrels," Tracy ordered. "And two boxes of cartridges. Now, if you peach on me, kid, you'll hear from me."

"I'll help you, Tracy," said Charles. "I'm kind of scared, but I'll help you."

So the boy could hear, Tracy turned to Mrs. Gerrells and said, "If he betrays me, I'll kill your other two children."

After Charles had set out on his mission, Tracy noticed that Mrs. Gerrells was terribly upset and had tears in her eyes.

"That was only a bluff," he said reassuringly. "Mother, you have nothing to fear from me. I have a mother. She is reading in the papers every day to see if I'm caught. When I last heard from her she was in Indiana. God knows where she is now. I wouldn't care about all this scrape I'm in if it weren't for her sake. God knows, lady, I wouldn't harm a hair on your head, let alone these innocent children."

Tracy let down his façade of iron-man bravado and tears formed in his icy-blue eyes.

A long embarrassing silence followed before Miss Baker finally changed the mood with a comment. "Why do you wear a moustache?" she asked. The hair on Tracy's lip was the only remnant of his month-old beard.

"Why do you ask?" queried Tracy.

"Have you a razor around here?" he asked after a laugh.

The hours he spent at the Gerrells house were to become the high point of the time since Tracy's escape from prison. At this home he was not only a daring and fearless outlaw, he also displayed qualities of sensitivity and compassion. His possible motive for this change in attitude was to charm Miss May Baker who was a pretty young woman with spirit to match. On the other hand, he exhibited enough of his tender side to make everyone in the Gerrells house feel that they would not be harmed. It would, of course, be a mistake to consider Harry Tracy a folk hero, but the characteristics he displayed while in the presence of a decent and normal family, seemed to fit that role more than at any other time during the manhunt. He was bold, he was chivalrous, he was daring, he was witty, he was clever, he was fearless and he appeared to not want to kill unnecessarily. The streak of violence which had exploded from the dark depths of his soul to the surface during the recent bloody gun battles seemed nowhere to be seen at the Gerrells. Indeed, had it not been for those gun battles and for the bloody, vindictive escape from the Oregon State Penitentiary, Harry Tracy might well have been considered to be the Robin Hood of the Pacific Northwest. If, for that one day, Harry Tracy was Robin Hood, then Gerrells house was his Sherwood Forest and Miss May Baker was his Maid Marion.

Mrs. Gerrells began a meal and Tracy pitched in to help; he cut kindling, carried water from the spring and offered to make himself useful in any way he could. It was on one of his trips to the spring that he saw a trainload of deputies, passing by the house. He had just enough time to disappear into the brush. The train stopped about a mile down the tracks and Tracy saw a group of men carrying rifles and shotguns jump down from the railroad car. He ran back to the house and watched from a window as the train moved to a position about one quarter mile from the Gerrells' yard.

Charles Gerrells, despite Tracy's threats, had gone to the sheriff's office in Seattle to report the outlaw's presence in his home. Only a handful of deputies had been in the office when the boy arrived. Deputy Sheriff McClellan, the same officer from Thurston County who had investigated the rumor of Tracy's appearance on the Blythe farm near Bothell, had taken along two other guards and a Seattle Post-Intelligencer reporter to investigate the report with Charles Gerrells showing them the way. The small posse had taken the Renton Streetcar at 9th Avenue and Washington telling the operator not to pick up any additional passengers in order to hasten their journey. McClellan had obtained the promise of Manager Osgood that the posse would be granted exclusive use of the car. However, the operator, stubborn and loyal to his regular passengers, refused to obey the order. By that time, the streetcar had arrived in Renton from the downtown terminus. It was crowded not only with regular passengers, but with those along the route who had seen the weapons of the deputies and wanted to go along to see the action.

At Renton, the small posse had boarded a caboose connected

to an engine and had started up the track toward the Gerrells home when they were seen by Tracy.

Two deputies were dropped off at the first stopping point and McClellan and the reporter stepped down at the other. As the men took their positions, they were unaware that Tracy knew of their presence. Although they were going to wait until Sheriff Cudihee and the main body of the posse arrived, the guards moved to vantage points around the house to prevent any attempt at escape. The Gerrells house was located between a river and the railroad tracks and seemed very easy to guard. The men settled in for wait that would stretch out for four hours.

Tracy returned to the house and looked out a window at the posse's movements.

Tracy said to May Baker, who was standing near him, "They had a red-haired reporter when they went up the track. I can always spot newspapermen. When I'm running from a posse, if I happen to look around, there is always a reporter about a mile in advance of the rest with a camera under one arm and big bunch of note paper under the other. I'm fleeing from interviewers, you know. I'm sorry but I can't take the time."

Turning from the view out of the window, Tracy stared at May Baker and asked, "What's your address?"

She shook her head.

"Tell me and I'll go downtown tonight and rob a jewelry store for you. Is there anything you would especially like?"

Before she could answer, Mrs. Gerrells called everyone for

dinner. Tracy went outside to retrieve Anderson and bring him in for some nourishment.

The two men sat on one side of the large dining room table and the three women sat on the other; the children sat around the ends. Tracy ate very little and seemed content to watch the children.

"This is just like home," he said. "You don't know how much I am enjoying your society."

"You spoiled our berry picking expedition," complained May Baker coyly.

"Well, we'll all go berry picking in a little while if like," said Tracy. "I'll help you."

"But we will be late getting back to Seattle," objected Mrs. McKinney, missing the joke.

"That's all right," returned Tracy. "I'll steal the best buggy in the whole neighborhood and drive you home."

Conversation continued throughout the meal and did not stop when everyone moved into the living room afterwards. Tracy picked up an old newspaper which described the Underwood manhunt (another search conducted by Sheriff Cudihee for a man who was wanted for killing his child).

"Now there is a man who, in my opinion, is one of the biggest cowards in the state," Tracy said. "Why, hanging is too good for Underwood. He should be shown no mercy. Some of the papers say that Tracy is a coward, but they don't know me. I kill men. I never harmed a woman or a child in my whole life."

"But Tracy," said May Baker, "you shot Merrill in the back."

"That is unjust," said Tracy, just a little hurt. "The papers have the wrong story. When the newspaper men come around to interview you about my visit, tell them I killed Merrill without treachery. He was a mean-spirited sort of man. When we quarreled and decided to fight, I was willing to be square. But I knew him and as we walked away ten paces from each other, I watched him over my shoulder. At the eighth step, he turned to fire. I jumped around and let him have it. As he reeled and fell, I shot him in the back. Then I walked up to his fallen body and shot him in the head."

"But you needn't have killed Breece," pressed Miss Baker.

"I had to. The newspapers have got the wrong story about the fight. I told Breece to fling down his gun. In a second we were locked in each other's arms. We struggled for a barely a second when I raised my revolver and shot him. The men with us started to run."

Tracy had the two men he shot in Fremont confused. The man he shot with the pistol was not Breece, but Rawley.

At 4:00 in the afternoon, Deputy Cook arrived with a small part of the main posse. He advanced up the track to a commanding position in front of the Gerrells house; the other men were distributed to cut off all escape routes. Shortly thereafter, Sheriff Cudihee arrived with the rest of the posse and Guard Carson with his bloodhounds.

"We can wait here until dark," said Tracy casually as he saw the gathering of the men. "Then we'll walk down the track together. I'll go with you as far as Renton. It'll be a nice moonlight walk in very pleasant company."

He took a long, low bow and looked directly at May Baker.

"Well, I don't know," she said. "It won't be very pleasant if those deputies are shooting at us."

"But I'll be safe," he said. "You ladies will form a cordon around me. You would do that for me, wouldn't you?"

"Oh sure," said Baker, "we would like to get ourselves killed for you - I don't think."

Tracy turned to Mrs. Gerrells and changed the topic of conversation. He asked her how she made the bread that she served for dinner.

"Why don't you take your wife in Portland along with you?" she asked. "She could do the cooking."

"The girl whom the police are watching in Portland is not my wife," said Tracy emphatically. "She is the sister of Dave Merrill. Her family are not treating her right. I took pity on her. She was sick. I sent her money so that she could get proper attention. She never got the money until I found out that it was being held back. Then I had to send it through a third person. No man could stand aside and see a woman badly treated. I know I couldn't and I don't suppose I would stand very high amongst most people. That's all there is to that story."

After a few hours, the time began to drag for everyone except Tracy. He seemed to be thoroughly enjoying the company and conversation. He seemed to give little thought to the mounting threat outside the house.

"Oh dear," said Baker, blunt as usual. "I feel tired of staying in the house all day and doing nothing. Can't we go out?"

"You bet not," said Tracy. "But do you dance?"

"Yes," she said, "I like to dance – sometimes."

"Does anyone here play?" asked Tracy pointing to the piano.

"But why do you ask?" queried Mrs. McKinney.

"Why, I thought we might have a little music and Miss Baker and myself could take a turn around the room."

Tracy continued to be nonchalant in his attitude even though the posse could be seen through the windows closing in on the house. There appeared to be no possible routes of escape that were not heavily guarded. With no orders from the sheriff, two men suddenly walked up to the front door of the Gerrells house. Both men were staggeringly drunk. The newspapers later referred to them as "meddling fools" and "idlers from Renton."

When they knocked at the door, Tracy took Miss Baker and Mrs. McKinney into the kitchen while Mrs. Gerrells went to see who it was that was foolish enough to endanger their lives. One of the men, a butcher from Renton, asked in slurred speech, "Is Tracy here?"

When Mrs. Gerrells answered negatively, he would not take no for an answer and strode into the house to look for himself. He proceeded to the door which led to the kitchen. The door was half open and he turned to Mrs. Gerrells and said, "Is Tracy in here, then?"

"What would Tracy be doing here?" she answered.

Shaking his head in disbelief, the butcher walked back into the living room and continued his questioning of Mrs. Gerrells. Noticing that the men who had come into the house were under the influence of alcohol - probably to build up their courage, Tracy whispered to the two women in the kitchen why he abstained from it.

"Liquor is a dangerous thing," he explained. "It should be avoided. I'm glad to say I've never been drunk. A man like myself dare not touch the stuff. It dulls the brain. It's almost a curse to humanity."

The two drunken men left the house still unconvinced that Tracy was not present but they were too befuddled to continue the search.

Mrs. McKinney, completely annoyed with outlaw's presence at first, was beginning to resign herself to the fact that her captor would not be leaving soon. She tried to make small talk to pass the time.

"What nationality are you?" she enquired. "I'm Scots-Irish."

"Why, so am I," said Tracy. "And you?" he asked pointing to Miss Baker.

"I'm of English descent," she said. "I was born in Texas."

"I knew you were a Southern girl," said Tracy. "I knew it by your speech and because you are so plucky."

The quoting of this statement by the newspapers earned Miss

Baker the title of "The Plucky Miss Baker" and it was a name that stayed with her the rest of her life (she died in 1971 at the age of 86). In the posse waiting outside the house, was her future husband, James McKinney the brother in law of Mrs. McKinney. Mr. Gerrells was also in the posse anxiously awaiting the release of his family.

As the afternoon became evening, Tracy began to show signs of wanting to leave. He watched out the window for increasing periods of time, yet he still showed no signs of concern.

"I wish my trousers were not so short," he said. "I think I'll go out and hold up one of the deputies. Do you see anyone on the track whose trousers would fit?" Tracy's eyes surveyed the countryside which was still in the wraps of a heavily dripping sky.

"You sure have beastly weather on Puget Sound," he said in disgust. "Why, it has rained all the time nearly since I landed here. I think this is unhealthy country."

The captives smiled at the double connotation of his words.

"No," said Tracy picking up the joke, "I mean in its ordinary sense."

"Well, of course," said Miss Baker in typical unruffled style, reacting like a Chamber of Commerce member to a visitor's complaint, "that was understood."

"I think I'll go to Seattle tonight," said Tracy ignoring Miss Baker's sarcasm. "I would like to see Clancy's place. Do you know where it is?"

"Of course we don't," replied Mrs. McKinney indignantly.

Tracy apologized with another southern gentleman bow and returned his attention to the window.

"The people are all after the reward," he said keeping his eye on the track. "They're all after the money."

Excusing himself, Tracy slipped out the back door of the house for a few minutes to check an escape route. He forded the small river behind the house without anyone in the posse detecting him and then swam back five minutes later. Reentering the house, he asked Mrs. Gerrells to take Anderson to the chicken coop; he joined her there and sent her back into the house for some straps to bind his former hostage to a post. After securing the straps so that Anderson could not escape, he returned to the house for the last time and said his farewells sadly

"Well goodbye," he said to the gathered hostages, "it was just like home."

Tracy exited the house and walked down to the river bank at the place he had found to be unguarded. He dropped to his hands and knees and plunged into a field of overgrown shrubs and shoulder high ferns. Slowly he crept through the wet green field until he reached the middle. Without a rustle, he boldly rose to his feet - his rifle in his hand - with his back toward the house. Several newspaper men saw him rise and mistook him for a deputy.

"There's a fool of a deputy exposing himself," said one of the reporters.

Tracy ducked down again into protection of the field and was lost from view. Deputies in the area where he had appeared, finally realized that their man was no longer in the house and gave an alarm. The volunteer posse members, eager for action after the long siege, instead of holding their positions, swarmed to the point where Tracy had been seen. Sheriff Cudihee tried to maintain discipline and yelled for the men to stay where they were, but, excited by the prospect of gunplay, they ignored the sheriff's pleas and pushed forward. In the wake of their movement, they left an unguarded corridor in a southerly direction. Tracy, who was periodically watching the posse's movements in his progress through the brush, saw the opening and threaded his way down the river bank toward it.

The carefully laid trap that had been patiently maintained for five hours was ruined by the posse's impetuosity.

Guard Carson, Secretary Lyons of Oregon, Deputy McClellan and half a dozen King County Deputies rushed into the Gerrells's home to check and see if everyone inside was unhurt. Mrs. Gerrells quickly stepped out and called for Anderson. The hired hand from Bainbridge Island who had been held captive for days rose trembling and was cut free from his bonds by a reporter. So grateful was Anderson to be free that although he moved his mouth, not a sound emerged from his throat; he was so choked by joyful emotion that he could not speak.

When he learned of Tracy's escaping the trap, Guard Carson brought his bloodhounds from the rear. They were given a piece of Tracy's discarded clothing to catch a scent.

The dogs, howling like hunting hounds close on the trail of a fox, took to a run down the trail near the river bank. When the trail ended one quarter mile down the river, Carson crossed over a bridge and put the hounds to a search on the other side. Quickly the dogs regained the scent and they began to bay even louder as the distance to between the hounds and their quarry was narrowing. The trail led due west toward the town of Belt Line and the large posse fell in eagerly behind the running dogs; it seemed as if the posse was on the verge of overtaking Tracy for the first time.

About half way between the Cedar River and Burrough's Boat House on Lake Washington, the dogs stopped dead in their tracks. They had run into a heavy dusting of cayenne pepper across the trail. The sniffing hounds had filled their sensitive nostrils with the spice and they began to wail in pain. It took Carson nearly ten minutes to relieve their discomfort by washing the pepper from their snouts. Even after having their noses cleaned, the dogs' sense of smell seemed hampered and they were not so eager.

However, after a few minutes on the trail, the bloodhounds regained the scent and they were once again closing in on the fugitive. Their deep-throated bellows rang through the forest.

Tracy knew that he had to take immediate action. He made a large circle around the posse through heavy timber and backtracked on his original trail. After accomplishing this maneuver, he headed straight north for Lake Washington.

The dogs managed to figure out his trick but on the shore of the lake they lost the scent entirely. Guard Carson and Sheriff Cudihee were bitterly disappointed. Tracy had eluded them again.

It was nearly dark. Rather than plunging blindly into the gathering gloom of the forest, the sheriff called off the search for the night and sent Carson and the dogs into Renton for a rest. The main body of the tired and frustrated posse arrived in Renton to seek shelter for the night. Shortly thereafter, a woodman named John Atwood arrived to tell the story of his recent meeting with Harry Tracy in the timber overlooking Lake Washington. He said that Tracy had asked him if the roads which skirted the area would lead him to a thoroughfare that could take him into Seattle. The woodman's story did little to arouse the tired posse, however, and most of the members returned to their homes for the night with the disheartening realization that even though the outlaw had been completely surrounded, he had still managed to escape with apparent ease.

Sheriff Cudihee returned to Seattle at about 10:00 that evening with John Anderson, the freed hostage. He wanted to question the man about his time with the outlaw. He also offered a new theory, not just a little bit tinged with the bitterness of his latest defeat.

"Tracy is not in his right mind after days of wandering in the woods. He has become demented and has no particular object in view. His only desire is to secure notoriety in the newspapers."

Cudihee's statement was given in the heat of disappointment and it was a point of view in which the sheriff himself did not believe. The constant days of stress and frustration which he had experienced had begun to take their effect.

Chapter 15:

The Near Miss

Many posse members went back to their farms and jobs after losing Tracy's trail near Renton. A few volunteers and regular deputies were guarding the main south King County roads, but no sightings were made and prospects looked dim.

A man who was trying to pass himself off as "Tom Tracy" was arrested by Deputy Sheriff McCloud in a crowd outside the offices of the Post-Intelligencer. The crowd, which had gathered once again to read the dispatches of the resumed manhunt's progress, was being disturbed by the man's loud abusive boasts of being Harry Tracy's brother. He was described by other people in the crowd as being "slightly under the influence of alcohol."

Deputy McCloud found him waving a picture of Tracy and Merrill he had clipped from the front page of a newspaper. He was shouting to the crowd about Tracy's right to shoot his pursuers because he was being hunted down like an animal in the woods. After a short period of questioning, the deputy let "Tom Tracy" go free; he assumed that the man who was a drunken boaster could not be telling the truth.

The entire population of King County was watching each and every stranger with a suspicious eye. Harry Tracy, the outlaw and fugitive, had proven that he might show up anywhere, at any time. Unidentified strangers took their chances.

At the Hillman home, near Kenwood Streetcar Station at Green Lake (close to the area where the search had been concentrated on July 3), a stranger carrying a Winchester walked in the door without knocking. He pushed Mrs. Hillman, who was standing in the way, out of the doorway and walked straight to the telephone. He was muttering something under his breath about needing to use it immediately. Grabbing the receiver, the man rattled the crank around a few times without asking for a number. Mrs. Hillman stepped outside to gather her two year old child and the man ran out the door and past her again mumbling something about the telephone not working.

Across the street from the Hillman house, Mrs. W. S. Rees saw the man leaving and called to her husband to go over and question him.

"What are you doing here?" demanded Rees. "Where are you going?"

"That's none of your business," snapped the stranger. But checking his harsh attitude, the man said, "Oh, I just came out to look for a couple of cows that I am missing. I believe they have been stolen. That's the reason I am carrying the rifle."

Mr. Rees stood at his front gate and watched as the stranger turned his back and walked off down the road.

Mrs. Hillman immediately notified the sheriff's office and Guard Carson and his bloodhounds were dispatched to the location. Carson took the dogs into the Hillman kitchen and other various places in the area. Cudihee was not convinced that the man was Tracy. He did not remove the guards in Renton. The greater part of the county was on alert, realizing that the outlaw might appear anywhere, given his past erratic and unpredictable movements.

Tracy was positively sighted for the first time since his escape from the posse in Renton by a farmer named Michael Dolan at the railroad crossing over the Green River two and one half miles northeast of Auburn. Dolan, on his way to visit a neighbor, saw a man answering Tracy's description crawling through the brush. Knowing that the outlaw was reported to be in south King County, he stopped the first person who happened down the road, George Hummel, who was on his way to deliver vegetables to market. Dolan was sure that it was Tracy he had seen. He took Hummel to the place where he had made the sighting while he was telling him the story.

"Now go into town as fast as you can," said Dolan, "and tell the members of the posse that Tracy is now lying in the brush just across the bridge. He has been there since noon. Don't give me away on this, as it might get back to Tracy's ears and then I'd be afraid to stay out here any longer."

With this information, Hummel whipped his team and headed toward Auburn. When Sheriff Zimmerman of Snohomish County to the north who happened to be in town at that point in time, heard the report, he found himself in a peculiar situation; every other member of the posse was farther away from Auburn than the position where Hummel had reported him to be. He first notified the King County Sheriff's Office in Seattle of what he had learned and what his intentions were. He then set out for the Green River railroad bridge accompanied only by a local newspaper reporter who did not want to miss the possibility of an exclusive story.

Sheriff Zimmerman and the reporter left Auburn in a borrowed horse and buggy. After covering half of the distance to the Dolan farm, the two men were met by James Dolan, the father of the man whom Hummel had reported had seen Tracy. The sheriff showed the old man his badge and asked him if knew anything about the outlaw.

The elder Dolan, who had a reputation for being ill-tempered and crotchety, looked at the badge and said in a bothered tone, "No, I don't know anything about him."

"Now Dolan," said Zimmerman, "your son has seen Tracy and has sent word to town to that effect. If you do know anything, it's your duty to tell it."

"Suppose I do know something," said the white-haired man drawing closer to the buggy. "What's there in it, if I tell?"

"What," shouted the sheriff, "do you mean to say that with a murderous villain like Tracy wandering around the countryside killing people and tying others, you'd want money to give any information assisting his capture? Why, man, Tracy might choose you as the next person to rob, bind and gag. He might even press you into his service as he did Anderson."

"Well, what's that to you?" said the old man. "You live by your brains, don't you? So do I. I know where he is, but I wouldn't tell you now if you gave me a mine."

"Why you ill-tempered old son-of-a-bitch," shouted the sheriff. "I ought to thrash your hide." He lifted his buggy whip in rage but the old man sensed some harm might be coming his way and ran off down the road to Auburn in a stiff-legged gait, cackling all the while.

"That man's cupidity and effrontery fairly paralyzes me," said Zimmerman in self-righteous indignation. "A few more men like that in this state and Tracy would never be caught. He evidently expected me to go down into my pocket and pay him a round sum for information that might protect him and his family."

The sheriff and reporter continued on to the Dolan farm where they found no one home. This added inconvenience added fuel to the fire of the sheriff's frustration and with a continuous stream of profanity he whipped the horse into a run toward the nearest neighbor's farm to ask where Dolan might be found. At the William Neely farm, one half mile away, the sheriff finally caught up with Michael Dolan. Zimmerman asked him to relate his information about Tracy.

Dolan appeared to be nervous and frightened.

"Say, are you sure I'm not going to get into trouble with Tracy if I tell you anything, am I?"

Sheriff Zimmerman had reached the end of his patience with the uncooperativeness of the Dolan family. He stately flatly that Dolan "very well better tell his story or some night he might be bound and gagged or forced into a similar fate as the one John Anderson had endured."

The warning loosened Dolan's tongue.

"I was going across a bridge to Neely's place," he said, "when my attention was attracted by a man making his way through the brush on the hillside about one hundred feet from the north end of the bridge. He was walking with his body bent over as if to screen himself with the bushes. At that distance, his clothing appeared to be black and he wore a black hat. In one hand he carried what looked like a white bundle. The other hand was held low so that if he had anything in it, I could not see the object."

"As soon as the man saw that he attracted my attention, he jumped behind a bush. I at once thought of Tracy and I was a little bit scared. In a moment or two, the fellow left his position and crawled to a more protected spot as I could tell by the moving brush. Then he rose to his feet and peered at me from behind a tree. I walked away and did not return home for some time. Shortly before 3:00, my wife and little girl were picking berries along the river, when they saw a man close to where I had caught sight of him. He was sitting down and eating something. My wife says that he is a dead ringer for the pictures published of Tracy."

With the correct story secured, Zimmerman left the newspaper reporter and another newsman who had followed the buggy on horseback to watch the bridge while he walked a mile up the Green River to get a better view of the scene. At a shallow point, he forded the river and climbed a steep hill. He continued along a ridge to a position where he could see the river valley below him. He waited in vain for two hours trying to locate the outlaw's hiding place.

When he returned to the bridge, he sent one of the reporters to

Auburn with the order for all available posse members to join him but no reinforcements arrived. At 6:00, he decided to return to Auburn himself to find out why no one had answered the call.

When Zimmerman reached town, he met Sheriff Cudihee who had just arrived from Puyallup with several deputies and Guard Carson with his dogs. Carson had made the journey all the way from Green Lake where he had been engaged in the wild goose chase the night before.

Since it was late in the day to start a full scale search, volunteers were called for to guard the roads leading from Auburn to the river. For some reason, no one was sent out to guard the bridge. Deputy Sheriff Berner, who had come from Seattle to answer Zimmerman's call for men, was sent with a posse of twelve men to guard the railroad track near Covington Station in the Cascade foothills in case Tracy might make a break to cross the mountains. Sheriff Hartman of Pierce County moved to guard the roads leading to Sumner and Palmer. Since both Covington and Sumner were on the main line of the Northern Pacific Railroad leading east, the men guarding the tracks were given permission by officials of the railroad to search every eastbound train.

However, the plans to head off Tracy's flight were once again too late. By the time the guards had taken their positions, he had slipped away into the night.

A farmer named Johnson who lived in the Green River valley hitched his team of horses at 6:00 AM the next morning. After getting his horses ready, he returned to his house to have the breakfast prepared by his wife before setting out for the fields. He had only begun to eat when the door to his kitchen was pushed open and a man strode boldly inside.

"I suppose you know who I am," said the man dressed in black with a Winchester dangling at his side.

"I guess I do," said Johnson giving a nervous look in the man's direction.

"My name is Tracy," said the man walking over to the stove to warm his hands.

"Yes," said Johnson trying in vain to swallow a mouth full of breakfast, "and you can have anything you want."

Tracy stood by the fire and let the heat penetrate his soaking clothes. He asked for a new suit and Mrs. Johnson ran into the bedroom. She returned a short time later in a very bothered manner throwing a set of underwear at his feet. Saying nothing, Tracy took the underwear and went into another room to change, but he put on his old suit.

Mrs. Johnson cooked breakfast and Tracy ate a large portion of eggs and bacon. After the meal he told Mr. Johnson that he wanted him to go into Tacoma and buy two Colt .45 revolvers. He started to make out a list of his exact needs, but checked himself as if realizing that he might be giving out positive proof of his whereabouts.

"Write it down yourself," said Tracy handing Johnson the paper and pen.

"But I am a poor talker," said Johnson in the same kind of

broken Swedish-English that had been spoken by John Anderson, "and I cannot write at all."

"Well, write it as well as you can," ordered Tracy, "and then (they) will understand it. Dig up what money you have and if that isn't enough - borrow it, get it done some way, and if you don't get the guns and come back alone, I'll kill your wife and children. I'll be watching from the bluff and if you bring back men with you, I'll shoot them and kill your wife."

As Johnson left the house, Tracy added, "I didn't kill the Gerrells boy because he was so young and then he had no money, but had to pawn watches."

Harry Tracy had once again thrown up a wall of sheer bravado to convince Johnson that he should not turn him in. The tactics he used, "bluffs" he called them, were most effective on poor men with families. In Tracy's mind, he did not plan to carry out the threats and, indeed, he never did. Because of his reputation and his fierce appearance, he was able to succeed with his intimidations without actually harming anyone, except, of course, the posse members who got in his way; he considered the men hunting him to be deserving of death for seeking his own.

Johnson said later that the reason he obeyed Tracy's instructions without going to the sheriff was, "I was afraid that if I didn't do as I was told, he would kill my family and I hurried to Kent and got some money from a friend and took the 7:00 train for Tacoma."

Once again Tracy had made a man do his bidding using only

words to compel him to comply with his orders.

As soon as Johnson had set out on his journey (with an admonition from Tracy to be back no later than noon), the outlaw assembled the other three members of the family, Mrs. Johnson, a seventeen year old daughter, Annie, and a fifteen year old son. He suggested that they all move to a point of vantage on the hill behind a house where he could watch all approaches to the farm. Although Tracy believed in his bluffing ability, like any good gambler, he wanted to keep other options open in the event that he was called to show his hand.

Annie pointed out a place about two hundred yards from the house which met Tracy's approval and the group of four walked slowly to it. When they were settled, Mrs. Johnson began immediately to plea for the lives of her family. She explained that it would be impossible for her husband to return from Tacoma by noon.

"Have you ever heard of me doing something bad to women and children?" asked Tracy.

"No, but we're afraid you'll take Papa along with you," said Mrs. Johnson.

Tracy declined to pledge that he would not carry out a threat to kill Mr. Johnson if the deputies arrived with him. To pass the time he started a new conversation.

"I feel sorry that I had to hold up the Gerrells family. I enjoyed my visit very much. Anderson told a lot of lies about how I treated him. I did tie him. It was necessary. I didn't strike or kick him, however, and didn't hold a gun on him while he was rowing me in the boat."

Tracy thought awhile and then mumbled, "I'll surely kill him now; he tells too many lies."

The outlaw then recounted a story about his exploits in Colorado with the legendary "Wild Bunch." He said that he had robbed five banks in quick succession with two other men, netting a total of over $36,000.

"But I had to give up my share," he sighed, "in order to protect my pals. Later an innocent man was sent to the penitentiary for thirty five years - convicted of a crime of which he knew nothing."

Mrs. Johnson asked what would happen if anyone came up to the farm while they were waiting for her husband to return.

"You all get behind the tree and keep out of sight. I'll stay and fight. I never run."

******

Johnson arrived in Tacoma and went to purchase a weapon at the gun store of K.A. Kimball. Tracy had ordered a Colt .45 with a six inch barrel, but unfortunately Kimball did not have one in stock. Instead, he sold Johnson a second hand Colt with a seven and one half inch barrel. Johnson said he knew nothing of guns, but that he was buying it for a friend and that it must be as good as new. To prove this, he had Kimball write on the bill of sale, "Guaranteed to be good as new." Johnson also bought a box of cartridges and a belt. The bill came to $11.00. Johnson had more money and could have bought another pistol at Kimball's but Tracy had told him not to buy more than one gun at one store.

Robert Young, a local advertising salesman, was in the gun store at the time and asked Johnson if he was going to hunt Tracy with the gun he had just purchased. Johnson turned bright red at the suggestion. He replied that he had no use for the gun and was only buying it for a friend.

While inspecting the pistol, Johnson found that one of the springs that worked the revolver mechanism was missing. Kimball asked Johnson to wait for an hour or two until he could find the time to repair it but Johnson did not want to chance taking the extra time. A clerk found a spare spring and Johnson left the store without putting the new part into position. The transaction had only taken five minutes but Johnson was already passed the noon deadline that Tracy had set for him. Hurrying as fast as possible, Johnson reached his home at 4:00 in the afternoon. Tracy saw him approach and sent the boy down to meet him. Johnson sent the pistol ahead with the boy and followed.

"This is just what I need," said Tracy before opening the package. When he removed the brown wrapping paper, his excitement lessened. "This isn't the right gun; where is the other one?"

Johnson tried his best to explain why he did not have two guns. He told Tracy that it was because he had been told not to buy more than one gun at a single location; when he had gone to another store, the owner told him he had no pistols left in stock. It was growing late by then and he thought that it would be best to be heading home.

"To show you that I'm honest and I didn't care about the cost," said Johnson, "here is the money the other one would have cost - take it."

"I don't want the money, Johnson," said Tracy in a disappointed tone. "Do you think I want to rob you? You did just right - it's all satisfactory - don't worry about it. However, I will take $2.00 from you as a loan and will return it when I can. Money is of no use to me, I only want revolvers to protect myself."

Johnson thrust the rest of the money, about $20.00, back at him.

Tracy pledged that it was just a loan and that sooner or later he would pay it back.

Everyone reentered the house and Tracy had Mrs. Johnson cook up some dinner. She fixed two dozen eggs, four pounds of ham and then bundled up three loaves of bread, a cup of salt, a roll of butter and some sugar in a flour sack for Tracy to take with him. After dinner, the outlaw sat by the stove and made a holster out of some old boot tops for his new revolver.

Before leaving, he asked for some paper, envelopes and stamps; Mrs. Johnson could not supply the paper but gave him two envelopes and two $.02 stamps.

Tracy shook hands with everyone at the door and mounted a white horse from the barn, promising to turn it loose in a mile or so after he reached the protection of the woods. He asked the boy about the moving of the railroad depot to Auburn and said that he would hold up a train there with his new revolver and force the crew to carry him anywhere he wanted to go.

Mrs. Johnson gave this account later:

"Tracy did not joke at my house. Twice he talked about his mother and I could see tears in his eyes each time. He told me that when he went to a house he always tried to pick out one owned by poor people as they thought more of their family than rich people and he not only liked their society but was surer of forcing their compliance with his orders."

Mrs. Johnson was impressed with Tracy's forcefulness and will to such an extent that she made a special plea to reporters which true to journalistic tradition, was not followed:

"Please don't write anything that is not what I told you, because it makes Tracy mad to see stories about him in the papers. He might come back and kill us. He said that he would kill Anderson. That man can do anything he says. I will never sleep in that house again until he is either dead or out of the country."

After leaving the Johnson house, Tracy headed for the mountains in an attempt to break through the cordon of men which had surrounded the Green River area.

Shortly after midnight, he was walking alongside the Northern Pacific Railroad tracks when he met the posse assigned to guard Covington Station. Deputy Sheriff Bunce and his son, Fred, were manning the outer guard line one mile west of the Covington Sawmill Company. They were located at the eastern end of a long gulley where the track entered the Cascade tunnel.

Deputy Bunce heard a man walking down the tracks and waited until he could hear the footsteps directly across from his position. Bunce ordered the man to halt.

"Hello," said a voice.

"Step forward," demanded Bunce. "What is your name?"

"My name is Anderson," said the man.

Before Bunce could decide what to do next, the man began to run. Thinking the man must be Tracy, Bunce and his son leveled their shotguns in the direction of the retreating man and emptied their barrels. They reloaded and fired again. It was a very dark and cloudy night; neither man could be sure if any of the shots had taken effect.

"Of course, it was so dark we could not see the sights," said Bunce in his report to Sheriff Cudihee, "but we were so close I don't see how we could miss him."

Harry Tracy took cover in the woods. He had been slightly wounded in the hip by the Bunce fusillade. Hobbling along farther up the track, he moved about fifty yards before running into Deputy T. E. Crowe. Crowe put his rifle to his shoulder and said, "Who goes there?"

"A deputy," replied Tracy with consummate calm.

Crowe lowered his gun, accepting the lie, and approached Tracy to talk with him. That outlaw kept up the ruse by suggesting that Crowe join him in heading off the fugitive's flight. Before Crowe could answer the suggestion, two bullets whizzed past his left ear as he felt the burning sting of powder on his cheek. He only survived because of the dark and the close quarters.

Tracy did not wait to see if his shots had found the mark; he jumped down into the brush below the tracks and plunged into the dark night.

Crow hurried to the telegraph station and sent news of the gun battle. He suggested that Sheriff Cudihee should bring the bloodhounds from Auburn now that they had Tracy cornered.

With both deputies and bloodhounds, Cudihee arrived at Covington Station shortly before 8:00 AM. Guard Carson put the bloodhounds to the trail at the spot where shots were fired and the dogs followed a scent for about a mile in circular path along the edge of the dense growth of timber. As had happened many times previously, the trail ended at a body of water. This time it was at the entrance to a shallow swamp. Tracy knew how to handle bloodhounds and he made them virtually ineffective with his scent-covering tactics.

At 10:00 that same morning, Tracy was reported to have been seen at a farmhouse five miles south of Covington Station. The bloodhounds were taken to the area escorted by eight deputies and Sheriff Zimmerman. Sensing a fresh trail, the dogs began to bark eagerly and set off down the path. They held the scent for over eight miles, their best effort of the manhunt. Don, the dog that had been following Tracy's scent throughout Oregon and Washington, was the most excited of the two animals, pulling and straining at the leash controlled by Guard Carson. The promising start fizzled out, however, when near the junction of the Columbia and Puget Sound

Railroad and Northern Pacific Railroad, two miles east of Leary, the trail suddenly ended, washing out in a small, swamp-like lake nestled in the foothills of the Cascade Mountains.

Sheriff Cudihee, staying in Black Diamond for the night, gave a statement for the press indicating his determination to remain on the outlaw's trail.

"So long as the outlaw is within the confines of Western Washington, my efforts will be directed toward his capture. Though we have met with defeat and unprecedented obstacles, there are many reasons why I yet believe the chase will terminate successfully. Chief among them is the fact that Tracy is now a mere wreck of his former physical self and also that hereafter deputies will meet rather than pursue him. Topographical conditions make this possible."

On Saturday, July 12, Harry Tracy appeared at a small house owned by the Portrauts, an older French couple. The house faced a county road and was bounded in the back by the Green River; across the river was a steep bluff. Mrs. Portraut saw Tracy limping up the road coming from Black Diamond. Painfully dragging his left leg, he made his way to kitchen entrance.

"I'm the man the posse is hunting," said Tracy in a tired voice.

Portraut was frightened and remained silent.

"I want something to eat," said Tracy walking inside the house, "and I don't want to talk outside."

Mrs. Portraut fixed a simple meal of bread, butter, pie and milk. Tracy was on the verge of physical exhaustion and could barely lift a fork. He was very thin and his face was more drawn and gaunt than ever. His wound seemed to give him constant pain, his left leg was nearly useless and his back appeared to be stiff.

"I got wounded in the back, just above the left hip," he told the old couple. "I was hit with buckshot. The wound is troubling me. I was shot last night."

Tracy appeared to be nervous and worried. He talked little and when he did, it was in short sentences. At one point, he looked out the window and saw five posse members drive by in a buggy.

"You have nothing to gain by giving me away," he said taking his Winchester in his hand and heading to the bedroom. His voice was soft, without a hint of threat. Once in the bedroom, he started to swear at the posse, but he checked himself when he saw that Mrs. Portraut could hear his words. With his hands clenched around the Winchester, he watched the posse drive on toward Auburn without guessing that their quarry was in the Portraut home. He walked back into the kitchen looking to the Portrauts like a man who had been face to face with death.

The old couple felt no fear in the outlaw's presence and even began to pity him for being forced to live on the run unceasingly, driven to the edge of physical collapse.

Before leaving, he asked for the distance to the towns of Enumclaw and Buckley and received estimates from Mr. Portraut.

"Have you seen any hunters?" he asked the man.

"No, we have seen no one," said Mr. Portraut.

"Well, don't tell them you saw me."

Tracy limped out the door and away from the house toward the river.

The Portrauts watched him until he entered the brush and disappeared from view. After waiting a few minutes to be sure that he had gone, the couple left the house and stood by the county road until a dairyman, Z. T. Rey, pulled up his wagon. Rey took the couple to his house and had his hired hand take the news of Tracy appearance to the posse in Black Diamond the next morning.

"He didn't look like a criminal," said Mrs. Portraut. "He treated us very nicely and it is hard to believe that he has such a black record."

A posse was sent to the Portraut home with ex-Deputy Woolery, Guard Carson with his bloodhounds and Deputy Berner. The bloodhounds were not able to follow the scent across the river, leaving the posse to scatter along two possible routes the outlaw might have taken. It was thought that Tracy probably had taken refuge on the overlooking bluff to gather strength while his wound healed. If that was the case, the posse felt sure that he had blundered into a death trap and that the manhunt would end within a few days.

Chapter 16:

Further Exercises in Futility

The notoriety of Harry Tracy had spread over the entire country and the progress of the manhunt was duly noted in every large newspaper in every major city in the country. There was a kind of nostalgic frontier innocence combined with rough brutality that had somehow captured everyone's imagination.

An interesting anecdote concerning President Theodore Roosevelt was spread throughout East Coast newspapers. While the existence of the conversation was hotly disputed by Cabinet Secretary Cortelyou, it demonstrated the scope of interest in the "Manhunt for Harry Tracy" as touted by many front page headlines.

Supposedly, Colonel Edward Emerson of the Venezuelan Army along with John A. Ryan and James Tracy of the Second Battalion of the New York National Guard, all former members of the President's Rough Rider Regiment, had called on Roosevelt dressed in their old uniforms. After the visit of several hours, the men recounted the President's interest in the case of Harry Tracy in the state of Washington. There had even been some discussion of the possibility that James Tracy might be a distant cousin of the outlaw. According to the three, Roosevelt had been following the progress of the manhunt very closely since the beginning and he was intrigued by the outlaw's constant ability to elude pursuers.

When these reports were printed in newspapers the next day, Cortelyou immediately denied that such a conversation had taken place. For a President of the United States to express such an interest in such a trivial thing as the exploits of an outlaw on the frontier fringes of an ambitious and budding empire, was far too frivolous an activity to be admitted publicly. However, given the sporting blood and hunger for action that was in the nature of "Teddy" Roosevelt, it was just the kind of adventure that he would relish.

******

Nearly two days had elapsed since Tracy's visit to the Portraut home. There was no further clue to his whereabouts. The "Death Trap" that he was supposedly caught in turned out to be another dead end. The outlaw had once again managed to slip through the lines of the posse and leave his pursuers to wonder at how he could have accomplished it.

Since the near miss at the Cascade Tunnel, Tracy's objective had been obvious: he was trying to cross the Cascade Mountains. Newspaper reporters set up their headquarters ahead of the posse in the town of Enumclaw and the posse itself concentrated their efforts on the area around the town of Kanaskat on the Palmer cut-off. It was supposed that Tracy would take either of the two routes to cross the mountains: Stampede pass, used by the main line of the Northern Pacific Railroad, or Naches Pass above the partially completed state road built in 1896.

Rumors again began to spread of Tracy's location. Near Black Diamond two guards, Deputy Sheriff Walter Collins and a butcher named Elmer McDonald, claimed to have seen both Tracy and Merrill together between the towns of Franklin and Kanaskat.

"McDonald and I watched the road near Kanaskat all last night," said Collins, "and did not leave there until 11:00 the next morning. I went to Leary and McDonald to Franklin. Hardly had I arrived at Leary before a wire from McDonald reached town to the effect that he had seen both Merrill and Tracy about midway between Kanaskat and Franklin. McDonald is honest and truthful and there must be something to his story." Apparently, neither of the two men had read the newspaper accounts about the demise of Merrill.

A man named Williams reported that he had been held up for a meal by Tracy and Merrill near Lake 32 not far from the town of Kangley. Another man, Fred Brooks, who lived about a mile from the Portraut house, told a story about being shot at by the outlaw, but when he was questioned by deputies, he admitted that his tale was just a jest; one of the many that continued to plague officials in their search.

When all hope of finding Harry Tracy's trail seemed lost, he was finally seen at 5:00 in the afternoon of July 13 by a ten-year old boy, Clarence Burke, one and one half miles east of Enumclaw. Tracy was sitting near the edge of a gravel pit, still dressed in his black clothes and hat, when the boy rode by on his bicycle. Tracy hailed the boy to the side of the road. The man appeared to be very tired; his head was drooping and he had dark circles around his eyes. Around the man's waist was a crude holster containing two pistols; in his arms was cradled a Winchester rifle.

"Can you tell me the road that leads to Buckley?" the man asked the boy.

"Yes, sir," said Burke in a quiet voice, guessing the man was Tracy but trying not to show it, "it is about two hundred yards farther down, and the road leading to the mills branches off from it."

"How far is it?" Tracy asked.

"Well, I think it's about three and one quarter miles."

"Thank you," said Tracy politely, taking up his rifle as he set off a quick pace down the road.

As soon as the man was out of sight, Burke rode his bicycle as fast as his legs could pump the pedals into the town of Enumclaw. He abandoned his bike on Main Street and ran up to a group of men standing in front of the saloon to tell them what had happened. Sheriff Hartman of Pierce County was notified (he was in town at the time) and he, in turn, notified Sheriff Woolery at Palmer. Hartman immediately requested that Guard Carson and his bloodhounds be sent to Enumclaw to take up the chase. Woolery, Guard Carson and the bloodhounds and a wagon load of deputies set out immediately for Enumclaw, while Walter Lyons, the irrepressible Oregon representative, followed later in a wagon sent to them from Enumclaw.

The bloodhounds were put to the scent at the point where the boy, Burke, had seen Tracy. They followed a trail for half a mile until it ended at yet another swamp. By that time it was dark and Sheriff Woolery decided to set up guard positions and wait for daylight.

Sheriff Cudihee was at Ravensdale and Woolery sent him a wire concerned the day's activities:

"No doubt that man seen on road is Tracy. Hounds took trail and followed it half mile to dusty road where they lost scent. Dogs were called off and party will start again at 4:00 AM. Cannot tell where Tracy is going although believed he is circling. Berner feels they are on the right track. Hartman with a strong guard is out tonight. We are guarding everything here and guards will be reinforced all along the line tomorrow."

To Sheriff Cudihee, it was the same old story. He refused to rush over to lead the posse; he had another strategy in mind.

Sheriff Brown of Kittitas County, the first county on the eastern side of the Cascade Mountains, began making plans to head off Harry Tracy if he happened to successfully negotiate the guards at the passes.

"Should Harry Tracy emerge from the cover of Puget Sound forest and head down the eastern slope," he said, "it will be a question of speed not strategy. Nature will not aid him in providing a safe retreat at every turn and field glasses rather than bloodhounds will come into requisition."

The guards in the passes, who were searching all trains heading east of the mountains, were beginning to draw the enmity of the railroad crews who were becoming fed up with the delays caused in their schedules. One train crew member announced to a group of indignant deputies, "Tracy would be a welcome guest on our cars across the Cascades even though he be minus the customary brakey's toll."

******

At Spanaway Park in Tacoma, the manhunt took on a different purpose: entertainment. The Sunday crowds were being amused by the stories of some the past victims of Harry Tracy's depredations. John Laird, the aged Scotsman from Olympia who had been forced to offer hospitality to the outlaw, John Anderson, the hired hand from Bainbridge Island who was forced to become his unwilling servant and hostage and Frank Scott who had met Tracy on his trip across Puget Sound on the *N & S*, all took turns telling their stories of the small part they each played in the drama of the "Manhunt For Harry Tracy."

******

Since all roads, passes and railroad tracks leading east were being heavily watched, Tracy did what no one expected him to do; he proceeded west. He doubled back on his tracks and headed back toward Auburn over old roads and Indian trails.

To understand how completely this plan of action outwitted the well-laid trap set by the posse, one must understand the lay of the land. There was a bluff overlooking the Green River Valley which led for several miles above the location of the Portraut house. Across the bluff in a westerly direction, was located the Muckleshoot Indian Reservation Mill. The bluff divided the Green River and White River which had their conjuncture at Auburn, eight miles away. On the other side of the Muckleshoot Reservation

Mill, the White River valley led up to the Cascade Mountains near Enumclaw. Tracy had moved from the bluff above the Portraut's house west to the mill, and then moved over the summit down to Enumclaw. Once in town, he had found his escape route into Eastern Washington blocked, and so he had followed one of the many old Indian trails back to the reservation mill.

On his backtrack across the bluff, Tracy was seen by a farmer named O'Neil. The farmer and his wife had just arrived at their home from a short buggy ride in the area. Mrs. O'Neil went inside the house and Mr. O'Neil began to feed his pigs. Out of the corner of his eye, he saw a stranger in black cross his field.

"I was standing about the middle of the hog pen," O'Neil said, "when I glanced up and saw the man emerge from the brush and come over to the fence. At the moment, I was yelling at the pigs and he looked up and saw me. He didn't realize, however, that I saw him. Like a flash he ducked under the fence and ran like a deer in a bent position to the old hop kiln. There I lost sight of him entirely."

"He carried something like a Winchester rifle and in general he answered to the description of the escaped murderer. If the convict had desired to continue to the Green River valley, nothing lay in his way. At Indian Agent Reynolds' house on Auburn Road, four roads cross. Two lead to Enumclaw and another is Whitney Road running to the Green River valley; the fourth, of course, goes to Auburn. This place is not guarded and if Tracy had continued on his journey after we left, there was nothing to prevent him taking any one of these thoroughfares."

O'Neill's story was corroborated by a Native American boy who saw Tracy on a road leading by the reservation.

******

On July 15, the mystery of what had happened to Dave Merrill, Tracy's partner, was solved. The body of Merrill was found near Chehalis within two hundred yards of the main line of the Northern Pacific Railroad, thrown behind a log beside a county road. The discovery was made by Mrs. Mary Wagoner of Napavine and her thirteen year old son, George. They were out gathering blackberries and were attracted to the spot by the stench of Merrill's rotting flesh. The story told by Tracy of killing his partner was fresh in their minds and they approached to investigate the smell. What they saw was two feet sticking up out of the brush. Without pursuing their curiosity any further, they notified he authorities in Chehalis of their find.

Sheriff Degeiller of Lewis County, the man in charge of the posse hunting Tracy and Merrill less than a month previously, took charge of the case and Deputy Coroner Meade impaneled a coroner's jury to pick up the body. Benjamin Merrill, the brother who had left the logging camp on Anderson Island with the stated purpose of joining his brother and Tracy to help them escape, was working at the time in a livery stable in Chehalis. He was satisfied that the body found by Mrs. Wagoner was that of his brother. Warden J. T. Janes of the Oregon State Penitentiary took the train to Chehalis and although he could not positively identify the body, he stated that it almost certainly had to be Merrill. S. W. Studebaker of Castle Rock had known Dave Merrill for years and he was also satisfied that the body was that of his friend.

However, not everyone was convinced. When Merrill's body was transported back to the penitentiary to be viewed by the prisoners, most of the inmates disagreed with the identification and swore it was the body of a different man.

The only articles in the possession of the man thought to be Merrill, were a briar pipe, some tobacco, an upper plate with four false teeth and seven 30/30 bullets. He was dressed in a prison uniform with pants cut off at the bottom as if they were too long, a red undershirt and heavy shoes slit open, presumably because they were too tight.

The most important find was not discovered on the body. On the road within a few feet of the log where the body was first discovered, were two 30/30 cartridges lying on the grass. Another cartridge was found eighteen to twenty paces to the north. By the placement of these empty cartridges, it was not so difficult to accept Tracy's story about how he had killed Merrill. If a duel had indeed been fought, then the position of the shells clearly indicated that Tracy and Merrill were sixteen paces apart, the step eight that Tracy had said he was fired upon. Evidently, he had ejected one shell at the stopping point and had either fired another shot at the same position and had not ejected it until he moved in for a close range shot, or he had walked to close range and fired two shots. Because of the placement of the wounds in the back and neck, it was reasonable to assume that two shots were fired at long range and one at close range, corroborating Tracy's story.

Mrs. Mary Wagoner, the woman who had discovered the body, put in a claim for the reward offered by the state of Oregon. Her claim was addressed by Governor Geer in a masterful piece of bureaucratic rationalization:

"The reward is offered for the capture and delivery of the convicts, dead or alive, in the hopes of inducing men to take great risk to affect their capture. One who simply discovers the body has not done this. He should receive some compensation, say $300 or $400, but is certainly not entitled to the full sum. The same holds should Tracy die from exposure or when driven to commit suicide. I think that anyone, even though he be a sheriff or a deputy, could claim the reward for the outlaw's capture and should a number of men be instrumental in effecting his capture, the reward should be divided. There might be some complications which the courts would have to decide, but I do not think that anyone (who) might bring in the dead body would be entitled to the full reward."

Mrs. Wagner did not receive a reward, not even the partial payment promised by Governor Geer.

******

Sheriff Cudihee issued a general order on July 14 at 5:00 PM for all posse members to meet at Auburn. He was thoroughly disgusted with futile results of the manhunt to that point; it had been a campaign of chasing rumors, trying to coordinate unruly posses, managing private bounty hunters and heavy travel for his deputies and him with little or no sleep. He decided to put a new plan into action.

At 3:00 on the afternoon of July 14, Tracy approached the Garner farm on Boise Creek three and one half miles from Enumclaw. He had once again decided to escape Western Washington over the Cascade Mountains. He entered the house without knocking and found Mr. Garner and two of his three sons sitting at the table; the other son was shaving.

"Gentlemen," said Tracy, "I'm Tracy and want something to eat quick."

The Garners had just finished with dinner and told the outlaw to sit down and help himself to leftovers. Before sitting down, he ordered the two eldest of the Garner sons to a corner of the room where he could keep an eye on them. The youngest boy was so upset that he could not continue shaving even when told to do so by Tracy. The outlaw wolfed down some food and then called to the boy, "Young man, come here and shave me."

The boy protested that he did not want to shave him because he was not good enough with a razor.

"That's all right," said Tracy. "I'm not particular and I don't kick if you needn't."

The boy gave in, lathered the outlaw's face and went about shaving off the nearly two week's growth of Tracy's scraggly beard. When the job was finished, Tracy helped himself to a pair of pants hanging on the wall, tucked them under his arm, said his goodbyes and quickly made his departure.

******

The few posse members who remained in the small Cascade foothills towns were at a loss about what to do. The bloodhounds were still being held at Auburn and no new orders had been issued by Sheriff Cudihee. It was assumed that the sheriff was working out the details of some tactic which did not require the assistance of large numbers of men in a posse. There was an aura of mystery about Cudihee's actions; even Undersheriff Corcoran confessed that he had not heard from his supervisor in over twelve hours.

There were some poignant stories among the seemingly abandoned posse members, some of whom had been in the manhunt since Salem. Many of the men were stranded in strange towns with little or no money and no prospects other than the promise of reward money for Tracy's capture.

Jake Williams, a reservation Native American from Oregon, had been following Tracy's trail almost continuously since the day the two fugitives had escaped from the Oregon State Penitentiary. The ravages of a month and half on the trail had begun to tell on his physical condition; he had become tired and thin and looked like a man being hunted rather than one of the hunters. He had spent every cent of his savings at the start of the search to defray the cost of guns and supplies. Since the sheriff had issued the general order cease the hunt, Williams had been wandering around the streets of Ravensdale without any means of support. He told reporters that despite his situation, he was determined to remain in the chase until Tracy had been run down.

Sheriff Cudihee's unexplained actions were not the result of exhaustion and frustration as many people who were critical of him thought. Instead, he had decided to act on peripheral indications that Tracy was being aided by a small group of confederates and friends from Seattle, as first revealed by John Anderson. An informant from Whatcom County, Louis Ward, claimed he knew the men who were aiding Tracy and could lead the sheriff and a small group of deputies to the place where they were all hiding out.

Ward was known to the newspaper reporters at the time only as the "Stool Pigeon" and his story seemed dubious while still containing elements of the truth. Ward told Cudihee that accomplices rumored to be north and south of Seattle were indeed assisting the outlaw at various times. They had rowed him to Port Madison, had met with him in Bothell and at Green Lake, and had traveled a short time with him near Renton. Ward's story intrigued Cudihee since he also suspected Tracy must have had some assistance in order to elude his deputies so completely for such a long time. The strangers who continually loitered around his headquarters and were just as continuously chased away at the point of a gun, had become familiar faces. In all of his days as a lawman, he had never seen an outlaw with such incredible luck, cunning intelligence and sheer bravado; his innate instincts told him that only a man with confederates could manage to accomplish such a total defeat of a posse.

The remainder of Louis Ward's story stretched into the realm of fantasy. He said that Tracy had hoped to place himself at the head of a local gang of outlaws who would perform criminal deeds so daring and profitable that the "feats of the James Boys, the Daltons or even Joaquin Murietta and his cutthroats would suffer by comparison." The reason, Ward claimed, that Tracy was wandering around the countryside was not to get food and weapons; this, he said, could have easily be accomplished by the confederates. The real purpose of his wanderings was to gain notoriety of such stature that the mere mention of his name would invoke instant fear. Ward insisted that Dave Merrill was not dead, but in Seattle waiting to join Tracy at the right moment so they could set up an outlaw gang which would have as its territory, the area from Salem to Seattle.

While Cudihee did not believe Ward's entire story, he thought there was a possibility that some of it might be true. He thought that perhaps there were men who were trying to assist Tracy and that they did actually believe that they could establish an outlaw gang of incredible proportions, since, after all, Harry Tracy's name was now infamous throughout the Pacific Northwest. The men might well be deluded by their own dreams.

Ward told Cudihee that he could lead him to a hideout where Tracy was recuperating from his wounds and where he was staying with a few trusted men. After thinking over Ward's offer for two hours, Cudihee made a bold decision: he would follow the informer's suggestions and see where they led. He had nothing to lose. Tracy had not been heard from since a logger had reported seeing him heading up the Gold Hill trail. The outlaw might be hiding anywhere while his wounds healed and Cudihee thought

Ward's plan was worth a try.

Ward went as far as suggesting the names of the men he supposed were assisting Tracy: Thomas Floyd, alias Tattoo Red, and an ex-convict named Simmons. Tattoo Red had spent two terms at the Washington State Penitentiary in Walla Walla. The first sentence was for burglary in Whitman County and the other was for stealing a horse in Vancouver. He was, at that time, wanted for the murder of Louis Grummota, a saloon-keeper from Lakeview near Tacoma on May 10. Red was supposed to have been the means of communication between Tracy and his friends in Seattle. Cudihee had been given reports that a man answering Tattoo Red's description had passed through the posse lines repeatedly during the manhunt and that he had once or twice attempted, when in close quarters with the posse as a volunteer, to impede the progress of the manhunt. Simmons had been implicated in the Hyams-Paulson money jar robbery in Seattle eight years previously and was known to frequent the saloons and brothels below Yesler, preying upon unsuspecting Yukon "boomers" and sailors on leave. Ward also mentioned a man named Miller. Miller had been seen in the vicinity of Buckley during the days when the posse was in the area. He had completed his term at the Oregon State Penitentiary shortly before Tracy and Merrill had broken out and Oregon officials were convinced that he was in some way responsible for placing the guns in the workshop which the convicts used to affect their escape. A man resembling Miller had been seen heading up the Gold Hill trail with a pack load of provisions.

Cudihee put his plan into motion. He took Ward with him to Covington Station and tried to convince the man to lead him to the place where Tracy was hiding. Ward protested that if he did so, he would be shot by the men for betraying them. However, Ward claimed to know the whereabouts of a cabin where the men were staying and he offered to go ahead to see if Tracy was still there.

Cudihee sent Ward on his mission and he disappeared into the forest for about eight hours before returning with information that he had found the men at a cabin on the shores of Lake Sawyer. He said that Tracy was there with Tattoo Red and Simmons. Refusing to join the chase due to concern for his own safety, he gave Cudihee directions to the cabin.

The sheriff chose twelve of his best deputies and the group left for Lake Sawyer with a guide, Jack Fraser, showing the way. The men had to literally cut their own trail because of dense undergrowth which had completely covered the original one. After wandering through the forest and getting lost at least twice, the posse finally emerged at a spot close to the cabin, although they could not see it in the dark. Daylight revealed their position near the cabin and Cudihee gave the order for a direct assault. The entire posse charged the cabin with pistols and rifles ready for action. When they burst open the door, they found the cabin empty. An old fire was discovered in one corner and a pile of rags with bloodstains was found in another but other than these two tenuous clues, there was nothing to suggest that Ward had told the truth about the cabin serving as a hideout.

With another disappointment in a long string of disappointments, Cudihee's spirit was broken. He retired from the search leaving a small complement of deputies in charge of the area near Ravensdale. He returned to his office in Seattle. A few additional men were stationed at the Lake Sawyer cabin where it was believed that Tracy had visited only days before the posse arrived. Cudihee told reporters in thoroughly disheartened address that he would not go into the field again until he heard definite news of Tracy's whereabouts from his deputies.

Chapter 17:
Into Eastern Washington

Frank Donnelly, foreman of Union Pacific Railroad switching crews in Denver, Colorado and Tracy's former fellow worker in the days in which both men were employed by the Northern Pacific Railroad in Seattle, was interviewed in his Denver home and was asked questions by the press about his past association with the now-infamous and yet un-captured outlaw, Harry Tracy.

"At one time Tracy and I worked together, he was a student - that is he was learning to become, a brakeman," Donnelly said. "He was given to having a good time and, while enjoying himself with the boys, never gave evidence of a man of vicious temper. He was popular rather than otherwise."

"Tracy is no worse than I am. His greatest characteristic is his coolness in a row, and I believe his work on the railroad and his training has helped him elude the officers of the law. I know nothing of his crime, but from my knowledge of him, I think he believed there was only one thing to do and he is doing it now in bending every energy to escape. That he is not an out and out degenerate is proved, I think, by his treatment of his temporary victims. While he has been harsh, he has not sacrificed life from mere wantonness."

As the days began to pass without any additional clues to Tracy's exact location, the immediacy of the threat to Seattle and King County decreased. With it, came the diminishing of his notoriety as the Daily Times and the Post-Intelligencer moved the story off the front pages for the first time in over three weeks, relegating it to the Northwest News sections.

Chief Deputy Sheriff of Pierce County left for Naches Pass on a solitary mission to hunt down the outlaw. He was equipped with a pack horse, a saddle horse, provisions for several weeks and enough weaponry to be protected against any attack.

The King County posse was disbanded and the search was put on hold. Guard Carson returned to Walla Walla with his ineffective and exhausted bloodhounds.

Harry Tracy had escaped the posse and defeated every effort to contain him in the Western Washington region.

On July 21, Charles Coombs, a rancher living three miles east of Enumclaw, reported that his sister had found that someone had entered her kitchen while she was away visiting and had taken food, a small frying pan and a gold watch. Coombs suggested that the thief might have been Tracy since no strangers had been sighted in the area.

A few days later, a miner named Elsner came into the Cascade Miner Newspaper office at Roslyn, a mining town on the eastern slopes of the Cascade Mountains, and stated that he believed Tracy had spent the nights of July 20 and 21 at Camp Creek. According to Elsner, Tracy had reached Easton by freight train and there had met friends who first took him to Lake Cle Elum for the night and then had taken him to Camp Creek where several miners were working their claims. The miners, according to Elsner, were in sympathy with Tracy and they had given him food and dressed his wound which they discovered was quite deep. He had slept at the mill near the creek and had caught eighteen trout there in the morning. Elsner bought newspapers from the past two weeks and he told the clerk that he was taking them back for Tracy.

Sheriff Brown of Kittitas County arrived in Roslyn that same day to investigate Elsner's story, but the miner had already left to return to his camp. Neither Brown nor the town marshal believed the tale and they dismissed it as just another one of many stories being told to stir up excitement about the search. Sheriff Cudihee agreed with the two lawmen and said he had proof that Tracy was definitely west of the Cascades as late as Saturday July 19. He had placed extra guards at Palmer and points east as well as on all of the trails leading to the Cascade Tunnel. He was confident that Tracy could not get over the mountains without being seen.

At Miller's logging camp near Kanaskat, a man calling himself Harry Tracy walked up and demanded a dinner. He was asked by one of the loggers why he had not taken advantage in the lull in the search to leave the Green River valley.

"I have some business to settle with Merrill's brother," the man said. "I understand that his brother wants to see me."

The men left the logging camp shortly after his meal and a report was sent to officials. The description the loggers gave of the man's appearance did not quite fit with that of Tracy even though he was said to have carried two pistols and a Winchester. It was generally assumed that the man was an imposter.

Charles Gerrells, the boy whom Tracy had sent into Seattle to buy pistols and instead had returned with a posse, was standing on the platform at the Union Street Station when a man who resembled Tracy walked up and stood beside him. The boy was so shocked by the similarity in appearance that he ran immediately to the sheriff's office to report his sighting. Deputies investigated but could not find the man and they simply did not believe that Tracy would be so stupid as to come into Seattle when he was so safe in the Cascades.

A man named William Nixon found himself in trouble when he tried to impress a woman performer at the Alhambra Music Hall by impersonating Harry Tracy. The Alhambra was the establishment owned by Joe Williams, the brother of the gravely wounded deputy sheriff who was still suffering in the hospital. Nixon had taken a liking to one of the dancers in the Alhambra show and he called her over to his table for a talk.

"Don't be surprised when I tell you I'm Tracy," he said in a whisper. "I know you don't believe me but don't give me away or you'll suffer the consequences."

Nixon made the frightened woman buy him two glasses of beer. After downing them, he left with an admonishment to the woman not to reveal his identity. It took the woman about a half an hour to summon up the courage to tell Williams, but when she did, he flew into a rage. He was terribly upset that the man who had shot his brother might have had the audacity to enter his saloon.

Knowing that nothing could be done that night, Williams laid out a plan for the man's next visit. Patrolman Chipman, the officer on the beat near the Alhambra, promised to arrest the man if he ever came back to the saloon. A few nights later, Nixon returned to the Alhambra and immediately sought out the same woman. As he talked to her, she signaled Williams behind the bar. Williams slipped out the back door to find Patrolman Chipman. When he did not find Chipman, Williams walked a few blocks north and found Patrolman Flanagan. He asked Flanagan to make an arrest of the man claiming to be Tracy who was in his saloon for the second time.

The two men proceeded to the Alhambra with Flanagan entering the back door and Williams strolling nonchalantly in the front door. Drawing his pistol, Flanagan approached Nixon and said, "Hands up, make a move and you die." Nixon was caught completely by surprise and he stood up to confront the voice behind him. The patrolman, not wanting to shoot a possibly innocent man, brought down his fist on Nixon's head.

A fight broke out between the two men and Williams grabbed the nearest beer mug and moved to join the melee. Nixon was knocked unconscious by multiple blows from Williams' mug, Flanagan's pistol butt and various customers' fists. The beaten man was brought to the city jail and was at once recognized as not being the outlaw he claimed to be. Because of his bloodied condition, Nixon was given only a light sentence of a few days in jail and then he was let go.

Harry Tracy emerged from his Cascade Mountain sanctuary on August 1. After nearly two months in the heavily forested and brush covered country of Western Washington, he was on the verge of entering the broad Eastern Washington, high desert plain.

The landscape in Eastern Washington was dramatically different than the western slope of the Cascades. It was a broad and relatively flat plain with the topography of a high desert more like Nevada than Western Washington. The forest thinned out from thick Douglas fir, first to pine trees and then to scrub brush. Farms in the area were limited to river valleys and were far more scattered than the more populated western slope. The smell of sagebrush filled the air, very warm in the steady August sun. Temperatures soared from the 60s in Western Washington to the 90s in Eastern Washington. It was a totally different place and a totally different environment than Tracy had been experiencing for the last two months.

On horseback for the first time since his breakout, Tracy worked his way from Blewett Pass down the ridge which lay on the western side of the wide Columbia River. The river, while not at its widest expanse farther down its relentless march toward the Pacific Ocean, was still a daunting obstacle to be overcome. As Tracy made his way to the town of Wenatchee, the ground flattened, the skies brightened and his spirits lifted.

This new country seemed to signify freedom compared to the close confines he had recently escaped. It reminded him of Colorado and his days as a member of the "Hole-In-The-Wall" gang. He thought he might return to the land of his wilder youth.

At 10:00 in the morning, he arrived outside the fruit ranch

owned by Wenatchee City Councilman W. A. Sanders and operated by his son-in-law, Samuel MacEldowney, with two good pack horses, a saddle horse and camp outfit common to a sheepherder.

Sanders was in the middle of packing apricots into a storage shed when he was approached by the stranger on horseback. Since his ranch was often encountered by men on the road, Sanders was not surprised by the visit.

"Good day," he said not looking up from his work.

"I'm Tracy, the Oregon convict," said Tracy in his usual blunt and unconcerned tone.

Sanders smiled at the joke and said, "Help yourself to apricots, Mr. Tracy."

"I see you don't believe me," said Tracy reaching under his coat and gently removing one of his revolvers, "but perhaps this will help you realize I'm telling the truth." He pointed the weapon at Sander's head. "I want you to give me a little assistance. And you must do just as I tell you."

"Very well, Mr. Tracy," said Sanders becoming more serious, "What do you want?"

"Well, for the present just keep quiet. I don't want any disturbance and I want a rest."

Climbing down from his saddle, Tracy entered the shed and stretched out near where Sanders was working. As Sanders continued his chores, Tracy struck up a conversation. He spoke nervously but seemed to be in good spirits. His physical condition, according to Sanders, was worn but still strong overall with no sign of the wound.

At 12:00, Sam MacEldowney came to the shed to call Sanders in for the midday meal. When he discovered that Sanders was talking to another man, he invited the stranger to eat with them.

"Mr. MacEldowney," said Sanders, "this is Mr. Tracy."

Thinking that it was just another normal introduction, MacEldowney nodded his acknowledgement and turned away.

"Wait, Sam," said Tracy, "I see you don't remember your old friends."

MacEldowney had lived near Portland, Oregon in previous years and he had known Tracy before he had been sent to the Oregon State Penitentiary. Suddenly, MacEldowney remembered the voice and the face and said, "My God, it's Harry Tracy."

The outlaw suggested that they should go into the house to eat the meal that MacEldowney had offered. When they entered the home, the rest of the family along with their two hired hands was sitting at the table waiting to begin the meal.

"My friends," said Tracy, "Mr. MacEldowney knows who I am and that what I say goes. Just do as I say."

Tracy sat at the end of the table nearest to the door while everyone else was crowded around the other end. The meal progressed quietly and when it was finished, Tracy told the group not to leave his sight.

They moved out to the porch and under the shade of the front yard trees to spend the hot afternoon. To pass the time, Tracy started a conversation.

"Everyone wants to know where I'm going," he said. "Well, I'm going to the 'Hole-In-The-Wall' country in Wyoming. There I can be a thief among thieves and safe."

Taking Sanders aside, Tracy asked the man what the town of Wenatchee was like and whether or not it had a bank. Sanders told him about the Columbia Valley Bank.

"Well, I think I'll go and make them a visit. I promised a fellow that helped me out of the penitentiary $6,000 inside of a year and I always keep my word. I don't want to harm poor people but I will hold up an express company or a bank. This seems to be a good chance and I think I'll take it."

Tracy walked over to MacEldowney and said, "Sam, I'm going to Wenatchee to hold up the bank and you're going with me."

"But there'll be a fight," protested MacEldowney. "If you don't get killed, I will. Even if I don't get killed, I'll be considered an accomplice, which is just as bad. I'm a poor farmer with a family to support."

Tracy gave in to his old friend. "Well, I guess I'll get my $6,000 at some other time."

Turning his attention to another subject, Tracy brought up the gun battle at the Van Horn house.

"Breece grabbed me and would surely have got me had I not killed him. After shooting Breece the second time, I jumped over a fence, almost into Cudihee's arms. He dropped his gun and ran. I picked it up and would have taken it but I could not get through the brush good with two guns."

Tracy was bragging in this conversation. He might have been trying to get even with Sheriff Cudihee for the tight pressure he had been exposed to in King County. If Tracy had jumped over a fence causing a man to drop his gun, then that man could not have been Cudihee since he was in a relatively remote position from the position where Breece and Rawley were shot. Once again, Tracy had Breece and Rawley confused; Rawley was the man he shot at close range.

Without stopping to dwell on his last thought, Tracy continued to ramble.

"At one time, the posse was lined up on a railroad track as thick as crows on a picket fence - within thirty feet of me. And later, when they thought I was wounded badly, I was on a hill and watched them surround a clump of timber. They would rather send dogs in than go themselves, though. Things were getting pretty warm for me over there and I made for this side. I came over the mountains like a rabbit crawling through the underbrush and working slowly through the timber. When I got on this side, I met a miner and he gave me an old broken down horse. Afterwards, I struck a sheep camp over near Ellensberg and got two other horses I have with me now."

Tracy allowed Mrs. MacEldowney to go into the kitchen in the late afternoon to prepare supper. The arrangement for the evening meal was the same as the afternoon with Tracy on one side and everyone else on the other. He appeared more nervous to the others at this meal, restlessly jumping up from his seat, pacing back and forth and then sitting back down at the table. He talked rapidly, almost hysterically at times, but still with enough caution not to reveal his future plans.

After supper, he sent the men to unsaddle his horses so he could inspect them. All three of the animals showed signs of being ridden hard and far. Tracy asked the men to once again saddle the horses when he saw that there were only work horses on the ranch and that he could use none of them to replace his own. When the saddling was completed, Tracy announced that he was leaving and wanted MacEldowney to accompany him as a hostage and a guide. Mrs. MacEldowney began crying at this suggestion and when the children joined in, Tracy relented. It was possible that Tracy, who had been virtually alone on the trail since leaving his hostage, John Anderson, wanted MacEldowney's company as much as his assistance. Perhaps the nostalgia of seeing an old friend from happier times had prompted his suggestion.

"Sam," said Tracy, "can get me a couple of good, fresh horses?"

"You can see for yourself what I have," he said.

"They won't do," said Tracy shaking his head. "I want good, fresh saddle horses and they must be shod. What have your neighbors got?

Within a short distance from the MacEldowney home was a pasture owned by a man named Lockwood. A number of horses stood grazing leisurely on the grass.

"Sam, are any of those any good?" asked Tracy.

"Yes, I think they are."

"Go get them for me."

MacEldowney walked to his neighbor's pasture and picked out three of the best horses. Tracy had the men saddle the new mounts. He then had MacEldowney mount each horse in succession in order to determine their ability. Satisfied by the demonstration that the horses were satisfactory for his purposes, Tracy prepared to leave.

"You people have been fair to me," he said. "Fairer than anyone I've met. I should take Sam with me but if you'll promise not to give away on me until I have time to get away, I'll let him off. You're the only people that I know in this neighborhood and if you stool I'll get even if it's the last thing I ever do."

Just as Tracy was ready to ride out of the corral, a neighbor, John Johnson, walked into the yard for an evening visit. Tracy wanted to take him along as a guide, but after a short talk, MacEldowney convinced him that Johnson was also a family man and that he could also not be put under risk. After warning everyone not to move from the property for at least twenty four hours, Tracy rode away.

The former hostages were properly threatened by Tracy's promise to return if they did not follow his orders. They waited in fear all night, wondering if Tracy might decide to return. In the morning, MacEldowney followed the trail left by the stolen horses far enough to satisfy himself that Tracy had taken the road down to the Columbia River before he proceeded into Wenatchee to relate the news of the outlaw's presence on the east side of the mountains.

After leaving the MacEldowneys, Tracy rode down to the Mottler ferry, twelve miles to the south. He arrived late in the day and had to wake the Mottler brothers to ask them to ferry him across the Columbia. Without identifying himself, Tracy put in his request for the ferry to be put in operation. The Mottler brothers, who resented being awoken from their night's sleep, retorted that it was impossible to cross the dangerous river at night.

Tracy did not sleep while waiting for daylight; he paced beside his horses, anxious to get some distance between himself and the inevitable pursuers he knew would be on his trail before long. At the first light of dawn, he woke the Mottler brothers and had them ferry him across the river before they had their breakfast. When he reached the eastern shore of the river, he marched his horses off the ferry (a rough-hewn craft constructed from pine planks) and announced that he was broke and that even if he did have the money, he would not pay the two brothers because they had been so uncooperative.

Once on the far side of the Columbia, Tracy headed into the rough, broken country of Moses and Grand Coulees, the dry beds of the ancient path of the river. With the numerous hills, ravines, washouts and eroded escarpments covered with scraggly brush and thin forests, central Douglas County offered the outlaw almost as much protection as he had in Western Washington.

Posses were quickly sent out from the small towns in the area as soon as the alarm was sent out from Wenatchee, but they were not of sufficient number to guard even a fraction of the possible routes Tracy might take on his journey.

On August 1, Sheriff Cudihee, surprised to learn that his man had crossed the mountains into Eastern Washington, left Seattle for Wenatchee with two deputies and Benjamin Merrill, who, after identifying his brother's body, had sworn to hunt down Harry Tracy.

The sheriff and his small posse took to the field the first morning after they arrived by train. They headed for Coulee City and Wilber where a farmer had reportedly seen the outlaw cross his property.

Cudihee and Friel of Waterville set out to follow a trail that led toward the town of Ephrata. Guard posts were established at Coulee City and Wilber on the main roads leading east in the hope of cutting off Tracy's forward movement. A farmer named Perkins, living three miles south of Almira, reported to Sheriff DeBolt of Douglas County that he had seen a rider with two pack horses cross his property. While DeBolt and Cudihee tried to pick up the trail leading from the Perkins farm, Sheriff Gardner of Lincoln County lent his assistance by providing men to guard the ferries that crossed the Columbia River and the road that led northwest to Spokane.

Tracy had, by that time, left the topographically advantageous coulee country and was well into the flat eastern plains that were dotted here and there with waving fields of wheat. The towns of this region were basically railroad depots for the shipping of grain to Seattle where it would be redistributed to other parts of the country. At intervals of ten to twenty miles on the railroad track, the communities were easily skirted by the outlaw who seemed to be avoiding all contact with farmhouses instead of preying upon them as he had done in Western Washington. Perhaps he felt more exposed in this region and preferred not to take his chances with any pursuing posse in this open country.

Eastern Washington had more of a Midwestern than Northwestern appearance. No doubt Harry Tracy felt a sensation of freedom in the wide, blue-sky openness of the land. Compared to the close, cloudy confines of the thick forests of the Puget Sound region, it must have seemed like a release from another kind of prison.

The wheat industry in that part of the state was a steadily growing business and the most important factor in that expansion was, of course, the railroads. In Davenport, the last in the line of wheat towns from the Columbia River to Spokane, a conference had been planned for August 3 to discuss the future possibilities of the wheat business. James J. Hill, the president of the Great Northern Railroad, was the featured speaker at the conference. Other dignitaries present there were President C. S. Mellen of the Northern Pacific Railroad and President Mohler of the Oregon Railroad and Navigational Company.

James J. Hill was one of the most successful of a number of railroad magnates at the beginning of the 20th century. He had completed his railroad line from Minneapolis-St. Paul to Seattle in 1893, had survived the depression caused by the financial "Panic Of

1893" and had been the only owner of a major railroad not to go bankrupt in the process. Because of his business acuity he had been given the nickname "The Empire Builder."

His nemesis at the time was President Theodore Roosevelt who came to power as a "trustbuster" and who had vowed to keep Hill and his partners from monopolizing the railroad business in the West. Hill was in the area to promote his railroad as the best and most efficient way to transport grain. He was reported to have uttered the famous line that referenced his single-minded determination to build the world's best railroad: "Give me snuff, whiskey and Swedes, and I will build a railroad to hell."

Hill had little interest in the unfortunate but minor disturbance caused by some wild-west era outlaw on the loose in the area.

The V.I.P.s at the conference planned only a short stay in Davenport, but the five thousand farmers and businessmen in attendance intended to stay on for some time, hopefully, to draft some detailed proposals.

Charles McCarthy, a rancher living twelve miles south of Wilber, reported that a man who resembled Tracy's description had stopped at his house on the morning of August 3 to ask for directions to Wilbur, Davenport, Reardon and Sprague. The rancher had talked with the man for almost ten minutes before he continued on his way. A Mrs. Craben had seen the same man that evening heading north on the road that led to Wilbur. Sheriff Doust of Spokane County headed west to join the other sheriffs in the manhunt, hoping to head Tracy off by setting up a guard post ahead of his reported location.

A note was found by C. V. Drazon, a prominent rancher living one mile north of Odessa and only a few miles from the Craben house. It was pinned to a wall where Tracy had watered his horses. The note was from Harry Tracy to the owner of the property and it concerned his dogged pursuer, Sheriff Cudihee.

The note read:

"To whom it may concern;

Tell Mr. Cudihee to take a tumble and leave me alone or I will fix him plenty. I will be on my way to Wyoming. If your horses was (sic) any good, I would swap with you. Thanks for the drink. Harry Tracy."

Chapter 18:

The Manhunt Ends

While out riding on the high divide in the Lake Country below the main line of the Great Northern Railroad, a nineteen year old young man named George Goldfinch came upon the camp of a lone man.

The man introduced himself as a miner and invited Goldfinch to sit with him and have some tea. When the young man accepted and sat down next to the fire, the stranger acted as if he had not had anyone to talk to in days. He insisted that Goldfinch should stay and have something to eat.

As the man fixed the meal, he talked incessantly in a nervous manner. He asked Goldfinch about the condition of the crops in the area, which, he replied, were fine, and wondered who had won the Jeffries-Fitzsimmons heavyweight championship fight. When Goldfinch told him that Jeffries had scored an upset knockout after nearly being beaten to a pulp, the man showed great interest and the two carried on a long discussion about who really was the best fighter.

Goldfinch explained that it was Jeffries' ability to absorb punishment and recover from a severe battering that won him the rematch for the title with Fitzsimmons, who was regarded as one of the hardest punchers in boxing history. The rematch with Jeffries occurred on July 25, 1902 in San Francisco. For nearly eight rounds Fitzsimmons subjected Jeffries to a vicious battering. Jeffries suffered a broken nose, both of his cheeks were cut to the bone, and gashes were opened above both of his eyes. It appeared that the fight would have to be stopped, as blood freely flowed into Jeffries' eyes. In the eighth round, Jeffries lashed out with a terrific right to the stomach, followed by a left hook to the jaw which knocked Fitzsimmons unconscious.

"Where is Tracy?" asked the stranger suddenly interrupting the story.

"Near Wilbur last anyone heard," answered Goldfinch.

"I am Tracy," said the stranger, matter-of-factly. "I want you to take me to the nearest ranch."

Tracy had Goldfinch lead the way, promising to shoot if he was being taken into a trap. At each obstacle in the way, the outlaw dropped behind a bush to prevent a possible ambush.

The two men reached the ranch of Lou and Gene Eddy, two bachelor brothers working the somewhat meager land of the rock-covered Lake Creek area. Tracy immediately identified himself. He announced to the Eddy brothers that he would be staying at their place for some time. Lou Eddy, who had hitched a team for a visit to a distant neighbor, Ben Hurley, abandoned his plan and went with his brother Gene and young Goldfinch to cut hay for Tracy's horses.

Before supper, Lou repaired the outlaw's makeshift holster, sharpened his razor and knife and mended his cartridge belt which had holes too large to hold his 30/30 shells.

The meal was quick and simple and afterwards Goldfinch

protested that he had better be going home if Tracy did not want his disappearance to arouse suspicion. Reluctantly, the outlaw let the young man go with a warning that he would kill both of the Eddy brothers if he so much as breathed a word to anyone that he was at the Eddy farm.

As the boy rode away, Tracy realized that for the first time, he had let someone out of his grasp without the hold of fear of a family member's death. He had violated his own crude sense of psychology. He knew that his intimidations only succeeded when the family was poor and had only each other to count on. He had let Goldfinch, who hardly knew the Eddy brothers, go free. He must have sensed that his generosity could be a possibly fatal mistake.

Goldfinch returned to the Eddy ranch on Tuesday morning. He expected Tracy to be long gone. Instead he found him helping in the building of the Eddy barn. Planning to leave shortly and thinking that he had sufficiently cowed Goldfinch into not revealing his whereabouts, Tracy let Goldfinch leave the ranch again that afternoon.

Goldfinch, after agonizing about what to do, decided to tell Mr. Blenz about his meeting with Harry Tracy. Blenz immediately sent the young man to the nearby town of Creston where he was told to telegraph Sheriff Doust in Spokane and Sheriff Gardner in Davenport. Goldfinch was overheard telling his story to the station manager by J. J. Morrison, a twenty two year old section foreman. Morrison was extremely excited at hearing the news that Harry

Tracy was in the area. He ran to tell his friend, Maurice Smith, a young man in his mid-twenties, who had served in the Spanish-American War and who had recently graduated from the University of Minnesota Law School.

The two men decided to discuss the possibility of forming a posse with their mutual friend, E. C. Lanter, a twenty three year old M. D. just out of medical school, just beginning his first job. Smith and Lanter had discussed earlier how they would capture the outlaw if they had a chance and that chance seemed to have come their way. Without much planning, the three men decided to move to the Eddy ranch and they invited Goldfinch to accompany them as a guide. Goldfinch declined the invitation, knowing that Tracy would be furious with him for disclosing his location and that he would be looking for revenge.

Morrison knew the country well enough to lead the men to the ranch by himself, but he suggested that they bring along Frank Lillengreen to help find the way. Lillengreen was a warehouse worker in Creston and Morrison's hunting partner. Both men owned high-powered hunting rifles which would be needed if the group met Tracy in a gun battle.

Smith borrowed a new Winchester from the hardware store, but Lanter had to make do with a 48.82 caliber black powder Winchester with a bullet lodged in the barrel. Lanter removed the bullet by the loading the rifle with a light powder charge, tying a string around the trigger, propping the ancient weapon up with a wooden barrel and discharging it while hiding behind a woodpile.

So armed, they proceeded to the livery stable of C. A. Straub who was also the town constable to procure both transportation and the necessary sanction of the law.

Morrison and Smith were both married and they had to return to their homes to make excuses to their wives. Both men were back at the livery stable within an hour. The rifles and ammunition were loaded onto a wagon and Dr. Lanter brought along his surgical bag in the chance that someone might be so unfortunate as to be hurt.

The driving forces in the make-shift posse were the young professionals, Lanter and Smith. Both men were from the East and had come to the unlikely city of Creston, Washington to begin their careers. It was their bold vision and reckless courage which prompted the other men to risk their lives against a man who had proven to be a formidable foe for even the most professional of lawmen. For these men to presume that they could capture the notorious outlaw, Harry Tracy, was an almost foolhardy assumption.

The young and inexperienced posse started out on the main road that led to the small town of Fellows between Creston and Davenport. At Fellows, the five men looked south over the open country and saw the slight outline of the Eddy ranch about three miles away. Goldfinch had told them that the Eddys were building a new barn which looked out over this approach; Tracy would be able to see for miles without revealing his position.

In order to have the advantage of surprise, which the men felt they needed in order to increase their odds against the more experienced outlaw, the Creston posse abandoned their wagon and walked cautiously toward the ranch under the cover of some low hills. As they approached, they separated in order not to raise an identifiable cloud of dust in the loose and arid soil. They made a wide circle around the Eddy barn so that they could move in from the south. This maneuver took an extra five miles of hard travel, but all concerned deemed it necessary in order to achieve total surprise.

At the point directly west of the barn, they decided to deploy themselves for action. Straub and Lillengreen were to remain behind to cover the others with their long range hunting rifles while Morrison, Smith and Lanter continued toward the barn.

The three frightened and excited young men crawled steadily across the ground until they were directly south of the ranch. Slowly they worked their way closer to the barn until they could hear the sounds of hammering from inside. At the top of a haystack, they could see a bedroll which they took as proof that Tracy was still on the ranch.

With painstaking care, they crept along in a crouch until they were only one hundred yards from the barn. Suddenly, the hammering stopped and all three men dropped to their stomachs full of dread that they had been seen and were shortly to be met with a steady stream of Tracy's deadly bullets. Hugging the ground in the hot still air, the men realized that they were in a very vulnerable position. Goldfinch had told them that the cracks in the barn wall had not yet been filled in with mortar and they were wide enough for a man to fire through. They wondered if Tracy was, at that moment, lining them up in his gun sights.

After what seemed to be an eternity of waiting, the three men crawled to a point behind a haystack to discuss the situation. Despite their fears, they still, obviously, had not been seen.

Talking in whispers, they decided to surround the barn because they saw that there was a thicket of trees on one side of the barn where Tracy would have been able to hide and fire in relative safety if they remained where they were. To accomplish this maneuver, they had to split up again. Morrison held the position behind the haystack while Smith and Lanter moved closer. The two friends slid on the ground, side by side, realizing that their fantasy about hunting down Harry Tracy had lost all of its romanticism and was now a matter of life and death. As amateurs in the "man hunting" game, they knew that their only hope lay in careful planning, their greater numbers and a lot of luck.

Whispering to each other in low tones as they moved, Smith and Lanter decided that if Tracy appeared and started shooting that they would concentrate on replying to the fire rather than trying to watch out for each other. The two men pressed ahead, despite their fear, and reached the edge of the Eddy barnyard without being detected.

George Eddy drove into the yard with his team hitched to a mower at about the same time as Lanter and Smith arrived at the edge. Tracy had permitted him to work in a field some distance from the barn, if he promised to keep in sight. While in the field, he had encountered Straub and Lillengreen and he had been questioned about Tracy's presence on the ranch. Eddy had not wanted to give any information about the outlaw, given his promise to exact revenge. However, he relented and admitted that Tracy was, indeed, in the barn. Smith and Lanter guessed that he knew about the posse members by the way he nervously unhitched the team from the mower.

After finishing the unhitching, Gene Eddy yelled, "Hello," toward the barn shed that was being used as a blacksmith shop and Tracy unsuspectingly stepped into the open. Smith and Lanter recognized him by his lean frame and by the clothes that Goldfinch had described to them. Harry Tracy, the object of a two month long search throughout the states of Oregon and Washington, was within the sight of the two young Creston men, only fifty yards away.

"Take a shot," whispered Lanter under his breath to Smith figuring that his own old black powder rifle would not be effective at that distance.

Smith, somewhat recklessly, decided to give the outlaw a chance to give himself up.

"Throw up your hands, Tracy," he yelled holding up his rifle to back up his order.

Tracy gave no answer and quickly ducked behind the Eddy horses for cover. Before Smith could get a clear shot, the outlaw dove into the barn where his rifle was stored. Goldfinch had told the Creston men that Tracy kept a saddled horse in the barn at all times. They expected him to take one of two possible escape routes: one leading north and the other leading south. Lanter ran to cover the southern exit and Smith moved to the top of a rocky gulley west of the barn to cover the northern exit. Both men waited patiently for Tracy to make a move.

From inside the barn, Tracy had been watching the men spread out. He decided to make a break for cover. Quietly sneaking out of the barn on the uncovered eastern side, he bent over and quickly walk-ran to a low, rock ridge. He was obviously heading for a draw that led south toward the Lake Creek basin, hoping that he would not be noticed. However, Lanter, sensing that something was happening, left his position and saw the outlaw trying to slip away.

Lanter rejoined Morrison and, pointing out Tracy's retreating form, both men began firing. Lanter's black powder rifle exploded in frightening roars, but neither he nor Morrison could bring their shots on target. Tracy returned the fire on the run, too exposed to engage in a stationary gun battle.

When he realized that he might be hemmed in on a ridge, Tracy veered away from his path and broke for a large rock shaped like a haystack on the edge of a barley field. The rock would be able to provide excellent protection since it was surrounded by a patch of trees and a clump of brush. Tracy ran directly for the rock, stumbled and fell. His rifle was sent crashing against a stone and, after retrieving the weapon, he recovered, picked himself up and managed to reach the rock before the pursuers could get a shot at him. Smith came running when he heard the shots from Lanter and Morrison. As he moved across the barley field, he could see

Lillengreen and Straub approaching the haystack rock from the southwest, drawing Tracy's fire. Smith could see the bullets raising little puffs of dust ten yards in front of their intended target. He could not understand such inaccuracy from a man reported to be such a crack shot, but he was too tied up in the immediate excitement to try to figure a reason why. Smith ran past Lanter and Morrison and took a position on an outcrop of a small gulley where he had a panoramic view of the entire area.

Lanter yelled for Smith to get down, but the young lawyer was still trying to spot the exact location of the outlaw. Smith saw a glint of the setting sun on a gun barrel behind the haystack rock and he knew that Tracy was in a vantage point that would allow him to fire from one side of the rock and then run to the other and fire again without exposing himself to a direct line of fire.

Again he saw Tracy's bullets fall harmlessly in the dusty soil ten yards short. He figured the problem must have been the setting sun in the outlaw's eyes, but even the bright, yellow-orange glow of an eastern Washington sunset should not have had that great an effect.

After a few minutes of exchanging fire with the outlaw, Smith called out, "One of you fellows go around the rock; get behind him," hoping that his call would dislodge Tracy from his nearly impregnable position behind the rock.

Tracy fell for the ruse and suddenly broke from the rock into the barley field. The men were so taken by surprise by the impetuous exit that they did not have time to fire until the outlaw was concealed in the tall grain. Once in the field, Tracy began to crawl on his hands and knees toward the Lake Creek basin. He followed the outline of a wash-out that was only filled in times of spring flooding and during the summer only held small pools of water in between grain stalks. Each time he crossed an area where the grain was not growing, the five Creston men opened fire, trying to mark their aim by the dirt puffs which flew up in front of and behind the fleeing outlaw.

Smith was in the most advantageous spot. The sights on the borrowed Winchester were new to him and his aim was too high in the beginning. But each time he caught sight of the outlaw through the barley, he tried to make corrections. Each shot he fired was marching steadily in on Tracy's running, stumbling form. On one particularly large open spot, which had dried completely over the hot, dry summer, Tracy pushed himself along on his back, sending shot after shot at the various members of the posse. Smith chose his shots carefully and each one was becoming progressively closer to the outlaw. The last shot that Smith took before Tracy disappeared back into the tall barley seemed to be right on target; he could see no puff of dust. At that point, Smith had emptied his rifle and he quickly reloaded sensing that he might have inflicted a wound on Tracy who was still crawling deeper and deeper into the heaviest part of the field. When Smith was ready to resume fire, Tracy had disappeared from sight.

With no guns blazing, the field was suddenly eerily quiet; not even a breeze rustled the still stalks of barley. Suddenly, Lanter and

Morrison saw some movement in the field near their position. Lanter fired his old black powder weapon in another explosion of smoke and fire and immediately a big hog let out a pained squeal and ran back for the safety of the barnyard. The tension had been so great for the posse over the time of the gun battle, that the sight of the squealing, frightened hog broke a floodgate of emotion. All five burst into an uncontrolled laughter. Though they tried to suppress their amusement, the comedic sight of the hog in the midst of such dire circumstances kept the men chuckling for more than ten minutes after it had occurred. Each time the laughter seemed to subside, some member of the group would not be able to contain himself and his muffled chuckles would cause the other men to begin laughing all over again.

Since nightfall was near, the posse members decided not to go into the barley field to track down the possibly wounded outlaw. Despite the possibility that he might escape under the cover of darkness, they planned to wait until morning to continue their pursuit.

Smith built a tower of stones and placed his hat on top, hoping to draw fire. But no shots issued from Tracy's supposed position. Darkness was rapidly spreading across the broad sky, when, out of the barley field, drifted the sound of a muffled report from a pistol.

"That was no rifle shot," said Lanter. "That was a pistol. Let's go in and see what happened."

"It could be a trap," said Morrison. "Let's wait until sunrise and some reinforcements."

The five men agreed to wait. They settled down to spend the night without leaving their position.

At 12:00 midnight, Sheriff Gardner and his son, Charles, arrived at the Eddy ranch. The Creston men filled him in on the day's action.

When the first light of dawn illuminated the white-gold barley field, Smith and Lanter decided to search the area. They invited Sheriff Gardner and his son to go along, but both men declined, not wanting to risk their lives unnecessarily. Before heading out into the waist high field of grain, the two young men looked at each other and nodded to themselves for support. They had come to the point where fantasy had become reality and their courage was not found wanting. Slowly they crept into the thick barley with just enough light filtering through the grey, morning skies to follow the bent stalks indicating the inch-by-inch progress that Tracy had made the previous day. About twenty yards from the last open space, where Smith had fired his last round in the outlaw's direction, Lanter stopped with a lurch and pointed ahead with his rifle; on the ground, stretched out in front of them, was the motionless body of Harry Tracy. He was covered with dirt and blood. His right leg appeared to have been broken by a bullet and there was a red hole where his right eye should have been. A closer inspection by the two men revealed another large hole in the outlaw's head where the bullet had split his skull upon exit.

From what Smith and Lanter cold see, Tracy's final moments were desperate. He had been hit by a bullet from one of the posse members, probably from Smith's last shot, in the leg; the force of the impact of the bullet had shattered his leg bones and had also severed an artery. Pushing on through the barley field, applying his belt as a tourniquet, he had crawled until he ran out of strength. At that point, he had raised himself up on his left elbow, placed the pistol to his right eye and had pulled the trigger with the thumb of his left hand.

The bullet had split his head in two but his right hand was found to be still gripping the Winchester that he had carried and inflicted so much damage with since his escape from the Oregon State Penitentiary. Smith took the rifle from Tracy's hand and discovered the reason why his shots had been falling so short of his desired targets; the filed-sight was dislodged, perhaps smashed against a stone when he had fallen on his flight from the Eddy barn to the haystack rock. The sharpshooter's weapon had been rendered ineffective by the fall. The "crack shot" had been foiled by a stroke of bad luck. All of the good fortune that Harry Tracy had in Western Washington had failed to follow him over the mountains.

When Sheriff Gardner realized that Smith and Lanter had found Harry Tracy's body, he rushed into the field waving his revolver and demanded to take charge of the corpse. The two men were understandably upset over such an order since the sheriff had done nothing to help. They relented, however, when Gardner said that all he wanted to do was to take the body to Davenport for embalming. He gave the Creston men his solemn promise that he would turn over the body of Tracy to them for the railroad trip back to Oregon where he had to be taken in order for the men to receive their reward.

An hour later, Sheriff Cudihee arrived on the scene. He was driven to the Eddy ranch by Mr. Hoople who Sheriff Gardner then enlisted to carry the body back to Davenport. None of the men from Creston knew how long and hard the King County Sheriff had toiled in exhaustion and frustration to capture the man who now lay in a grisly posture of death.

Cudihee stood staring at the body, not knowing what to do or say. The manhunt, which had become his personal and obsessive quest over the past month, was over. But for the sheriff, this seemed to be the wrong ending; he felt no spirit of exacted revenge, no joy in the fact that his man was now dead. To the other men present at the Eddy ranch, he appeared quiet and sullen, not satisfied with the sight that lay before him.

Chapter 19:

Aftermath

When the body of Harry Tracy was brought into Davenport, the story of his death had preceded him; hundreds of local people had heard the news and had gathered on the city streets to catch a glimpse of the final parade of the dead desperado. Many of the curious were still in town from the conference on the future of the wheat industry in the state of Washington and they pushed and shoved at each other to try to touch the body of the man who in life had evoked sheer terror by the mere mention of his name.

The "Tracy relic-hunters" as they came to be known, were carried away with excitement and turned into an ugly mob. As the wagon rumbled down the dusty Davenport street, a few people reached out and pulled off some buttons, then others began ripping off strips of clothes, finally a near-riot broke out and by that time no one wanted to be stopped from getting a souvenir.

The wagon managed to reach the coroner's office and the crowd gathered around it. Windows were broken and the crowd stormed through the door. The mob was yelling and screaming as they rushed inside the office. "Bedlam reigned" as clothes, hair and even pieces of skin were ripped and cut from the body. In less than ten minutes, Tracy's body was stripped naked and was dotted with bloody patches where hair and skin had been hacked away. The clothing was divided up "as if it was Christ's robe" by the unruly gathering in front of the coroner's office.

The Creston posse, who had just arrived in Davenport in time to see the mob in action, had to struggle against the surging mass of humanity in order to protect the body from being completely destroyed. Although the Davenport Times, the local newspaper, maintained later that the descriptions of mob activity were greatly exaggerated, eyewitness accounts by the Creston posse validate the chaotic situation that day. To the town's credit, most of the participants in the near-riot, were not from Davenport, and were, instead, out of town attendees of the wheat conference, thus salvaging some vestige of local pride and explaining the extent of the irrational activity.

Sheriff Cudihee was present in Davenport to witness the events and was reportedly so overcome with emotion at the sight of such morbid depravity that he broke down in tears. Perhaps it was a release of tension that had built up inside of him over the personally dissatisfying month long manhunt and then again, perhaps it was because he might have held a measure of respect for the man who had so boldly and intelligently eluded his posses and his plans - a measure of respect that could not countenance such shabby treatment - even to an outlaw and murderer. Whatever the reason, nothing further was heard from Sheriff Cudihee in regards to the disposition of the body, although he could have claimed it and he could have taken it back to Seattle by virtue of a valid warrant.

Cudihee quietly and unobtrusively bowed out and returned home by train. The bond between the sheriff and the outlaw, between the hunter and the hunted, between the respected and the disrespectful, between two adversaries of a drama that could have only been played out in the last vestiges of the frontier west was finally and summarily broken. The bond had nothing to do with body mutilations, souvenir hunting or disputes over who was to receive the reward money. The forces of collective progressivism and civilization had won out over the depredations of a single desperate man, as inevitably they must. An amateur posse, led by two men whose professions would propel them into the forefront of the region's emergence as a full-fledged economic power in a nation thirsty for imperialism, had finally tracked down and killed one of the last, true outlaws of an already by-gone era.

Cudihee's career would suffer for his failure to successfully lead the King County posse to capture Harry Tracy; he was voted out of office in the next election. Personally, however, he seemed to profit. His brusque manner mellowed and he opened a small livery stable that soon was bustling with activity. He had been a bachelor all his life, not wanting to subject a wife and family to the ridiculously long hours that needed to be spent in devotion to the job. In 1909, at the late age of 56, he finally married. He ultimately had his final vindication as a lawman when he was elected to a third term as King County Sheriff in 1912.

******

Constable Straub, not being able to locate Sheriff Cudihee because of his abrupt departure, sent a wire to Undersheriff Corcoran in Seattle.

"We, the posse who caught Tracy have been instructed by

Oregon officials to hold the body for further orders. We desire permission from you."

Corcoran, unaware of Cudihee's journey-in-progress back to the city, received the message and immediately contacted Governor McBride.

"Tracy killed last night near Creston, Washington. His body is at Davenport. Suggest you notify coroner and sheriff at Davenport to deliver Tracy's body to Sheriff Cudihee to be taken to Seattle for identification. Tracy is well known here and you will want positive identification which to base payment of reward offered by you. Cudihee now in Davenport, holds warrant charging Tracy with murder in first degree."

Governor McBride also received a telegram from Governor Geer of Oregon.

"I suggest you have Tracy's body brought to Seattle for identification for the Washington reward and forwarded at once to Salem for the same purpose. Perhaps the body should be embalmed. Deputy Sheriff at Seattle suggests same. Answer your opinion."

Governor McBride decided that identification by the Oregon officials would be sufficient enough proof for the Washington reward of $2,500. He sent telegrams to both Governor Geer and Undersheriff Corcoran to that effect. He felt that the identification procedure in Seattle would be extraneous and that the appearance of the body in the city that had suffered from his presence for almost a month might prove as disruptive as it had been in Davenport.

After the Seattle authorities refused to accept the body, a dispute over who was to take possession of it arose in Davenport. Sheriff Gardner demanded to have the right to deliver the body to Salem and claim the reward because it was within his jurisdiction that the outlaw had committed suicide. The Creston posse was unwilling to let Gardner have anything to do with the body since he had done nothing except show up at the Eddy ranch after all of the action was over. Dr. Lanter, in order to protect the Creston men's claim, stood guard over the body with same black powder Winchester that he had used in the gun battle with the outlaw. The fact that it was basically an ineffective weapon, made as little difference at that point as it did when he was in the shoot-out with Harry Tracy. His zeal in itself was enough to stop Sheriff Gardner from enforcing his claim. The matter was finally settled when Governor Geer wired Constable Straub to take possession of the body and to bring it to Salem.

A coroner's jury was quickly formed by the Lincoln County Coroner, B.P. Moore, to determine the exact circumstances of Harry Tracy's death. The jury made an inspection of the body and released this report:

"We, the undersigned duly sworn by B. P. Moore, Coroner of Lincoln County, as coroner's jury to inquire (sic) into the cause of death of the body of a person before us, after inspecting the body and hearing testimony of witnesses find as follows:

That the body is that of Harry Tracy, the escaped convict from the Oregon State Penitentiary; that said Harry Tracy came to his death at the ranch of Lou Eddy in Lincoln County, Washington on August 5, 1902 by means of a gunshot wound from a pistol in his possession and held in his own hands after first being wounded by party or parties unknown. That Harry Tracy was an escaped convict from the Oregon State Penitentiary, and at the time of his death was fleeing from officers and posses in pursuit; that none is blamable for his death, but that all efforts to effect his capture were praiseworthy and fully in accordance with the laws of Washington."

Before the body was put on the train for Oregon, muriatic acid was poured on the face to discourage body snatchers from attempting to steal Harry Tracy's remains for public display. On August 9, the corpse, in a plain zinc-lined pine coffin, was placed on a train bound for Salem. Constable Staub sat on the box for the entire trip, holding a loaded gun. If he had not, according to a later interview with the Spokane Spokesman Review, "souvenir hunters would have cut so many chunks off it that there wouldn't have been much left."

The reward offered by the state of Oregon could only be awarded on delivery of Tracy, dead or alive to Salem.

"The Creston Party of five men claim all of the reward," The Spokesman-Review reported two days after Tracy's death. "George Goldfinch claims a good share, and Sheriff Gardner, who says he was at the scene of battle, also claims a share. Maurice Smith, of the Creston party, said, 'Gardner is not entitled to one cent. He did not get to the scene of action until about two hours after Tracy committed suicide. Young Goldfinch is not legally entitled to any of it. I do not say whether we, if we get it, will give him any of it.'"

The matter of the reward resulted in a lawsuit, the outcome of which was reported by The Spokesman-Review in the following December 9, 1903, wire story from Olympia:

"After a lapse of 16 months, the reward of $2,500 for the apprehension of the outlaw, Harry Tracy, will be paid by the state of Washington. The payment of the reward has been delayed because of conflicting claims for shares of it. It will now be divided among Maurice Smith, Charles A. Straub, Joseph Morrison, Frank Lillengren and E. C. Lanter. They are the men who cornered Tracy on a farm in Lincoln County a year ago last August, took part in a running fight with him and finally wounded him so severely that he committed suicide rather than surrender. The continuing claimants were Richard Gemring, Sheriff Gardner and son and others who arrived after the smoke of the battle cleared away. A lawsuit involving the rights of different claimants was decided last June in favor of the men who took part in the actual battle, and Gemring et al, having taken no appeal, the reward will be paid."

In Portland, Oregon, a crowd was waiting for the train from Spokane that was carrying Harry Tracy's body. As it pulled into the station, the crowd clamored for a view. In order to protect the coffin, the Creston men were forced to stay awake on guard duty throughout the night. The next day they were met by another crowd in Salem, where the manhunt had begun over two months previously. The local police could do little to help the Creston posse as they transferred the body from the railroad car to the prison wagon. The curiosity seekers surged forward and smashed the side of the cheap coffin, taking with them splinters and strips of skin as souvenirs. Extra police were called in to quell the disturbance and to let the tired posse finish their job.

Harry Tracy was ironically buried next to Dave Merrill, his partner in crime and victim in a duel, in the prison cemetery. Penitentiary officials were still angry over his escape and the murder of their colleagues. They were not anxious to have any reminder of the events of the past weeks and they did not want any visitors coming to view his grave. Quick lime was poured over the remnants of the body to hasten its disintegration. It was unceremoniously dumped into an unmarked grave. The burial area was later covered over in an expansion of the prison facility.

During the following weeks, more than a dozen women appeared at Portland and Seattle police stations claiming to be the dead outlaw's widow. A medium priced cigar was named the "Tracy Cigar." However, it soon disappeared from the market due to diminishing sales as his notoriety faded. A bartender with a black sense of humor named one of his concoctions the "Tracy Cocktail - three shots and you're out" (of prison). There was a quickly put-together melodrama that was performed in Seattle with Harry Tracy cast as the "lovable, if misunderstood, hero." Audiences did not respond with overflow crowds. Several dime novels were written in the same year as his death in order to cash in on his brief but dramatic notoriety. Over the years, numerous accounts of his life have been written in various books, newspapers and magazines.

There have been two films that have dealt with his story: *Tracy the Outlaw*, a silent film produced in 1928 which tried, somewhat unsuccessfully, to recount the true story, and a more recent 1982 film called *Harry Tracy, Desperado*, which did not bother to try to tell the real story and attempted to recount a more thrilling version which bore little resemblance to what really happened.

The furor that Harry Tracy created in the months in which he had been hunted slowly died down, even in the places that he had passed through on his mission to escape. Today there are few markers on his trail of mayhem, no placards where he shot it out with deputies or held hostages for days. The man who so boldly and brazenly marched across five hundred miles of thick underbrush, tall grass and dense forests, has left only the impression of a memory. People living in the areas where he appeared on his circuitous pursuit of freedom, held vivid remembrances of the circumstances throughout their lives. Today, all of those who remembered are gone. It is their descendants who keep only a memory of a memory.

Perhaps it is fitting that this outlaw, no matter how bold and daring, has left little or no trace (no pun intended) on the landscape of the Pacific Northwest. His deeds and exploits should not be overly aggrandized, since he was, in fact, a convicted criminal, a thief and a cold-blooded murderer. He was also very polite, courteous to women, not a wanton killer but a self-justifying dispenser of his own crude code of frontier justice with a keen though rough-hewn sense of humor.

The story remains as a moment in the factual history of the growth of a region: the Pacific Northwest. It is still the same land that it was it was in Harry Tracy's time. Even though it is now widely settled and much of the dense undergrowth and timber has been cleared, the countryside still retains its basic wildness and overgrown nature. It does not take much neglect for the rain-soaked climate and fertile soil to reclaim its prominence over any kind of civilized activity. It was within this cover that the outlaw Harry Tracy hid from capture and eluded every posse that was dispatched to capture him. It was perhaps only in the Pacific Northwest that Harry Tracy could have been able to become a legend, however fleeting.

Bibliography

The accounts in this book are mainly taken from the pages of the daily newspapers that reported on the events associated with Harry Tracy's story and, as such, are part of the public domain.

Historical background information was obtained from the following publications:

Newspapers and Publications

1. The Portland Oregonian

2. The Vancouver Independent

3. The Seattle Daily Times

4. The Lincoln County Times

5. The Aspen Times

6. Steamboat Magazine

Books

1, Northwest Manhunts, Hollis B. Fultz, 1955, 229 pages, Fulco Publications, Elma, WA.

2. The History Of Tracy, W. Carter, 1902, 296 pages, Laird and Lee, Chicago, Illinois.

3. Harry Tracy: King Of The Outlaws, Harry Hawkeye, 1908.

4. The Wild Bunch, James d. Horan, 1958, 191 pages, The New American Library Inc. - Signet, New York, New York.

5. Thirteen Years In The Oregon Penitentiary, Joseph Kelley, 1908, 142 pages, n. pub, Portland, Oregon.

6. An Illustrated History Of The Big Bend Country, 1024 pages, 1904, Western Historical Publication, Spokane, Washington.

Printed in the USA
CPSIA information can be obtained
at www.ICGtesting.com
LVHW021954230624
783811LV00001B/17